DER HANDSCHUH
Mehr als ein Mode-Accessoire
THE GLOVE
More than fashion

Herausgegeben von / Edited by
Inez Florschütz
in Zusammenarbeit mit / in cooperation with
Leonie Wiegand

Mehr als ein Mode-Accessoire
More than fashion

DER HANDSCHUH
THE GLOVE

arnoldsche

DEUTSCHES LEDERMUSEUM

Contents

9
A big hand
for the glove

16
Shoes for the hands

26
Glove types

34
Clerical gloves

42
Royal gloves

50
The gauntlet

60
Falconry glove

70
Love token

78
Sports gloves

86
Driving gloves

96
The glove box

106
Glove sizes

114
Glove accessories

122
Perfumed gloves

132
The muff

142
Etiquette

150
Disposable gloves

158
Protective and work gloves

168
High-tech gloves

178
Object of desire

186
Trademark

198
Production of
leather gloves

201
Pantopia

202
Pantopia
Ideas for a firm hold

217
Bibliography

220
Acknowledgments

222
Imprint

223
Photo credits

Inhalt

6
Hand in Hand mit dem Handschuh

14
Schuhe für die Hand

24
Handschuhtypen

32
Klerikale Handschuhe

40
Königliche Handschuhe

48
Der Fehdehandschuh

58
Falknerhandschuh

68
Liebespfand

76
Sporthandschuhe

84
Autofahrhandschuhe

94
Das Handschuhfach

104
Handschuhgrößen

112
Handschuhzubehör

120
Parfümierte Handschuhe

130
Der Muff

140
Etikette

148
Einmalhandschuhe

156
Schutz- und Arbeitshandschuhe

166
High-Tech Handschuhe

176
Objekt der Begierde

184
Markenzeichen

194
Die Herstellung von Lederhandschuhen

201
Pantopia

203
Pantopia
Ideen, die Halt geben

217
Bibliografie

221
Dank

222
Impressum

223
Bildnachweis

Hand in Hand mit dem Handschuh

Seit einigen Jahren haben Modedesigner*innen für sich ein ganz besonderes Accessoire wiederentdeckt: den HANDSCHUH. Lange Zeit waren Handschuhe als elegantes Kleidungsstück in Vergessenheit geraten und dienten fast ausschließlich als Kälteschutz. Nun sind sie wieder da. Bei den internationalen Modenschauen in Paris, Mailand oder New York sehen wir Handschuhe in allen Farben, Formen und Längen sowie aus allen denkbaren Materialien. Auf den Laufstegen bei Gucci, Fendi, Prada oder Valentino tauchen die ausgefallensten Kreationen in Leder, Samt, Seide, Cashmere oder Wolle, verziert mit Federn, Perlen oder Nieten auf. Besonders im Sommer 2022 wurde der Modetrend, lange Handschuhe, sogenannte Opera-Handschuhe, zu ärmellosen Kleidern oder Oberteilen zu tragen, vermehrt von Designer*innen wiederbelebt. Hinter der Renaissance des Handschuhs, der nun vielfach mit Opulenz und Glamour auftritt, mag sich aber auch aufgrund der seit Anfang 2020 weltweit verbreitenden Covid-19 Pandemie verstärkt der Wunsch nach hygienischem Schutz verbergen. In der Serie *AND JUST LIKE THAT* streift sich Carrie Bradshaw, eine der Hauptfiguren, beim Betreten eines Lifts schicke, glitzernde Handschuhe über und drückt den Liftknopf mit der Bemerkung: „Das habe ich mir seit der Pandemie so angewöhnt." Mode und Hygieneschutz können durchaus zusammenkommen. Wir alle greifen wieder öfters zum Handschuh – in welcher Ausführung auch immer.

    All diese Entwicklungen haben uns angeregt, sich mit dem Thema HANDSCHUH näher zu befassen. Zu Beginn der Planungen stand – wie fast immer bei der Vorbereitung eines Ausstellungsprojekts im Deutschen Ledermuseum – die eigene Sammlung als Ausgangspunkt im Zentrum. Schnell merkten wir, dass wir aus dem zwar kleinen, aber exquisiten Bestand unseres Hauses die Vielfalt dieses häufig unterschätzten Accessoires aufzeigen können. Daraus leitet sich auch der Titel für Ausstellung und Publikation DER HANDSCHUH: Mehr als ein Mode-Accessoire **ab.**

Wir wollen darstellen, dass der Handschuh seit vielen Jahrtausenden für den Menschen ein ebenso nützlicher, wie modischer Begleiter ist. Bereits in der Antike war Handbekleidung vorwiegend bei der Garten- und Feldarbeit oder bei sportlichen Betätigungen üblich. In dem 1922 entdeckten Grab des 1323 v. Chr. verstorbenen Tutanchamuns fand man erstaunlicherweise 27 Exemplare. Ab dem 8. Jahrhundert wurde der Handschuh vermehrt als ein Herrscher- und Rechtssymbol beim Klerus, aber auch im Gerichts- und Lehnswesen verwendet. Seit der Krönung von Kaiser Friedrich II. im Jahre 1220 gehörten Handschuhe zu den kaiserlichen Insignien. Im Spätmittelalter wurde der Handschuh dann zum Modeartikel sowohl bei Herren wie Damen der höheren Stände. Eine differenzierte Etikette, wann und für welche Angelegenheiten Handschuhe getragen werden sollten, bildete sich zu Beginn der Neuzeit heraus. Bis in die 1960er Jahre war es für eine Dame fast ein Muss, beim Verlassen des Hauses Handschuhe zu tragen. Die kürzlich verstorbene Königin Elisabeth II. soll bei einem dreitägigen Besuch in Deutschland 50 Paare – passend zu jedem Outfit und zu jeder Tageszeit – im Gepäck gehabt haben. Berühmt wurden die Fotos von Audrey Hepburn mit langen Handschuhen in dem Film *Frühstück bei Tiffany* oder die schwarzen, häufig mit Nieten verzierten des Modeschöpfers Karl Lagerfeld. Er wusste wohl, dass kaum ein Körperteil des Menschen mehr das Alter verrät als die Hände, davon wollte er vermutlich mit dem Tragen dieses Accessoires – zumeist in einer Halbfingervariante – ablenken.

Auch in der Kunst waren Handschuhe immer wieder ein Thema. Im Werk der Surrealistin Meret Oppenheim tauchen sie mehrfach in Varianten auf. 1985 schuf sie in einer Edition von 150 Exemplaren Handschuhpaare aus Ziegenleder, die in Siebdrucktechnik mit den roten Adern ihrer Hand, die in den Handschuhen stecken könnten, bedruckt sind. Hiermit kehrte sie das Innere, das Verletzliche, nach außen. Der Schutzcharakter des Handschuhs wird inszeniert. Diese Funktion zieht sich ebenfalls durch die Geschichte und ist heute fester Bestandteil von Berufsbekleidungen etwa im medizinisch-hygienischen Bereich. Bei den unterschiedlichsten Sportarten wie Boxen, Cricket oder Golf kommen Handschuhe ebenfalls zum Einsatz.

In Ausstellung und Publikation stellen wir mit über 90 Handschuhen beziehungsweise Handschuhpaaren die vielen Facetten dieses Accessoires vor. Ergänzt werden die eigenen Bestände durch gezielte Leihgaben. Im Rahmen der Ausstellung kooperiert das Deutsche Ledermuseum darüber hinaus erstmals mit dem deutschlandweit einzigen Studiengang für Accessoire Design der Hochschule in Pforzheim. Die ausgewählten Positionen der Studierenden zeigen ein breites Spektrum der Gestaltungsmöglichkeiten auf: von fragilen Gebilden aus Tüll oder Schnüren über Halbfingerhandschuhe verziert mit (Trocken-) Blumen, langen Lederhandschuhen mit Applikationen oder wuchtiger Polsterung bis hin zu einem Handschuh aus dem 3D-Drucker. Wir freuen uns über diese variantenreichen Entwürfe der engagierten Studierenden.

Mit all den Beispielen möchten wir ein oftmals unterschätztes Accessoire wieder in den Mittelpunkt stellen und hoffen, dass auch Sie daran Gefallen finden. Die Auswahl der vorgestellten Handschuhe soll die historische und funktionale Bandbreite darstellen und folgt einer spannungsreichen Anordnung. In 20 Kapiteltexten erläutern wir das Bekleidungsstück in seiner Entwicklung und Fülle. Wir wünschen Ihnen mit der vorliegenden Publikation ebenso anregende wie abwechslungsreiche Einblicke in das **Thema** DER HANDSCHUH: Mehr als ein Mode-Accessoire. Mögen Sie dieses Accessoire für sich (wieder-) entdecken!

Dr. Inez Florschütz
Direktorin des Deutschen Ledermuseums

Some years ago now, fashion designers rediscovered for themselves a rather special accessory: the GLOVE. For a long time, gloves were forgotten as an elegant piece of clothing and served almost exclusively as protection against the cold. Now they are firmly back. At the international fashion shows in Paris, Milan, or New York we see gloves in all colors, shapes, and lengths – and made of every conceivable material. On the catwalks at Gucci, Fendi, Prada, or Valentino we witness the most extraordinary creations in leather, velvet, silk, cashmere, or wool, decorated with feathers, beads, or studs. In summer 2022, specifically the fashion trend of wearing long gloves, so-called opera gloves, with sleeveless dresses or tops was increasingly revived by designers. Behind the renaissance of the glove, which now often appears with opulence and glamour, there may also be an increased desire for hygienic protection, given the Covid-19 pandemic that has been spreading worldwide since early 2020. In the series *AND JUST LIKE THAT*, one of the main characters, Carrie Bradshaw, slips on fancy, glittery gloves when entering an elevator and presses the elevator button, saying it's "a little something I started during the pandemic." Fashion and hygiene protection can definitely go hand in hand, and we're all reaching for the gloves more often again – whatever form they may take.

All these developments have inspired us to take a closer look at the subject of GLOVES. At the beginning of the planning process – as is almost always the case in the preparation of an exhibition project at the Deutsches Ledermuseum – we focused on our own collection and took it as our starting point. We quickly realized that we could present the diversity of this often-underestimated accessory from our museum's small but exquisite holdings. And it was with this in mind that we came up with the title for the exhibition and publication: **THE GLOVE: More than fashion**.

We want to show that the glove has been a useful and fashionable companion for people for many millennia. Back

A big hand for the glove

in ancient times, gloves were in common use mainly for horticulture and field work, or for sports activities. Following its discovery in 1922, the tomb of Tutankhamun, who died in 1323 BCE, was found to contain an astonishing 27 such items. From the 8th century onwards, gloves were increasingly used as a symbol of sovereignty and law by the clergy, but also at court and as part of the feudal system. From the coronation of Emperor Frederick II in 1220 onwards, gloves formed part of the imperial insignia, then in the late Middle Ages the glove became a fashion item for both gentlemen and ladies of the upper classes. A complex etiquette as to when and for what purposes gloves should be worn emerged at the beginning of the modern era, and until the 1960s a lady virtually couldn't leave the house without wearing gloves. The recently deceased Queen Elizabeth II is said to have had 50 pairs – suitable for every outfit and time of day – in her luggage during a three-day visit to Germany. The photos of Audrey Hepburn wearing long gloves in the film *Breakfast at Tiffany's* became legion, as did the black gloves, often decorated with studs, sported by fashion designer Karl Lagerfeld. He was probably aware that almost no part of a person's body betrays age more than the hands, and he probably aimed to distract from that by wearing this accessory – usually in a half-finger version.

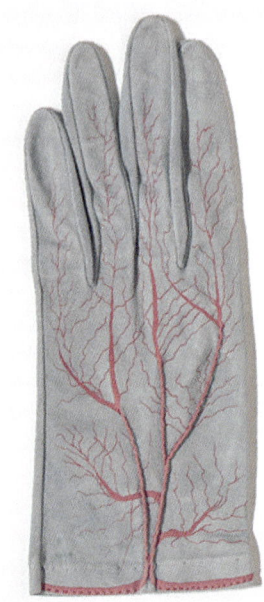
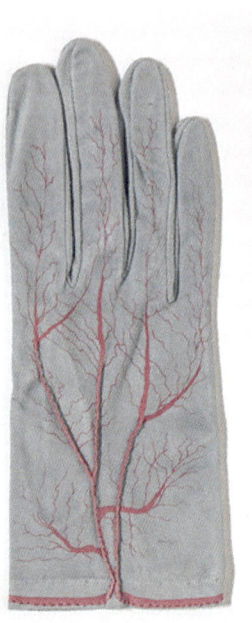

Meret Oppenheim, *Der Handschuh*, 1985, Edition *Parkett* Nr. 4, feines Ziegenwildleder, paspeliert, Siebdruck, Museum of Modern Art, New York
Meret Oppenheim, *The Glove*, 1985, edition for *Parkett* magazine, issue 4, goatskin suede, piped, silkscreen, Museum of Modern Art, New York

Gloves have likewise been a recurring theme in art, appearing several times in different variations in the work of surrealist artist Meret Oppenheim. In 1985, she created pairs of gloves made of goatskin in a limited edition of 150, on which she screen-printed the red veins of her hands as if they were in the gloves. She thus turns the inside, the vulnerable, to the outside, and in this way stages the glove's protective aspect. This function also runs through history and is now an integral part of professional clothing, for example in medicine and hygiene. Gloves are also used in a wide variety of sports, such as boxing, cricket, or golf.

In exhibition and publication we present this accessory's many facets with over 90 gloves or pairs of gloves, while loans from elsewhere round out the items from our own collection. As part of the exhibition, Deutsches Ledermuseum is also collaborating with the Accessory Design course at Pforzheim University, the only one of its kind in Germany. The selected positions of the students show a broad spectrum of design possibilities: from fragile structures made of tulle or cord to half-finger gloves decorated with (dried) flowers, and from long leather gloves with appliqué or bulky padding to a glove made by a 3D printer. We are delighted by the sheer variety of the designs that the dedicated students have created.

With all the examples, we aim to bring an often-underestimated accessory back into focus and hope you find it all as fascinating as we do. The gloves on display have been selected to represent the historical range and the diversity of functions, and are arranged to tell a fascinating story over the course of 20 chapter texts that explain the garment in its development and abundance. We wish you both stimulating and exciting insights into the subject of **THE GLOVE: More than fashion** with this publication. May you (re)discover this accessory for yourself!

Dr. Inez Florschütz
Director of the Deutsches Ledermuseum

HANDSCHUHE, *Manicure Gloves*, **A.W.A.K.E. MODE, Europa, 2021** / Obermaterial: Leder; Futter: Polyester / L: 22 cm, B: 10 cm / Inv.-Nr. 21480; Provenienz: Ankauf von A.W.A.K.E. MODE, London, 2022 GLOVES, *Manicure Gloves*, A.W.A.K.E. MODE, Europe, 2021 / Outer material: leather; lining: polyester / L: 22 cm, W: 10 cm / Inv. no. 21480; provenance: purchased from A.W.A.K.E. MODE, London, 2022

Schuhe für die Hand

Die deutschsprachige Bezeichnung ‚Handschuh' lässt schmunzeln, hat doch der Handschuh mit dem Schuh, der in der Regel eine stabile Umhüllung für den Fuß darstellt, wenig gemein. Im Gegensatz zum Schuh, der auch ohne Fuß darin zumeist in Form bleibt, fällt der Handschuh ohne die Hand, die er umkleiden soll, in sich zusammen.

Das Wort *Hondscio(h)* lässt sich bereits im 8. Jahrhundert im angelsächsischen *Beowulf*-Epos, allerdings als Eigenname eines Kriegers, nachweisen.[1] Für Handbekleidung waren zu dieser Zeit andere Begriffe gebräuchlich. Seit dem 7. Jahrhundert diente der lateinische Ausdruck *manicae* für Handschuhe.[2] Parallel erscheint auch das Wort *wantus*, im Plural *wanti*, in den Quellen. Das Lehnwort stammt aus dem Germanischen und beschrieb ursprünglich Fäustlinge, wurde sodann aber auch für Fingerhandschuhe verwendet.[3] Beide Begriffe waren im frühmittelalterlichen Sprachgebrauch üblich.[4] Bei dem Ausdruck *hantscuoh*, der ebenfalls im 8. und 9. Jahrhundert aufkam, handelte es sich um eine junge Wortbildung, die sich schließlich im Neuhochdeutschen allein durchsetzen sollte.[5]

Die semantische Verwandtschaft zum Wort *scuoh*, das den Schuh als Fußbekleidung meinte, und ursprünglich wahrscheinlich eher Schutzhülle oder Bedeckung bedeutete, wird an dieser Stelle deutlich. Der *hantscuoh* bezeichnete somit die bedeckte Hand analog zum *scuoh* als Fußbedeckung.[6]

‚Handschuhe' für die Füße gibt es im Übrigen auch: Bei Barfußschuhen, auch Zehenschuhe genannt, wird jeder Zeh gesondert umhüllt, wie die Finger bei einem Fingerhandschuh.

---

[1] Ebenso taucht in dieser Schriftquelle das Wort *glôf* für Fausthandschuhe auf, was eventuell mit dem gotischen *lôfa* „flache Hand" zusammenhängt. Es ist heute noch im Englischen *glove* enthalten. Vgl. Loschek 1993, S. 288 f. und Schwineköper 1937, S. 5. Siehe auch für die englische Wortherkunft Collins 1945, S. 52.

[2] Vgl. Schwineköper 1937, S. 15.

[3] Das franz. *gant*, ital. *guanto* sowie span. und port. *gante* gehen auf *wantus* zurück. Vgl. Schwineköper 1937, S. 11. Für Fausthandschuhe wurde hingegen der lat. Begriff *muffula* gebräuchlich. Vgl. Loschek 1993, S. 289. Im Niederländischen bezeichnet *want* nach wie vor den Fausthandschuh. Vgl. Schwineköper 1937, S. 12.

[4] Neben den beiden Wörtern gab es noch weitere Bezeichnungen wie etwa *chirotheca*, die vorerst für liturgische, dann für Fingerhandschuhe im Allgemeinen verwendet wurden. Siehe für eine ausführliche Darstellung der Verwendung der verschiedenen Begriffe Schwineköper 1937, S. 9–16, hier S. 13 f.

[5] Der Ausdruck stammt als Lehnwort aus dem Nordischen und hatte im Alt- und Mittelhochdeutschen verschiedene Nebenwörter. Siehe dazu ebenda, S. 14 f.

[6] Gall leitet den bedeckenden Charakter von dem gemeinsamen Wortstamm von „Schuh" mit Scheune ab. Vgl. Gall 1970, S. 118. Siehe für die Semantik des Worts Schuh als Schutzhülle https://www.duden.de/rechtschreibung/Schuh.

Collins sieht eine Verbindung zu der Übersetzung des Alten Testaments von Levy, bei dem Handbekleidung als Idiom zum deutschen Handschuh, als Schuh für die Hand, übersetzt wurde. Siehe dafür Collins 1945, S. 52.

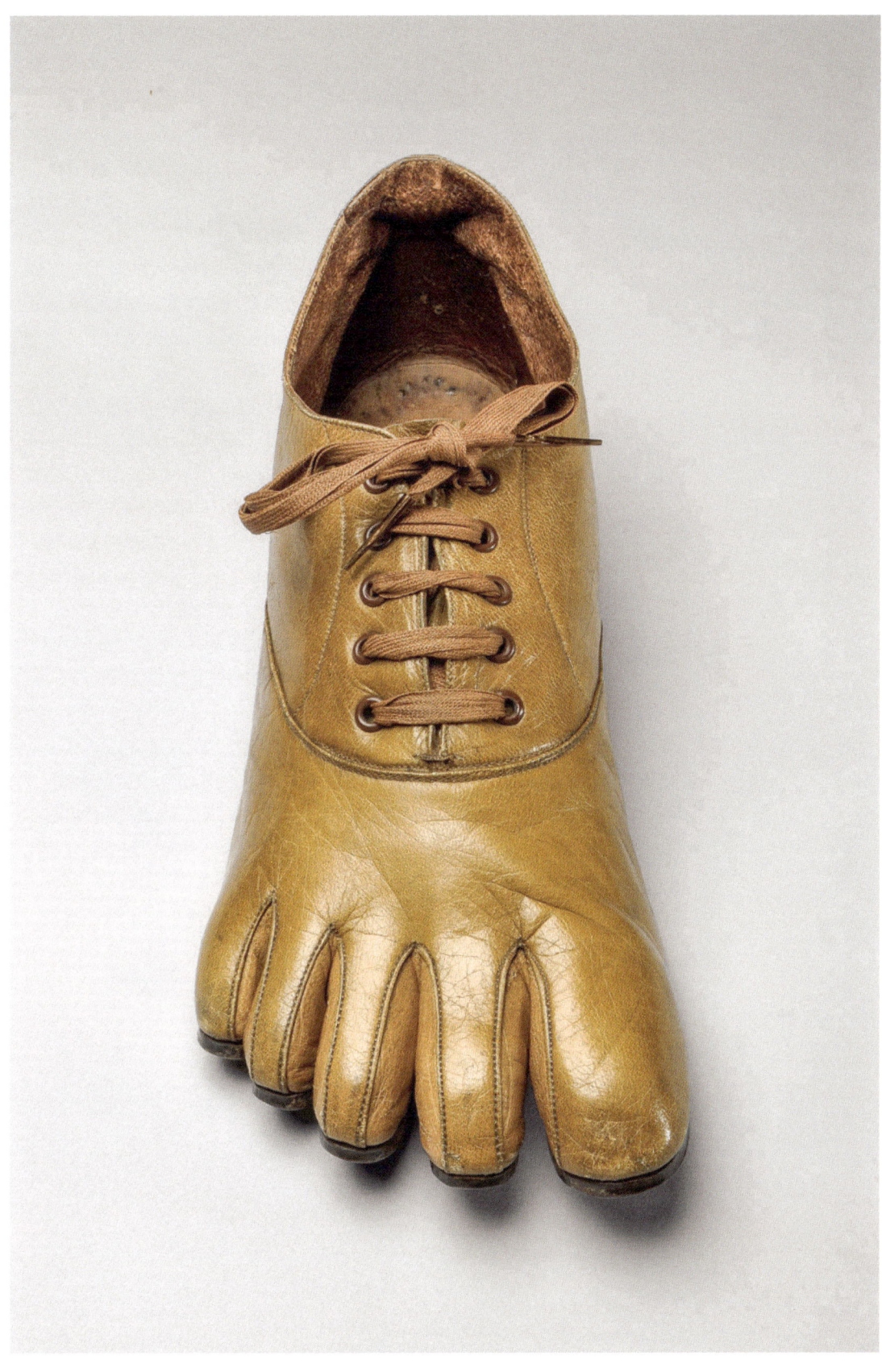

Zehenkammerschuh, Max Mannesmann, 1907, Deutschland, Deutsches Ledermuseum, Dauerleihgabe der Salzgitter AG | Konzernarchiv, Mannesmann-Archiv, Mühlheim an der Ruhr
Five-toe shoes, Max Mannesmann, 1907, Germany, Deutsches Ledermuseum, on permanent loan from Salzgitter AG | corporate archive, Mannesmann Archive, Mühlheim / Ruhr

Shoes for the hands

The German word for glove, "Handschuh", literally meaning a "hand shoe", is rather comical in that gloves have little in common with shoes, which tend to be more solid as coverings for feet. Unlike shoes, which usually keep their shape even without feet inside them, gloves collapse without the hands they are supposed to encase.

The word "Hondscio(h)" can be traced back to the 8th century in the Anglo-Saxon epic poem *Beowulf*, albeit in that case as the name of a warrior.[1] At that time, other terms were in use for hand garments. Since the 7th century, the Latin term *manicae* had been used for gloves.[2] In parallel, the word *wantus*, plural *wanti*, also appears in the sources. The loan word comes from the Germanic and originally described mittens but was then also used for finger gloves.[3] Both terms were common in early medieval usage.[4] The term *hantscuoh*, which also appeared in the 8th and 9th centuries, was a young word formation that would eventually become established in New High German alone.[5]

The semantic relationship to the word *scuoh*, which meant the shoe as footwear and originally probably meant something closer to a protective cover or covering, becomes clear at this point. The *hantscuoh* thus referred to the covered hand, similar to the *scuoh* as a foot covering.[6]

Incidentally, there are also "gloves" for the feet: In barefoot shoes, also called toe shoes, each toe is wrapped separately, like the fingers in a finger glove.

---

[1] The word *glôf* for mittens likewise appears in this scriptural source, possibly related to the Gothic *lôfa* "flat hand". It is still contained today in the English *glove*. Cf. Loschek 1993, p. 288 f., and Schwineköper 1937, p. 5. For the English word origin, see also Collins 1945, p. 52.

[2] Cf. Schwineköper 1937, p. 15.

[3] The French *gant*, Italian *guanto*, and the Spanish and Portuguese *gante* go back to *wantus*. Cf. Schwineköper 1937, p. 11. For mittens, however, the Latin term *muffula* became common. Cf. Loschek 1993, p. 289. In Dutch, *want* still denotes the mitten. Cf. Schwineköper 1937, p. 12.

[4] In addition to the two words, there were other terms such as *chirotheca*, which were first used for liturgical, then for finger gloves in general. For a detailed account of the use of the various terms, see Schwineköper 1937, pp. 9–16, here p. 13 f.

[5] The expression originates as a loan word from the Norse and had various secondary words in Old and Middle High German. See ibid., p. 14 f.

[6] Gall derives the covering element from the common root of the German words "Schuh" (shoe) and "Scheune" (barn). Cf. Gall 1970, p. 118. For the semantics of the word "Schuh" as a protective cover, see https://www.duden.de/rechtschreibung/Schuh. Collins sees a connection to Levy's translation of the Old Testament, in which the covering for a hand was translated as an idiom to the German "Handschuh", a shoe for the hand. For this, see Collins 1945, p. 52.

Bunt gestreifte Zehensocken
Colorfully striped toe socks

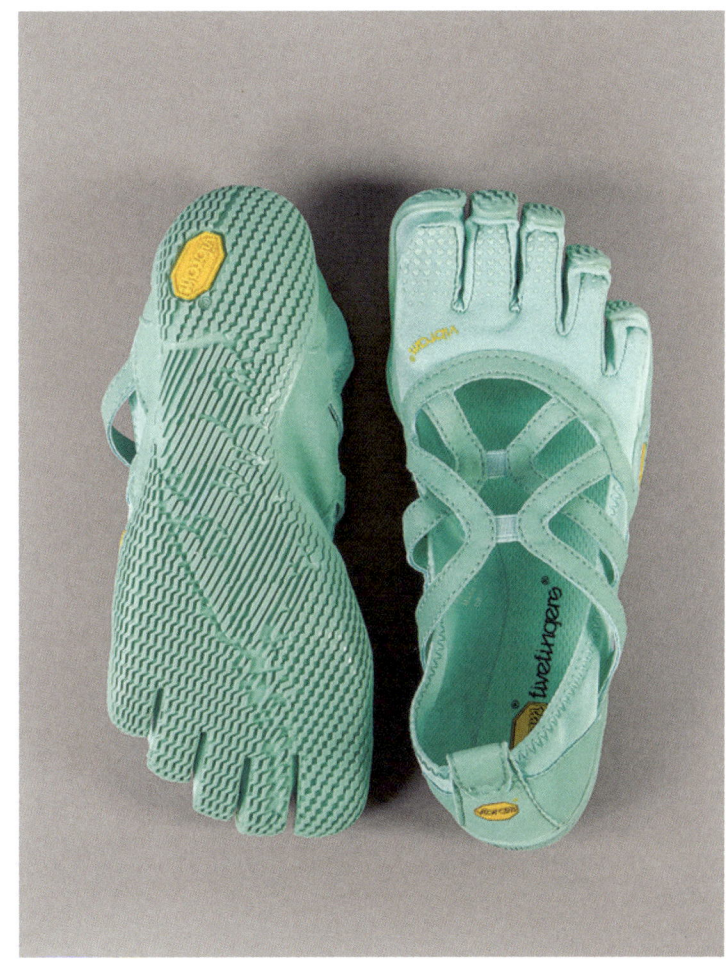

Barfußschuhe, ALITZA LOOP, FiveFingers, VIBRAM, 2019, München, Deutsches Ledermuseum
Barefoot shoes, ALITZA LOOP, FiveFingers, VIBRAM, 2019, Munich, Deutsches Ledermuseum

HALBFINGERHANDSCHUH, VEB Erzgebirgische Lederhandschuhwerke Johanngeorgenstadt, Erzgebirge, DDR, 1980/90/Lammleder, perforiert, Metall, Kunststoff/L: 16 cm, B: 11 cm/Inv.-Nr. 15416; Provenienz: Schenkung Erzgebirgische Lederhandschuhe GmbH, Johanngeorgenstadt, 1991 HALF-FINGER GLOVE, VEB Erzgebirgische Lederhandschuhwerke Johanngeorgenstadt, Erzgebirge, East Germany, 1980/90/Lambskin, perforated, metal, plastic/L: 16 cm, W: 11 cm/Inv. no. 15416; provenance: donated by Erzgebirgische Lederhandschuhe GmbH, Johanngeorgenstadt, 1991

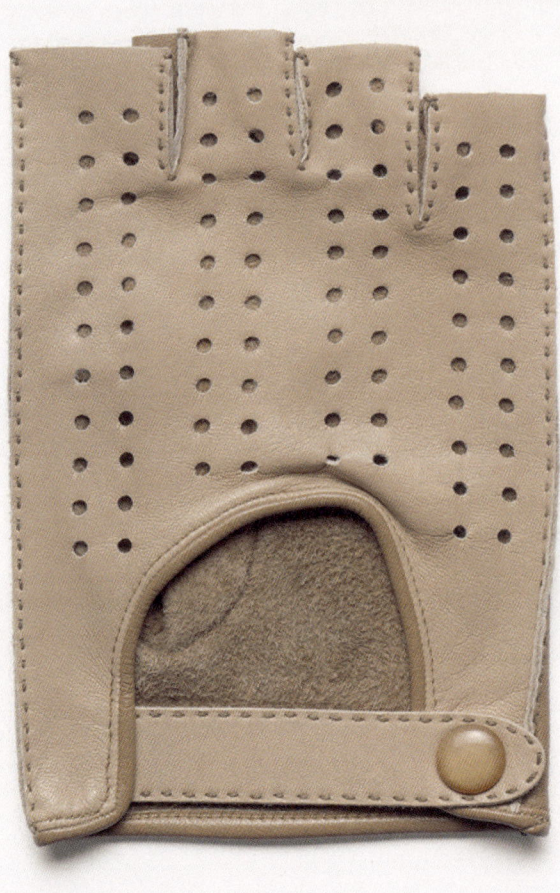

FAUSTHANDSCHUHE, Nachbildung der *Bernie Mittens*, Ulrike Janssen nach Jen Ellis, Offenbach am Main, 2022/Oberhand: Wolle; Innenhand: Fleece; Strickbündchen/L: 28 cm, B: 18,5 cm/Inv.-Nr. 21488; Provenienz: Ankauf von Ulrike Janssen, Offenbach am Main, 2022 MITTENS, replica of *Bernie Mittens*, Ulrike Janssen after Jen Ellis, Offenbach/Main, 2022/Back: wool; palm: fleece; knitted cuff/L: 28 cm, W: 18.5 cm/Inv. no. 21488; provenance: purchased from Ulrike Janssen, Offenbach/Main, 2022

ABENDHANDSCHUHE, Deutschland, 1950/60 / Glacéleder, Metall / L: 58 cm, B: 15 cm / Inv.-Nr. 21476; Provenienz: Schenkung von Marion Postlep, 2017 EVENING GLOVES, Germany, 1950/60 / Glacé leather, metal / L: 58 cm, W: 15 cm / Inv. no. 21476; provenance: donated by Marion Postlep, 2017

REITHANDSCHUH, Mexiko, vor 1924 / Leder, Applikationen / L: 32 cm, B: 15,5 cm / Inv.-Nr. 3159; Provenienz: Ankauf von Julius Konietzko, Hamburg, 1924 RIDING GLOVE, Mexico, before 1924 / Leather, appliqués / L: 32 cm, W: 15.5 cm / Inv. no. 3159; provenance: purchased from Julius Konietzko, Hamburg, 1924

HALBHANDSCHUHE, Deutschland, 19. Jh. / Baumwollgarn, eingestrickte Glasperlen / L: 16,5 cm, B: 12 cm / Inv.-Nr. 7766; Provenienz: Ankauf von Martha Günther, München, 1940 HALF GLOVES, Germany, 19th c. / Cotton yarn, knitted-in glass beads / L: 16.5 cm, W: 12 cm / Inv. no. 7766; provenance: purchased from Martha Günther, Munich, 1940

Handschuhtypen

Bei der Handbekleidung werden zwei Grundformen[1] unterschieden, denen im Laufe der Zeit auch verschiedene Bedeutungen zukamen. Während der Fingerhandschuh bereits im Alten Ägypten ein Luxusgut und Statussymbol darstellte – die ältesten überlieferten Handschuhe sind die Leinenfingerhandschuhe von Pharao Tutanchamun[2] –, stand beim Fausthandschuh stets der praktische Nutzen im Vordergrund. Letzterer leitete sich von der Urform des Handschuhs, einer Art Säckchen mit keiner oder nur für den Daumen vorgesehenen Unterteilung ab.[3] Der Fausthandschuh, auch Fäustling genannt, diente vor allem als Schutz gegen Kälte und bereits in antiken Kulturen bei schwerer körperlicher Arbeit vor Verletzungen.[4] Da er in seiner Machart einfacher und somit auch kostengünstiger in der Fertigung als ein Fingerhandschuh war, wurde er vor allem von Kindern und Angehörigen der niederen Stände getragen. Im europäischen Mittelalter war Bäuerinnen und Bauern nur das Tragen von Faust- und zweifingrigen Handschuhen erlaubt.[5]

Einen weiteren Handschuhtypus bildet der fingerlose Halbhandschuh, der im 15. Jahrhundert aufkam und sich in der Folgezeit in der höfischen, sodann auch in der bürgerlichen Damengarderobe großer Beliebtheit erfreute. Die zumeist auf dem Handrücken spitz zulaufenden Handschuhe bedeckten zwar die Unterarme ähnlich eines Pulswärmers, waren aber primär als dekorative Zierde, die aufgrund ihres Schnitts die Hände schmaler wirken ließen, gedacht.[6] Im 18. und 19. Jahrhundert erlebten die in Frankreich auch *Mitaines* genannten Handschuhe eine Hochphase und wurden sowohl in der Öffentlichkeit als auch im privaten Bereich getragen.[7] Heutzutage feiern sie ein Comeback und lenken als modisches Statement die Aufmerksamkeit auf die Hände ihrer Träger*innen und vor allem auf sich selbst.[8]

---

[1] Es wird zwischen dem Fingerhandschuh, bei dem jeder Finger umhüllt ist, und dem Fausthandschuh, bei dem eine Hülle die vier Finger und ein separates Abteil den Daumen umfasst, unterschieden. Auf den Fingerhandschuh soll hier nicht weiter eingegangen werden, da sich die weiteren Texte dieser Publikation überwiegend mit ihm befassen.

[2] Siehe dazu Redwood 2016, S. 7 und Green 2021, S. 18.

[3] Siehe etwa Kment 1890, S. 7. Fellumwicklungen, die vor Witterung und Verletzungen schützten, werden bereits in der steinzeitlichen Epoche vermutet. Vgl. Loschek 1993, S. 83.

[4] Der Fausthandschuh speichert im Vergleich zum Fingerhandschuh effizienter die Körperwärme, indem er die einzelnen Finger nicht voneinander getrennt umhüllt und den Fingern mehr Raum lässt, die so mehr Wärme abstrahlen können. Auch die Verwendung von Materialien wie Felle und Wolle bietet eine bessere Isolierung als die häufig aus Leder oder Seide gefertigten Fingerhandschuhe.

[5] Siehe auch Loschek 1993, S. 83 und Boehn 1928, S. 78. Kleiderordnungen, die sowohl Materialien als auch Schnitte für die jeweiligen Stände bestimmten, spiegelten die streng hierarchische Gesellschaftsstruktur wider.

[6] Die Länge der Handschuhe orientierte sich an der Ärmellänge der Kleider der jeweiligen Mode; gemein war ihnen, dass so wenig Haut wie möglich gezeigt werden sollte. Siehe für unterschiedliche modische Ausführungen von Halbhandschuhen etwa Cumming 1982, S. 46–50.

[7] Das Repertoire an Materialien umfasste Seide, Samt, Spitze sowie Glacéleder. Im 19. Jh. wurden Halbhandschuhe darüber hinaus auch selbst nach Vorlagen aus Frauenmagazinen gehäkelt oder gestrickt und mit kleinen bunten Glasperlen bestickt. Die Halbhandschuhe wurden im Häuslichen getragen und auch beim Speisen nicht ausgezogen. Siehe dazu Gall 1970, S. 124.

[8] Im 20. Jh. erhielten fingerlose Handschuhe vor allem durch die populären Modelle zum Autofahren oder Golfen ein sportliches Image. Heute tauchen sie prominent in Szene gesetzt als Modeaccessoire in Serien wie *Emily in Paris* (Netflix, 2022) auf.

Dame und Herr im Gespräch, beide tragen Handschuhe, *Journal des Dames et des Modes*, Costumes Parisiens, 1832
Lady and gentleman in conversation, both wearing gloves, *Journal des Dames et des Modes*, Costumes Parisiens, 1832

Alexander Roslin, *Die Dame mit dem Schleier*, **1768, Öl auf Leinwand, Schwedisches Nationalmuseum, Stockholm**
Alexander Roslin, *The Lady with the Veil*, 1768, oil on canvas, Nationalmuseum of Sweden, Stockholm

Lawrence Oates, Birdie Bowers, Robert Falcon Scott, Edward Adrian Wilson und Edgar Evans am Südpol, Antarktis, 1912, National Portrait Gallery, London
Lawrence Oates, Birdie Bowers, Robert Falcon Scott, Edward Adrian Wilson and Edgar Evans at the South Pole, Antarctica, 1912, National Portrait Gallery, London

Glove types

Where hand apparel is concerned, a distinction is made between two basic forms[1], which have also acquired various significances over the course of time. While finger gloves were already a luxury item and a status symbol as far back as in Ancient Egypt – the oldest surviving gloves are the linen finger gloves of Pharoah Tutankhamun[2] – in the case of mittens, practical use was always the main focus. The latter developed from the original form of a glove as a kind of small bag with no subdivision, or solely one for the thumb.[3] Mittens served primarily as protection against the cold and, even back in ancient times, also guarded against injury during hard physical labor.[4] Since they were simpler and thus less expensive to manufacture than finger gloves, they were worn primarily by children and members of the lower classes. In the European Middle Ages, peasants were only allowed to wear mittens and two-fingered gloves.[5]

Another type of glove is the fingerless half-glove, which appeared in the 15th century and subsequently enjoyed great popularity in the courtly, and then also in the bourgeois women's wardrobe. The gloves, which usually tapered to a point on the back of the hand, covered the forearms in a similar way to a wrist warmer, but were primarily intended as decorative ornaments with a cut that made hands appear more slender.[6] In the 18th and 19th centuries, such gloves, which were also known as *mitaines* in France, experienced a heyday and were worn both in public and in private.[7] Nowadays, they are making a comeback as a fashion statement, drawing attention to the hands of their wearers and, above all, to themselves.[8]

---

[1] A distinction is made between the finger glove, in which each finger is enclosed, and the mitten, in which there is one section enclosing the four fingers and another enclosing the thumb. The finger glove will not be discussed further here, as it features largely in the other texts in this publication.

[2] See Redwood 2016, p. 7, and Green 2021, p. 18.

[3] See, for example, Kment 1890, p. 7. Fur wrappings, which protected against weather and injuries, are assumed to have existed as early as the Stone Age. Cf. Loschek 1993, p. 83.

[4] Compared to the finger glove, the mitten is more efficient in retaining body heat, since it does not enclose the individual fingers separately and therefore leaves more space for the fingers to radiate more heat. Also, the use of materials such as skins and wool provides better insulation than the leather or silk often used for finger gloves.

[5] See also Loschek 1993, p. 83, and Boehn 1928, p. 78. Dress codes that determined both materials and cuts for the respective classes reflected the strictly hierarchical social structure.

[6] The length of the gloves was based on the sleeve length of the dresses of the respective fashion; what they had in common was that as little skin as possible was to be shown. For various fashionable half-glove designs, see for example Cumming 1982, pp. 46–50.

[7] The repertoire of materials included silk, velvet, lace, and glacé leather. In the 19th century, women also knitted or crocheted the half-gloves themselves according to patterns from women's magazines and embroidered them with small colorful glass beads. The half-gloves were worn in the domestic sphere and were not removed even at the dinner table. See Gall 1970, p. 124.

[8] In the 20th century, fingerless gloves gained a sporty image, especially through the popular models for driving or golfing. Today, they appear prominently as fashion accessories in series such as *Emily in Paris* (Netflix, 2022).

Handschuh des Pharao Tutanchamun, um 1330 v. Chr., Ägyptisches Museum, Kairo
Glove of Pharaoh Tutankhamun, approx. 1330 BCE, Egyptian Museum, Cairo

August Beckert, *Kinder beim Skifahren*, 1920/30, Bayerische Staatsbibliothek, München
August Beckert, *Children skiing*, 1920/30, Bayerische Staatsbibliothek, Munich

Lily Collins in ihrer Rolle als Emily in *Emily in Paris* mit Halbfingerhandschuhen, Netflix, USA, 2021
Lily Collins in her role as Emily in *Emily in Paris* with fingerless half-gloves, Netflix, USA, 2021

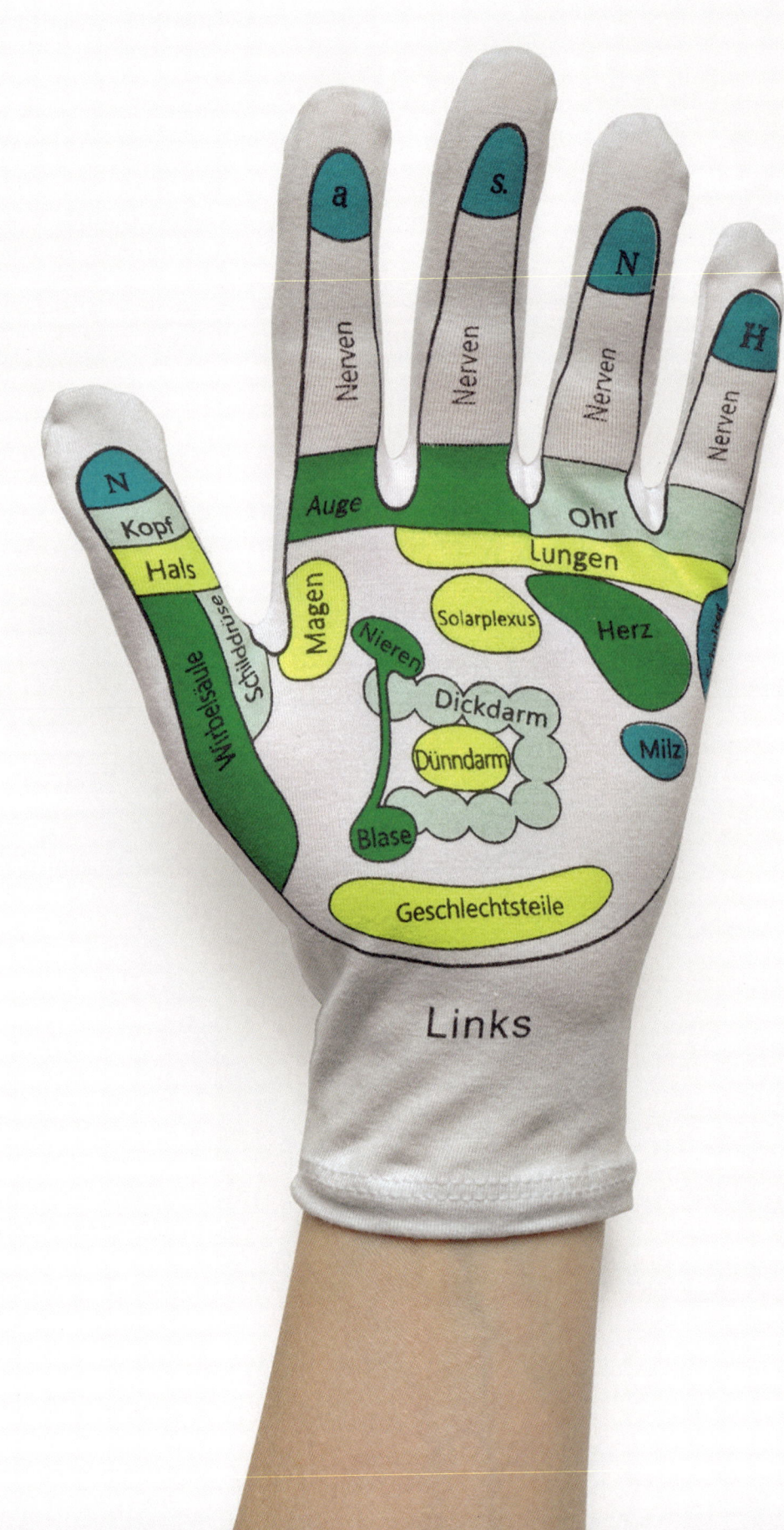

HANDSCHUHE MIT REFLEXZONEN, TrendShed GmbH, o. O., 2021/22 / Textil, bedruckt / L: 20,5 cm, B: 11,5 cm / o. Nr. **REFLEXOLOGY GLOVES**, TrendShed GmbH, place unknown, 2021/22 / Textile, printed / L: 20.5 cm, W: 11.5 cm / No number

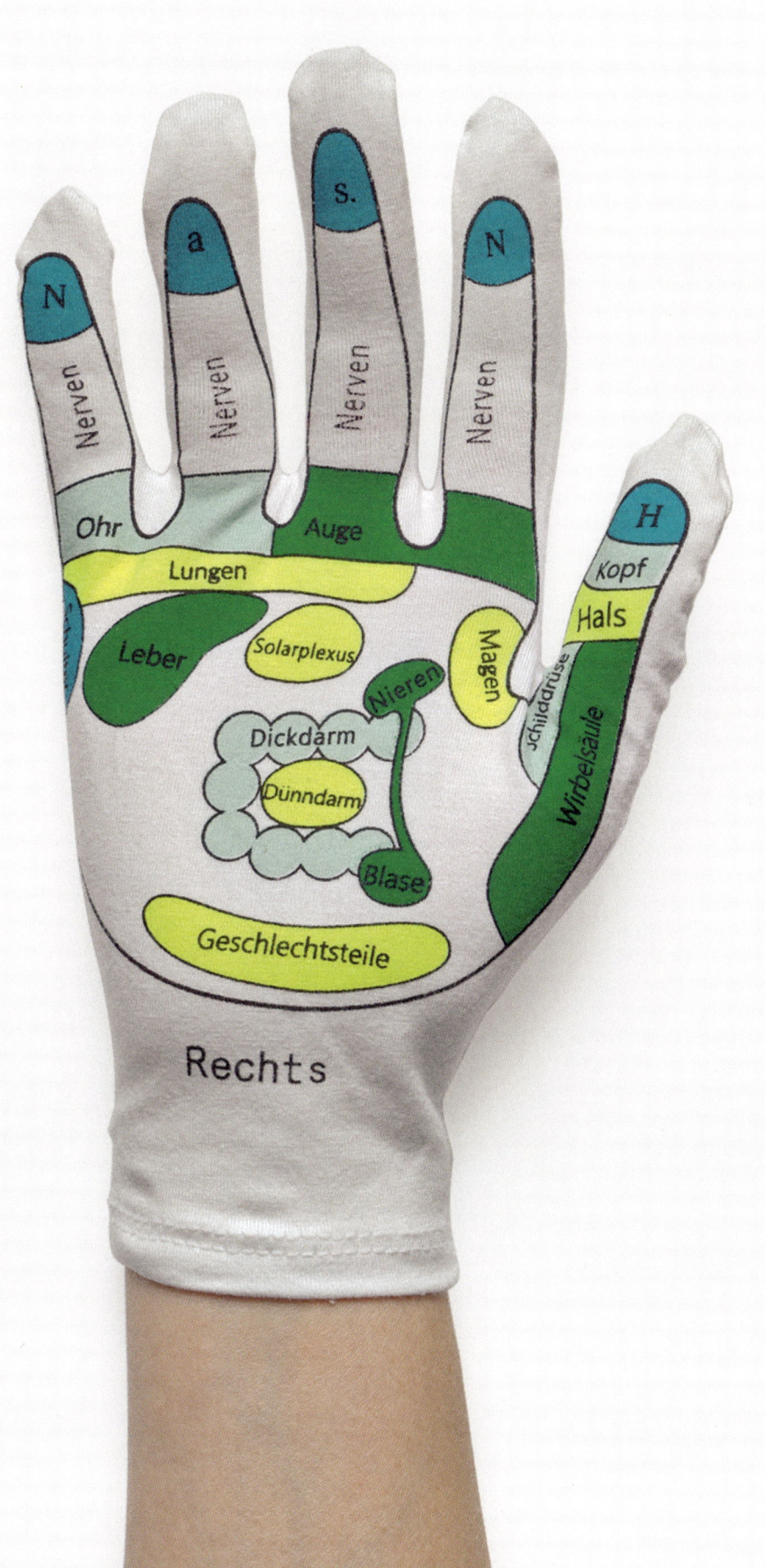

HANDSCHUH, VEB Erzgebirgische Lederhandschuhwerke Johanngeorgenstadt, Erzgebirge, DDR, 1980/90 / Lammleder, perforiert / L: 25 cm, B: 11 cm / Inv.-Nr. 15420; Provenienz: Schenkung Erzgebirgische Lederhandschuhe GmbH, Johanngeorgenstadt, 1991 GLOVE, VEB Erzgebirgische Lederhandschuhwerke Johanngeorgenstadt, Erzgebirge, East Germany, 1980/90 / Lambskin, perforated / L: 25 cm, W: 11 cm / Inv. no. 15420; provenance: donated by Erzgebirgische Lederhandschuhe GmbH, Johanngeorgenstadt, 1991

PONTIFIKALHANDSCHUHE, Rom, Italien, vmtl. 18. Jh./Seidengarn, gestrickt, Metallstickerei, Pailletten/L: 28,5 cm, B: 14,5 cm/Inv.-Nr. 8835; Provenienz: Ankauf bei der Galleria Sangiorgi, Rom, 1942
PONTIFICAL GLOVES, Rome, Italy, probably 18th c./Silk yarn, knitted, metal embroidery, sequins/L: 28.5 cm, W: 14.5 cm/Inv. no. 8835; provenance: purchased from Galleria Sangiorgi, Rome, 1942

Klerikale Handschuhe

Im mittelalterlichen Europa avancierte der Handschuh zum Amtszeichen geistlicher Würdenträger.[1] Bereits zuvor trugen Mitglieder des Klerus Handschuhe etwa als schützende Kleidungsstücke bei der Arbeit oder gegen die Witterung, bei liturgischen Handlungen sowie als luxuriöse, schmückende Garderobe.[2] Die Verwendung bei Gottesdiensten geht auf den altertümlichen *Ritus der verhüllten Hände* zurück, bei dem göttliche oder geweihte Gegenstände nur mit verhüllten, reinen Händen berührt werden durften.[3] Mit dem Mainzer *Ordo Romano-Germanicum* von St. Alban 960 n. Chr. änderte sich der Gebrauch des klerikalen Handschuhs insoweit grundlegend, als er in diesem offiziell zur Insigne des bischöflichen Ornats bestimmt wurde.[4] Fortan war es nur noch Bischöfen, Kardinälen und dem Papst vorbehalten, Fingerhandschuhe vor allem bei der heiligen Messe als Zeichen der Reinheit und des göttlichen Segens zu tragen.[5] Ausnahmen galten vereinzelt für Äbte, die beim Papst Privilegien und eine Sondererlaubnis erwirkten.[6]

Die Pontifikalhandschuhe waren in der Regel aus Seide gestrickt und gewirkt sowie zumeist mit einer Stulpe versehen. Aufwendige Gold- oder Silberstickereien zierten die Handrücken mit christlichen Motiven wie Lamm, Kreuz oder segnenden Händen. Ebenso gebräuchlich war das in einer Glorie aus kleinen Metallplättchen gefasste Monogramm IHS als Abkürzung für den Namen Jesus.[7] Farblich orientierten sich die Handschuhe in der Neuzeit an den liturgischen Gewändern der unterschiedlichen Festtage und Zeremonien; zuvor waren vor allem violett-, weiß- und rotfarbene Modelle sehr beliebt. Der Bischofsring, ebenfalls würdevolles Attribut und Standeszeichen, wurde über dem Handschuh getragen.

---

[1] Abgeleitet aus den religiösen Kulten altertümlicher Kulturen stellte der Handschuh zunächst ein Machtattribut der kirchlichen Elite dar, bevor er auch zum Status- und Machtsymbol der weltlichen Herrscher*innen wurde. Siehe hierzu S. 40 dieser Publikation.

[2] Schwineköper legt dar, dass innerhalb des Stands des Klerus teilweise geschlechtsspezifisch unterschieden wurde, wer Handschuhe tragen durfte. So war es Mönchen erlaubt, Nonnen nicht immer. Vgl. Schwineköper 1937, S. 22.

[3] Zugleich schützten sich die Berührenden auch vor den magischen Kräften der heiligen Gegenstände. Siehe dazu etwa Loschek 1993, S. 79.

[4] Im Ordo war auch festgehalten, wie die Handschuhe dem Bischof bei seiner Weihe unter Sprechen eines bestimmten Gebets zu übergeben waren. Nachdem das Werk von Mainz nach Rom gelangte, wurde der Handschuh als allgemeinverbindliche Pontifikalinsigne vorgegeben. Siehe dazu Schwineköper 1937, S. 29 f.

[5] Abweichungen bildeten Messen am Karfreitag sowie Totenmessen. Diese wurden mit bloßen Händen abgehalten. Siehe dazu Latour 1947 I, S. 2610.

[6] Wie bedeutend das Privileg war, Handschuhe tragen zu dürfen, verdeutlicht der Umstand, dass päpstliche Urkunden mit Sondergenehmigungen für Äbte häufig gefälscht wurden. Siehe dazu Schwineköper 1937, S. 36 und Gall 1970, S. 120.

[7] Im Mittelalter war die Abkürzung IHS für den Namen Jesus gebräuchlich. Die drei griechischen Buschstaben Iota (I), Eta (H) und Sigma (Σ) bilden die Kurzform des Namens Jesus (griech. IHΣOYΣ); IHS ist die Übertragung in das lateinische Alphabet. Ebenso wurde das Kürzel besonders ab dem 16. Jh. von der Ordensgemeinschaft der Jesuiten mit der Bedeutung „Iesum Habemus Socium" – „Wir haben Jesus als Gefährten" häufig verwendet.

Michael Pacher, Detail des Hl. Wolfgangs am Hochaltar in der Wallfahrts- und Pfarrkirche St. Wolfgang, 1471–1481, Holz, Österreich
Michael Pacher, detail of St. Wolfgang on the high altar in the St. Wolfgang pilgrimage and parish church, 1471–1481, wood, Austria

IHS-Monogramm in einem Strahlenkranz, Detail eines Pontifikalhandschuhs, vmtl. 18. Jh., Deutsches Ledermuseum
IHS monogram in a sunburst, detail of a Pontifical glove, probably 18th c., Deutsches Ledermuseum

Antonio Pisanello, *Papst Martin V.*, 15. Jh., Galeria Colonna, Rom
Antonio Pisanello, *Pope Martin V*, 15th c., Galeria Colonna, Rome

Clerical gloves

In medieval Europe, gloves became the official symbol of clerical dignitaries.[1] Even before that, members of the clergy wore gloves as protective garments at work, for example, or against the weather, during liturgical acts, and as luxurious, decorative clothing.[2] Their use in religious services goes back to the ancient *rite of veiled hands*, in which divine or consecrated objects could only be touched with covered, clean hands.[3] With the Mainz *Ordo Romano-Germanicum* of St. Alban in 960 C.E., the use of clerical gloves changed fundamentally insofar as they were officially designated the insignia of the episcopal regalia.[4] From then on, only bishops, cardinals, and the Pope were allowed to wear finger gloves, especially during holy mass, as a sign of purity and divine blessing.[5] Exceptions were made occasionally for abbots who obtained privileges and special permission from the Pope.[6]

The pontifical gloves were usually woven and knitted from silk and usually had a cuff. Elaborate gold or silver embroidery decorated the backs of the hands with Christian motifs such as the lamb, the cross, or blessing hands. Equally common was the monogram IHS set in a highlight of small metal plates as an abbreviation for the name Jesus.[7] In terms of color, the gloves took their cue from the liturgical vestments of the various feast days and ceremonies in modern times, while previously purple, white, and red-colored models were the most popular. The bishop's ring, also a stately attribute and sign of status, was worn over the glove.

---

[1] Derived from the religious cults of ancient cultures, gloves initially represented an attribute of power for the ecclesiastical elite, before they also became a symbol of status and power for secular rulers. See p. 42 of this publication.

[2] Schwineköper explains that within the status of the clergy, gender-specific distinctions were sometimes made as to who was allowed to wear gloves. Thus, monks were allowed to wear gloves, but nuns were not always. Cf. Schwineköper 1937, p. 22.

[3] At the same time, wearers also protected themselves from the magical powers of the sacred objects they touched. See, for example, Loschek 1993, p. 79.

[4] The Ordo also specified how the gloves were to be presented to the bishop at his consecration during the citation of a specific prayer. After the work reached Rome from Mainz, the glove was prescribed as a generally binding pontifical insignia. On this, see Schwineköper 1937, p. 29 f.

[5] Deviations were masses on Good Friday and masses for the dead. These were held with bare hands. See Latour 1947 I, p. 2610.

[6] The importance of the privilege of wearing gloves is illustrated by the fact that papal documents with special permissions for abbots were often counterfeited. See Schwineköper 1937, p. 36, and Gall 1970, p. 120.

[7] In the Middle Ages, the abbreviation IHS was common for the name Jesus. The three Greek letters Iota (I), Eta (H), and Sigma (Σ) form the short form of the name Jesus (Greek IHΣOYΣ); IHS is the translation into the Latin alphabet. Likewise, the abbreviation was frequently used, especially from the 16th century, by the Jesuit religious order with the meaning "Iesum Habemus Socium" – "We have Jesus as a companion".

Simone di Giovanni Ghini, Grabplatte Papst Martin V., nach einem Entwurf von Donatello, 1435, Bronze, Erzbasilika San Giovanni in Laterano, Rom
Simone di Giovanni Ghini, tombstone of Pope Martin V, after a design by Donatello, 1435, bronze, Archbasilica of San Giovanni in Laterano, Rome

Portrait von Papst Pius VI., **18. Jh., Öl auf Leinwand, Château de Versailles, Frankreich**
Portrait of Pope Pius VI, 18th c., oil on canvas, Château de Versailles, France

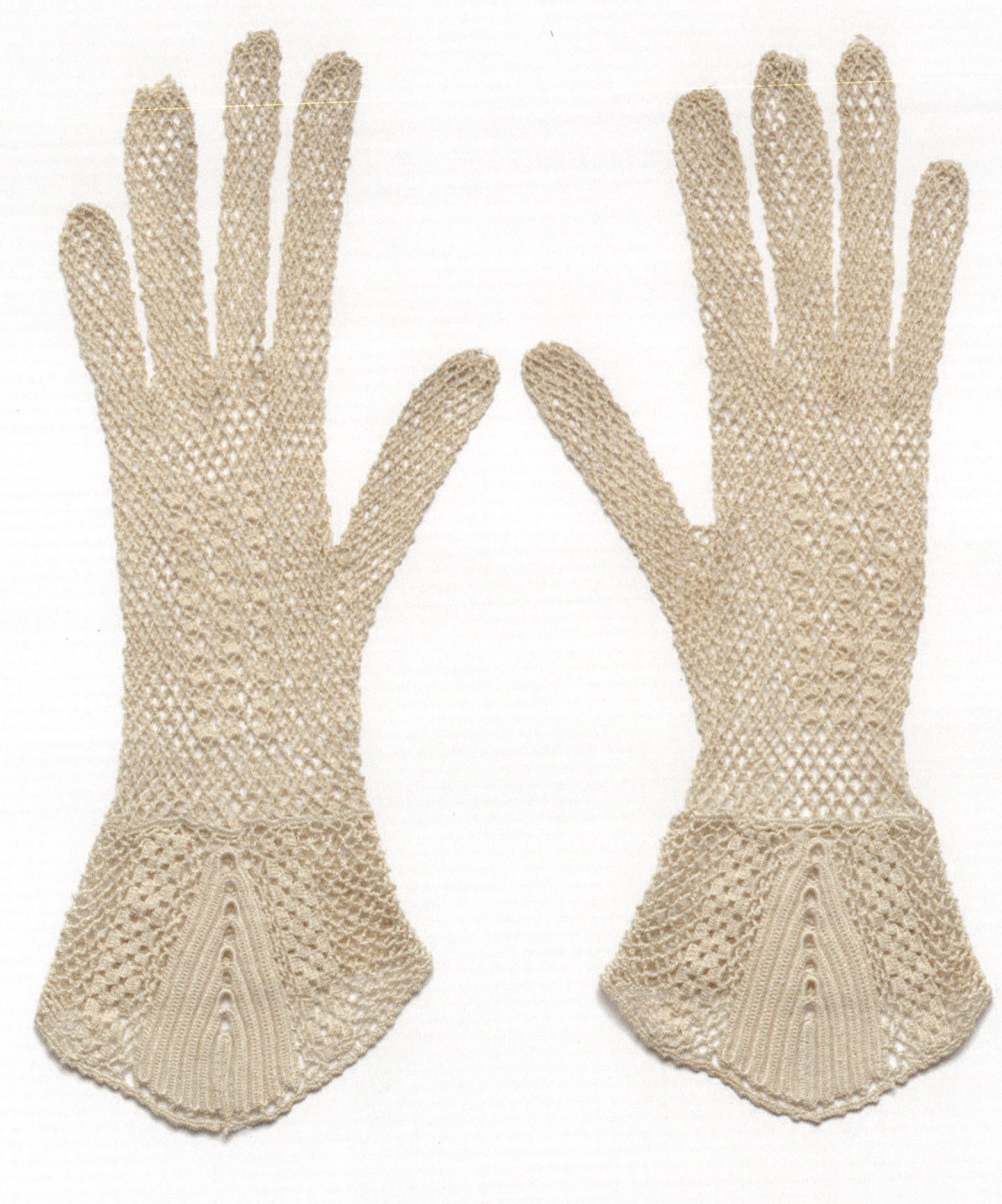

HANDSCHUHE, Deutschland, 1. Hälfte 20. Jh./Garn, gehäkelt/L: 26 cm, B: 10 cm/Inv.-Nr. 21481; Provenienz: Schenkung von Martina Gillich, Bad Emstal, 2022 GLOVES, Germany, first half of 20th c./Yarn, crocheted/L: 26 cm, W: 10 cm/Inv. no. 21481; provenance: donated by Martina Gillich, Bad Emstal, 2022

FAUSTHANDSCHUHE, *Eagle Gloves*, Issey Miyake Inc., Japan, 2018/Obermaterial: Wollmischung, plissiert, Wollflor, Schafleder; Futter: Webpelz, wattiert/L: 32 cm, B: 17 cm, T: 7 cm/Inv.-Nr. 21459; Provenienz: Ankauf von Vestiaire Collective, Paris, 2020 MITTENS, *Eagle Gloves*, Issey Miyake Inc., Japan, 2018/Outer material: wool blend, pleated, wool pile, sheepskin; lining: woven fur, padded/L: 32 cm, W: 17 cm, D: 7 cm/Inv. no. 21459; provenance: purchased from Vestiaire Collective, Paris, 2020

HAUSHALTSHANDSCHUH, Asien, 2022 / Latex / L: 30,5 cm, B: 11,5 cm / o. Nr. HOUSEHOLD GLOVE, Asia, 2020/21 / Latex / L: 30.5 cm, W: 11.5 cm / No number

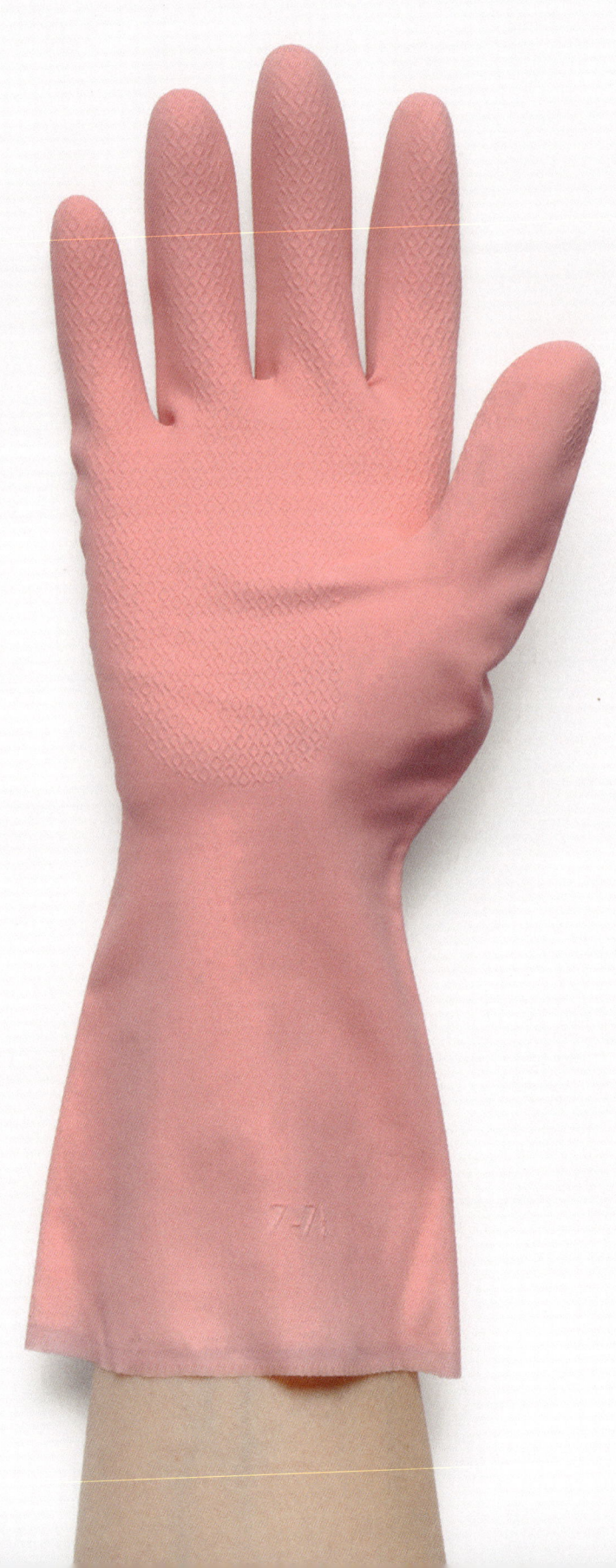

HANDSCHUHE, Europa, 17./18. Jh./Leder, Goldstickerei, Pailletten, Textilapplikationen/L: 32 cm, B: 16 cm/Inv.-Nr. 9114; Provenienz: Ankauf von Erich Junkelmann, München, 1943 GLOVES, Europe, 17th/18th c./Leather, gold embroidery, sequins, textile applications/L: 32 cm, W: 16 cm/Inv. no. 9114; provenance: purchased from Erich Junkelmann, Munich, 1943

Königliche Handschuhe

Als Kleidungsstück, das Autorität und Wohlstand verkörperte, gehörten Handschuhe nicht nur zu den klerikalen Amtszeichen, sondern auch zur Garderobe der weltlichen Herrschenden. Bereits die Karolinger- und Salierkönige trugen sie als statusträchtiges Standeszeichen und Symbol ihrer Macht.[2] Seit der Krönung von Friedrich II. zum römisch-deutschen Kaiser des Heiligen Römischen Reichs 1220 waren fortan die prunkvollen, mit Edelsteinen besetzten Handschuhe auch Bestandteil des Krönungsornats und der Kaiserinsignien.[2]

Im Mittelalter kam dem königlichen Handschuh darüber hinaus eine sinnbildliche Stellvertreterfunktion zu. Er fungierte als Rechtszeichen und symbolisierte die königliche Hand und damit des Königs Zustimmung beziehungsweise seinen Schutz. So ist etwa aus dem *Sachsenspiegel*[3] bekannt, dass das Marktrecht einer Stadt durch den am Marktkreuz aufgehängten rechten Königshandschuh angezeigt wurde und Rechtsgültigkeit erhielt.[4]

Als prestigeträchtiges Würde- und Amtszeichen war das Accessoire in der höfisch-ritterlichen Kultur vorerst nur den Männern vorbehalten. Ab der Jahrtausendwende auch zum festen Bestandteil der Damenmode geworden,[5] avancierten Handschuhe im 14. Jahrhundert zum kostbaren Luxusgut der höheren Stände und zierten bis ins 18. Jahrhundert die adeligen Hände.[6]

Auch wenn die Modelle heute deutlich schlichter gehalten sind als die ihrer Vorgänger, werden Handschuhe von Mitgliedern der Königshäuser bei öffentlichen Auftritten weiterhin getragen. Die Garderobe von Königin Elisabeth II. von England wurde immer von einem Hut und Handschuhen komplementiert.

---

[1] Auch bei anderen europäischen Königsgeschlechtern nahm der Handschuh als Herrschaftssymbol sowie während des Krönungszeremoniell eine bedeutende Rolle ein. Siehe Latour 1947 I, S. 2610 und Green 2021, S. 25 ff.

[2] Vgl. Loschek 1993, S. 80. Die Handschuhe befinden sich heute mit den anderen Reichskleinodien in der Sammlung der Wiener Schatzkammer. Bereits vor dem 13. Jh. waren Handschuhe schon Insigne und Bestandteil des offiziellen Gewands deutscher Könige. Die Kaiser Otto III. und Heinrich III. wurden mit ihren Handschuhen bestattet. Siehe dazu Gall 1970, S. 120.

[3] Der *Sachsenspiegel* ist ein in der ersten Hälfte des 13. Jh. entstandenes, illustriertes Rechtsbuch und gilt als eine der ältesten Quellen der Rechtsprechung im deutschen Mittelalter.

[4] Im Laufe des Mittelalters diente das Kleidungsstück in verschiedenen Kontexten als Rechtssymbol und -pfand. Siehe dazu Schwineköper 1937.

[5] Vgl. Loschek 1993, S. 83. Siehe zur historischen Modeentwicklung insbesondere beim Adel Latour 1947 IV, S. 2636 ff. Collins widmet in seinem Buch dem Aussehen, der Mode und der Bedeutung von Handschuhen von Königinnen wie auch von Königen jeweils ein Kapitel. Siehe dazu Collins 1945, S. 22–33 und S. 34–43.

[6] Rechnungen und Kleiderordnungen geben Aufschluss über den großen Bedarf der Adeligen an Handschuhen. Boehn nennt etwa allein für den französischen König Karl VI. in den Jahren 1386/87 die Nachfrage von 251 Paar Handschuhen. Vgl. Boehn 1928, S. 76.

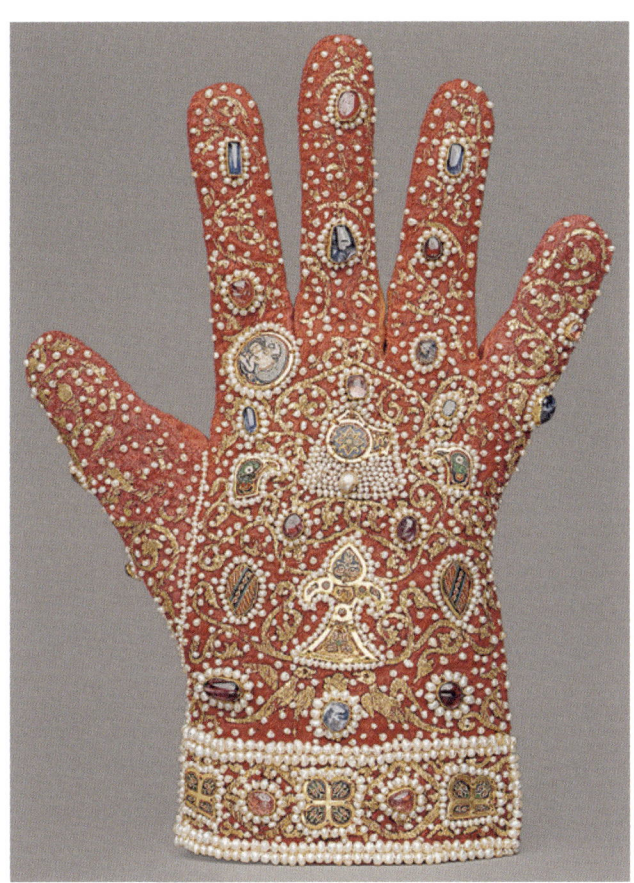

Handschuh des Krönungsornats der deutschen Kaiser, vor 1220 vmtl. in Palermo gefertigt, Kunsthistorisches Museum Wien, Kaiserliche Schatzkammer, Wien
Glove of the coronation regalia of the German emperors, probably made in Palermo before 1220, Kunsthistorisches Museum Wien, Kaiserliche Schatzkammer, Vienna

Königin Elisabeth II. von England, 1960
Queen Elizabeth II of England, 1960

Detailansicht aus dem *Sachsenspiegel* mit dem Königshandschuh am Marktkreuz
Detailed view from the *Sachsenspiegel* with the king's glove on the market cross

Royal gloves

As garments that embodied authority and wealth, gloves were not only clerical signs of office, but also part of the wardrobe of secular rulers. As far back as the Carolingian and Salian eras, royalty wore them as a status symbol and sign of the king's power.[1] From the coronation of Frederick II as Roman-German Emperor of the Holy Roman Empire in 1220, the magnificent gloves set with precious stones were henceforth also part of the coronation regalia and the imperial insignia.[2]

In the Middle Ages, the royal glove also had a symbolic, representative function. It was a legal symbol and signified the royal hand and thus the king's approval or protection. It is known, for example, from the *Sachsenspiegel*[3] that the right to hold a market in a town was indicated and lent legal validity through the suspension of the right royal glove from the market cross.[4]

As a prestigious sign of dignity and office, the accessory was initially reserved for men only in courtly culture and chivalry. From the beginning of the 11th century, gloves also became an integral part of women's fashion,[5] advancing in the 14th century to become a precious luxury item of the higher classes and adorning the hands of the nobility until the 18th century.[6]

Even if, today, the models are much simpler than those of their predecessors, gloves are still worn by members of royal families during public appearances. The wardrobe of Queen Elizabeth II of England, for example, was always complimented by a hat and gloves.

---

[1] The glove also played an important role for other European royal dynasties as a symbol of rulership and during coronation ceremonies. See Latour 1947 I, p. 2610, and Green 2021, p. 25 ff.

[2] Cf. Loschek 1993, p. 80. Today, the gloves are in the collection of the Vienna Treasury along with the other imperial regalia. Even before the 13th century, gloves were an insignia and part of the official garb of German kings. The emperors Otto III and Henry III were buried with their gloves. See Gall 1970, p. 120.

[3] The *Sachsenspiegel* is an illustrated book of law written in the first half of the 13th century and is considered one of the oldest sources of jurisprudence in the German Middle Ages.

[4] Throughout the Middle Ages, the garment served as a legal symbol and pledge in various contexts. See Schwineköper 1937.

[5] Cf. Loschek 1993, p. 83. On the historical development of fashion, especially among the nobility, see Latour 1947 IV, p. 2636 ff. Collins devotes a chapter each in his book to the appearance, fashion, and significance of gloves worn by queens as well as kings. See Collins 1945, pp. 22–33 and pp. 34–43.

[6] Invoices and dress codes provide information about the great demand for gloves among the nobility. Boehn cite the demand for 251 pairs of gloves for the French King Charles VI in 1386/87 alone. Cf. Boehn 1928, p. 76.

Nicolaes Eliaszoon Pickenoy, *Portrait einer jungen Frau*, **1632, Öl auf Tafel, The J. Paul Getty Museum, Los Angeles**
Nicolaes Eliaszoon Pickenoy, *Portrait of a Young Woman*, 1632, oil on panel, The J. Paul Getty Museum, Los Angeles

Detail eines Abendhandschuhs mit königlichem Allianzwappen, Ende 19. Jh., Grenoble, Deutsches Ledermuseum
Detail of an evening glove with the royal arms of alliance, end of 19th c., Grenoble, Deutsches Ledermuseum

Tizian, *Mann mit Handschuh*, **1523, Öl auf Leinwand, Louvre, Paris**
Titian, *Man with Glove*, 1523, oil on canvas, Louvre, Paris

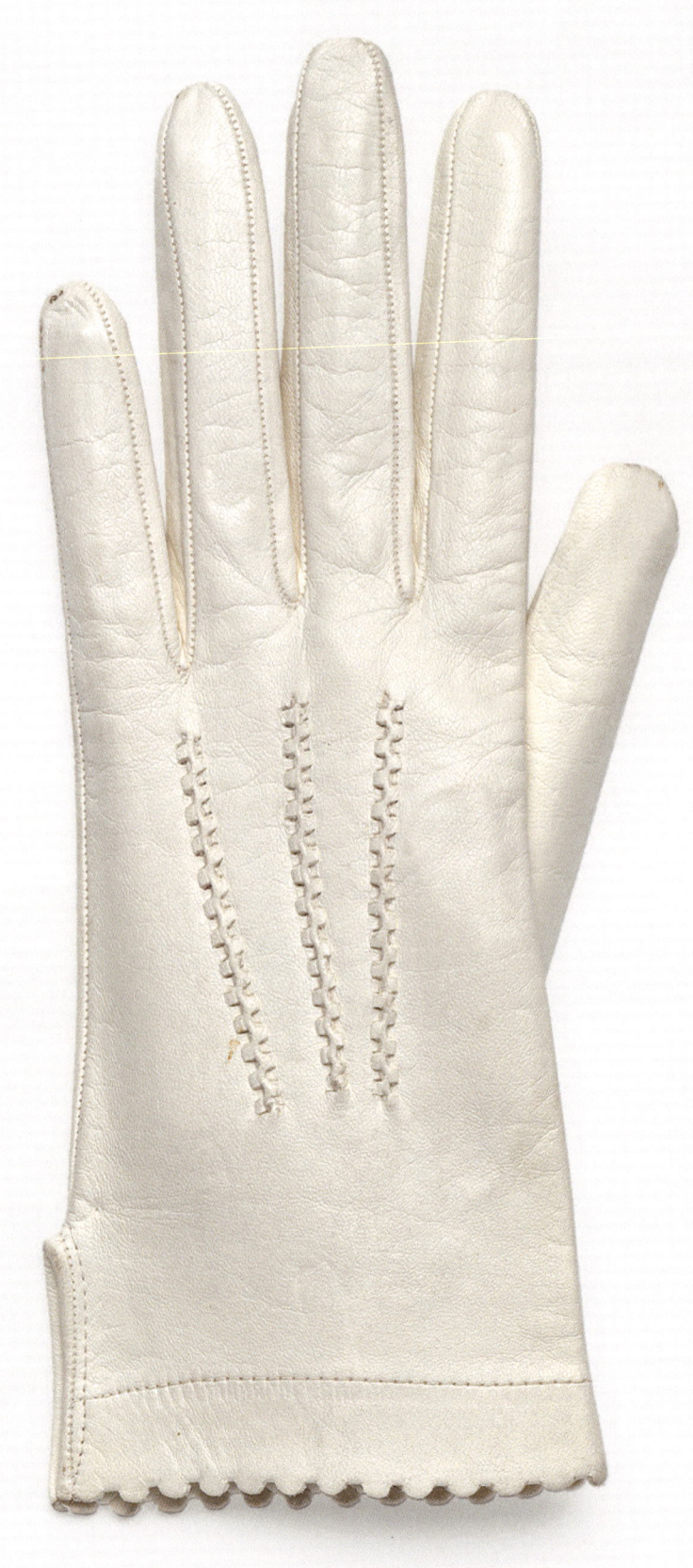

HANDSCHUHE, Deutschland, 2. Hälfte 20. Jh./Glacéleder/L: 23 cm, B: 9,5 cm/Inv.-Nr. 21487; Provenienz: Schenkung von Margareta Menzel, Heusenstamm, 2002 GLOVES, Germany, second half of 20th c./ Glacé leather/L: 23 cm, W: 9.5 cm/Inv. no. 21487; provenance: donated by Margareta Menzel, Heusenstamm, 2002

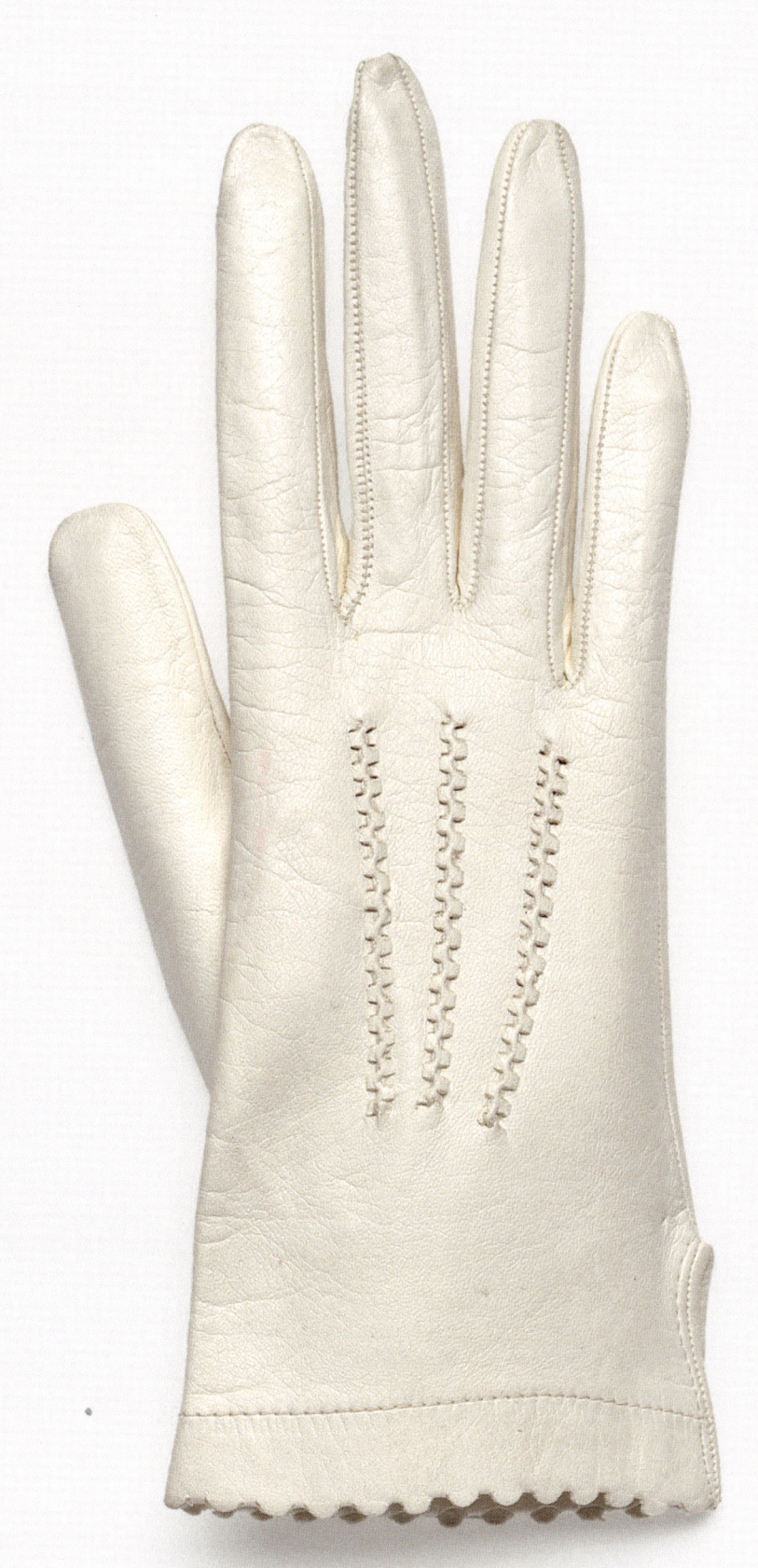

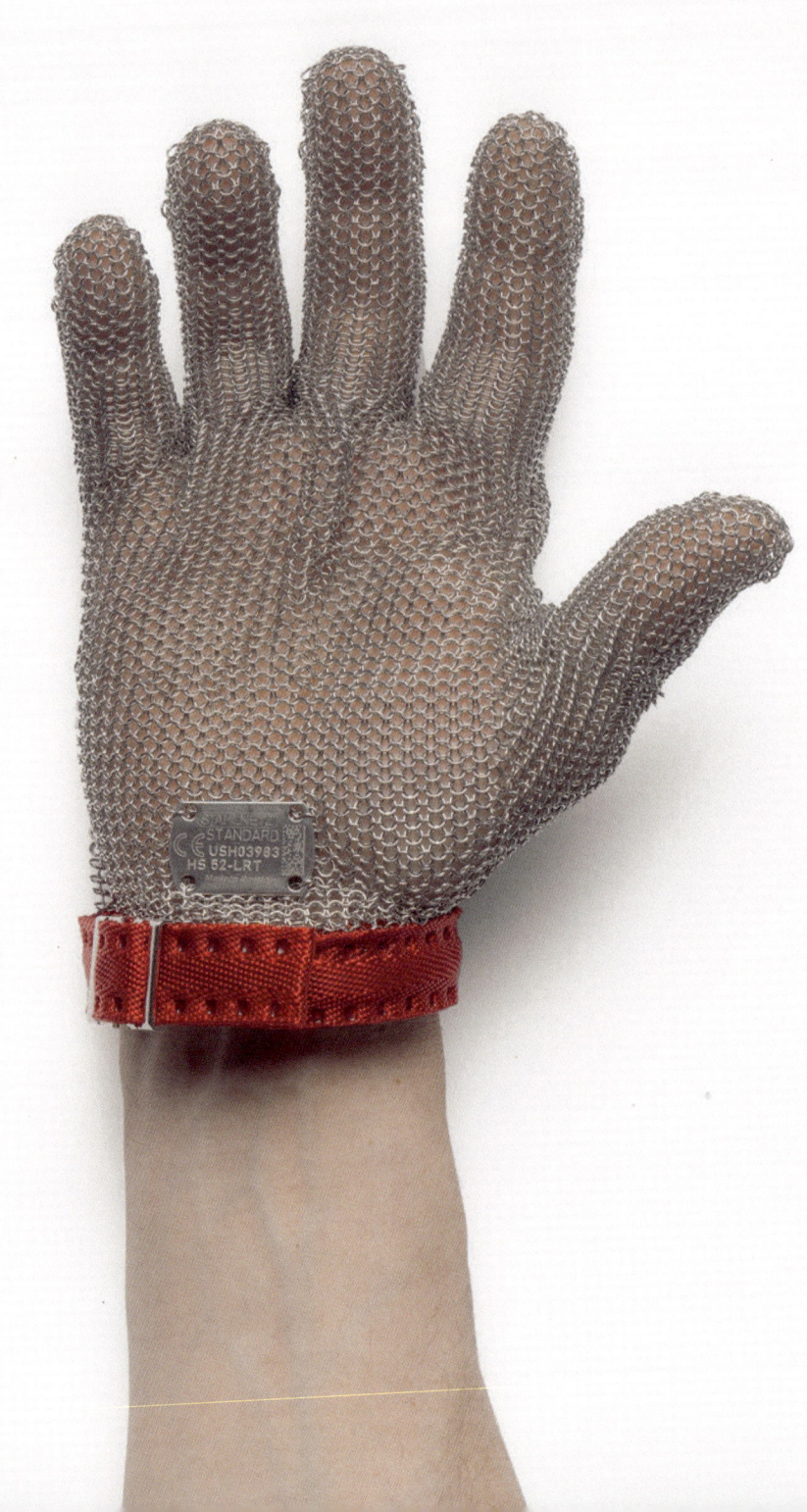

AUSTERNHANDSCHUH, *PALIO*, Carl Mertens, Solingen, 2021/22 / Edelstahl-Kettengeflecht, Textil / L: 20 cm, B: 21,5 cm, T: 6,5 cm / Inv.-Nr. 21483; Provenienz: Ankauf von Carl Mertens, 2022 OYSTER GLOVE, *PALIO*, Carl Mertens, Solingen, 2021/22 / Stainless steel chain mesh, textile / L: 20 cm, W: 21.5 cm, D: 6.5 cm / Inv. no. 21483; provenance: purchased from Carl Mertens, 2022

PANZERHANDSCHUHE EINER RITTERRÜSTUNG, Frankreich oder Deutschland, 1. Drittel 17. Jh./Eisen oder Stahl, Leder/L: 31 cm, B: 17 cm, T: 17,5 cm/Leihgabe des Hessischen Landesmuseums Darmstadt, Inv.-Nr. W 61:278 **(zugehörig)** ARMORED GLOVES OF A KNIGHT'S ARMOR, France or Germany, first third of 17th c./Iron or steel, leather/L: 31 cm, W: 17 cm, D: 17,5 cm/On loan from Hessisches Landesmuseum Darmstadt, inv. no. W 61:278 (associated)

Der Fehdehandschuh

„Der Kaiser ist mein Herr, nicht Ihr – Frei bin ich
Wie Ihr geboren, und ich messe mich
Mit Euch in jeder ritterlichen Tugend.
Und stündet Ihr nicht hier in Kaisers Namen,
Den ich verehre, selbst wo man ihn schändet,
Den Handschuh wärf [sic] ich vor Euch hin, Ihr solltet
Nach ritterlichem Brauch mir Antwort geben."[1]

‚Den Fehdehandschuh werfen' – diese Redewendung findet ihren Ursprung in einer Sitte der höfisch-ritterlichen Kultur im europäischen Mittelalter und zeigt eine ehrenhafte Aufforderung zu einem bewaffneten Zweikampf an. Das Hinwerfen des Handschuhs vor die Füße der Kontrahenten stellte somit eine Kampferklärung dar. Mit dem Annehmen des Handschuhs galt die Herausforderung als offiziell angenommen und die gegnerischen Parteien verpflichteten sich formell zur Austragung des Zweikampfs. Es war seinerzeit allgemein üblich, den Abschluss eines Vertrags mit der Übergabe von Handschuhen zu besiegeln. Das Kleidungsstück diente in diesem Fall als Rechtspfand und verkörperte die ritterliche Ehre.[2] Ebenso war das Überbringen eines Fehdebriefs eine gängige Praxis der Kampferklärung.[3] Das Austragen eines solchen Privatkriegs, der sogenannten Fehde, auch mit tödlichen Waffen war ausschließlich freien Männern vorbehalten und ein rein adliges Privileg.[4]

Der Begriff des Fehdehandschuhs selbst war indessen im Mittelalter nicht gebräuchlich, sondern ist eine neuzeitliche Wortschöpfung. Die Redewendung ‚den Fehdehandschuh werfen' wird heute noch verwendet.[5]

---

[1] Schiller, Wilhelm Tell, III. Akt, 3. Szene, zitiert nach Thalheim 2005 II, S. 166.

[2] Vgl. Loschek 1993, S. 82 sowie Latour 1947 I, S. 2612. Nach Schwineköper konnte der Handschuh auch an einen Kampfrichter übergeben werden, unter dessen Urteil man sich beim Zweikampf stellte. Siehe dazu Schwineköper 1937, S. 97.

[3] Vgl. Grathoff o.J.

[4] Vgl. Frevert 1991, S. 21.

[5] In der Popkultur ist die Form der Duellaufforderung nach wie vor zu finden. So handelt etwa Folge *Duell bei Sonnenaufgang* der amerikanischen Zeichentrickserie *Die Simpsons* davon, dass Homer Simpson mehrere Personen mit einem Handschuhschlag zum Duell auffordert. Auch in der Musik spielt der Fehdehandschuh eine Rolle, beispielsweise ist ein Battlerap-Track von Creutzfeld & Jacob feat. Kool Savas nach ihm benannt.

**Wilhelm von Diez, *Fehdehandschuh*, um 1885,
Öl auf Holz**
Wilhelm von Diez, *Gauntlet*, approx. 1885,
oil on wood

***Der Fehdehandschuh*, Sammelbildchen der Serie *Der Handschuh*,
Fa. Liebig's Fleisch-Extract, Farblithografie, 1904**
The Gauntlet picture card from the series *Der Handschuh/The Glove*,
a collection of cards published by Fa. Liebig's Fleisch-Extract, color lithograph, 1904

The gauntlet

"The emperor is my lord, not you! I'm free
As you by birth, and I can cope with you
In every virtue that beseems a knight.
And if you stood not here in that king's name,
Which I respect e'en where 'tis most abused,
I'd throw my gauntlet down, and you should give
An answer to my gage in knightly fashion."[1]

"Throwing down the gauntlet" – this expression originated in a custom of courtly chivalry during the European Middle Ages and indicates an honorable invitation to an armed duel. Throwing down a glove at the feet of an opponent thus represented a declaration of combat. Acceptance of the glove meant official acceptance of the challenge, and the opponents thus formally committed themselves to the duel. It was also common practice at the time to seal the conclusion of a contract with the handing over of gloves. In such cases, the garment served as a legal pledge and embodied knightly honor.[2] Delivering a letter of feud was likewise a common way of declaring combat.[3] Fighting a private war like this – the so-called feud which could also involve deadly weapons – was reserved exclusively for free men and was a purely noble privilege.[4]

The reference to the gauntlet itself, however, was not in use in the Middle Ages but is a modern neologism, and the phrase "throwing down the gauntlet" is still used today.[5]

---

[1] Schiller, Wilhelm Tell, Act III, Scene 3, quoted from Martin 2014.

[2] Cf. Loschek 1993, p. 82, and Latour 1947 I, p. 2612. According to Schwineköper, the glove could also be handed over to a referee under whose judgment one placed oneself during the duel. See Schwineköper 1937, p. 97.

[3] Cf. Stefan Grathoff n.d.

[4] Cf. Frevert 1991, p. 21.

[5] The form of challenging someone to a duel can still be found in popular culture. Episode *E-I-E-I-(Annoyed Grunt)* of the American animated series *The Simpsons*, for example, is about Homer Simpson challenging several people to a duel with a flick of his glove. The gauntlet also plays a role in music, for example, a German battle-rap track by Creutzfeld & Jacob feat. Kool Savas is named "Fehdehandschuh", meaning "The Gauntlet".

Michiel Jansz van Mierevelt, *Portrait von Maurice, Prinz von Oranien*, um 1613–1620, Öl auf Tafel, Rijksmuseum Amsterdam, Amsterdam
Michiel Jansz van Mierevelt, *Portrait of Maurice, Prince of Orange*, approx. 1613–1620, oil on panel, Rijksmuseum Amsterdam, Amsterdam

John Leech, *Lord John Russell „God defend the right"* (Gott verteidige das Recht), Serie *Punch*, um 1854
John Leech, *Lord John Russell "God defend the right"*, series *Punch*, approx. 1854

Graf Marshall fordert den Grafen von Derby mit dem Wurf des Handschuhs zu einem Duell heraus, in den Jean Froissart Chroniken, 1470, Frankreich
Earl Marshal challenges the Earl of Derby to a duel by throwing down the gauntlet, in Jean Froissart Chronicles, 1470, France

HANDSCHUHE, Fa. Johann Ludwig Ranniger & Söhne, Altenburg, um 1890/1900 / Links: Glacéleder, Tambourstickerei / L: 35 cm, B: 8,5 cm / Rechts: Glacéleder, Seidenstickerei / L: 32 cm, B: 8 cm / Beide: Leihgabe des Historischen Archivs der Roeckl Handschuhe & Accessoires GmbH & Co. KG GLOVES, Johann Ludwig Ranniger & Söhne company, Altenburg, approx. 1890/1900 / Left: glacé leather, tambour embroidery / L: 35 cm, W: 8,5 cm / Right: glacé leather, silk embroidery / L: 32 cm, W: 8 cm / Both: on loan from the Historical Archive of Roeckl Handschuhe & Accessoires GmbH & Co. KG

52

HANDSCHUHE, Prag oder Wien, Mitte 20. Jh./Schlangenleder, Leder, Metall/L: 23,5 cm, B: 9,5 cm/Inv.-Nr. 20955; Provenienz: Schenkung von Ute Maria Etzold, Wolfenbüttel, 2009 GLOVES, Prague or Vienna, mid-20th c./Snakeskin, leather, metal/L: 23.5 cm, W: 9.5 cm/Inv. no. 20955; provenance: donated by Ute Maria Etzold, Wolfenbüttel, 2009

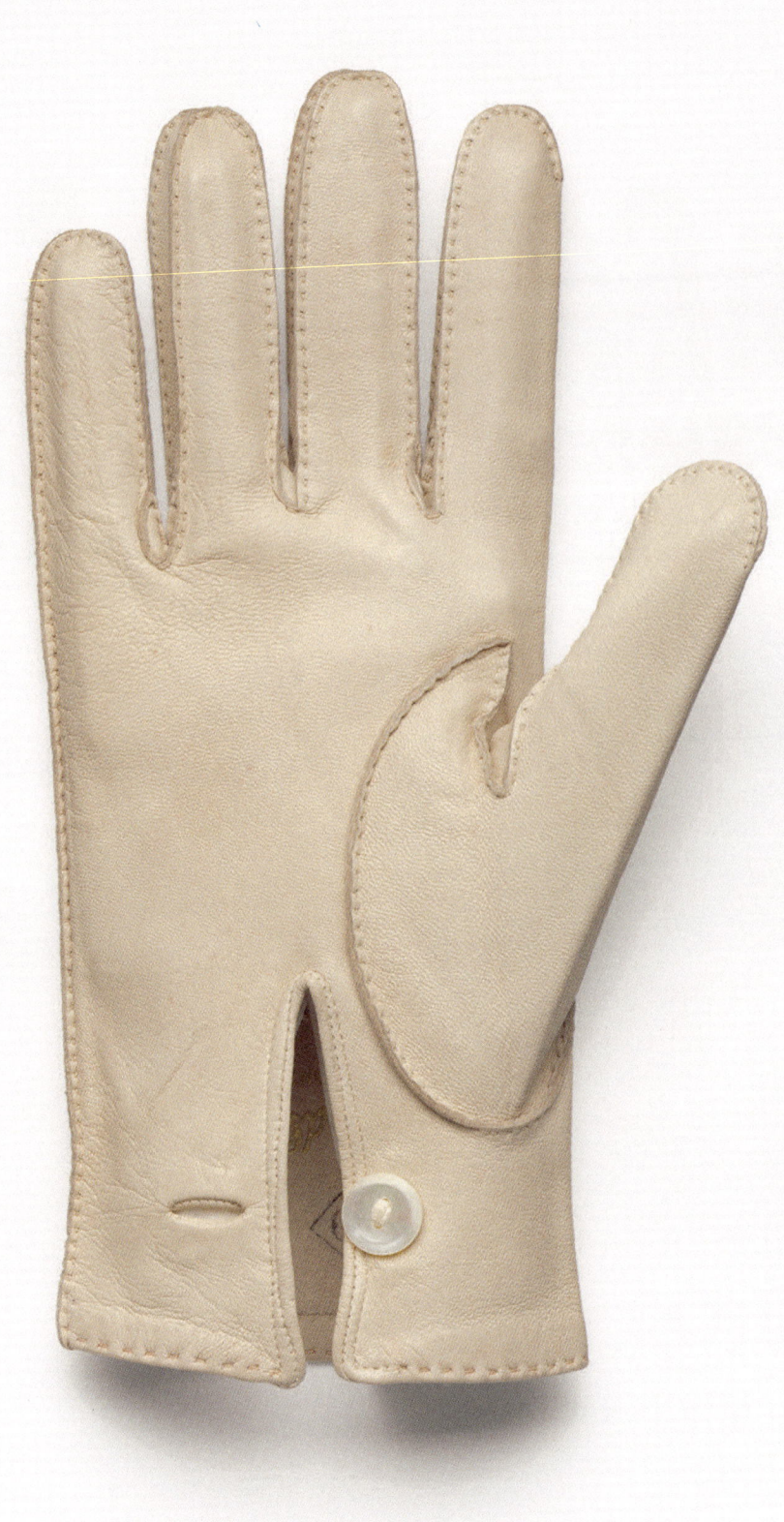

HANDSCHUH, Ober- und Unterhand, *Bryan's Gloves*, **England, 2. Hälfte 20. Jh./Leder, Perlmutt/L: 26,5 cm, B: 10,5 cm/Inv.-Nr. 16363; Provenienz: Nachlass von John Frederick Uihlein, Milwaukee, 1993** GLOVE, upper and lower hand, *Bryan's Gloves*, England, second half of 20th c./Leather, mother-of-pearl/L: 26.5 cm, W: 10.5 cm/Inv. no. 16363; provenance: estate of John Frederick Uihlein, Milwaukee, 1993

BOXHANDSCHUH, Bolivien, vor 1931 / Filz, Rohhaut, geflochten, Stein / L: 20 cm, B: 15 cm, T: 10,5 cm / Inv.-Nr. 4325; Provenienz: Ankauf von Julius Konietzko, Hamburg, 1931 **BOXING GLOVE,** Bolivia, before 1931 / Felt, rawhide, braided, stone / L: 20 cm, W: 15 cm, D: 10.5 cm / Inv. no. 4325; provenance: purchased from Julius Konietzko, Hamburg, 1931

FALKNERHANDSCHUH FÜR HABICHTE, Europa, 2022 / Nubuk, Metall / L: 35 cm, B: 19 cm / Inv.-Nr. 21491; Provenienz: Ankauf von Falknereigeraete Gerold During, Guben, 2022
FALCONRY GLOVE FOR HAWKS, Europe, 2022 / Nubuck, metal / L: 35 cm, W: 19 cm / Inv. no. 21491; provenance: purchased from Falknereigeraete Gerold During, Guben, 2022

Falknerhandschuh

Eine Handschuhart, die ebenso wie der metallene Handschuh der Ritterrüstung mit dem europäischen Mittelalter assoziiert wird, ist der Falknerhandschuh. Die Beizjagd, bei der mithilfe von abgerichteten Greifvögeln Jagd auf Beute gemacht wird, steht in einer jahrtausendealten Tradition. Ihre Wurzeln werden bereits vor 3.500 Jahren in Asien vermutet.[1] In Europa erlebte die Beizjagd ihre Blütezeit im Hochmittelalter, in dem die prestigeträchtige Jagdform Privileg des Adels war. Der auf der behandschuhten Hand sitzende Vogel avancierte in dieser Zeit selbst zum Statussymbol, das auch auf Herrschaftsbildnissen wiedergegeben wurde.[2]

Für die Jagd ist ein Falknerhandschuh essentiell. Wenn der Vogel nicht in der Luft ist, ruht er auf der Hand der Falkner*in. Um diese, in der Regel linke, Hand vor den scharfen Krallen und dem Schnabel des Vogels zu schützen, bedarf es eines besonders robusten Lederhandschuhs. Dieser ist häufig aus gewalktem Büffel- oder Hirschleder gefertigt, in mehreren Lagen verstärkt beziehungsweise unterfüttert.[3] Die Schaftlänge des Einzelhandschuhs variiert hingegen; die meisten sind mit einer langen Stulpe ausgestattet, die den Unterarm der Träger*innen bis zur Hälfte abdeckt und somit schützt. Aktuelle Modelle sind oftmals zusätzlich mit einem kleinen Ring versehen, um den Vogel mit einer Langfessel sichern zu können.

Heutzutage spielt die Falknerei etwa auch an Flughäfen zum Vergrämen von Vogelschwärmen eine wichtige Rolle.

---

[1] Siehe zur Geschichte der Falknerei etwa Niesters 2012.

[2] Vgl. Niesters 2012, S. 162. Die Verbreitung des Wissens zur Beizjagd und deren Popularität geht insbesondere auf Kaiser Friedrich II. mit seiner Schrift *Von der Kunst zu beizen* aus der Mitte des 13. Jh. zurück. Diese galt bis in die Neuzeit als wichtigstes Traktat in der europäischen Literatur zur Vogeljagd. Vgl. ebenda.

[3] Siehe Latour 1947 V, S. 2650 sowie Loschek 1993, S. 84.

**Hans Makart, *Die Falknerin*, 1880, Öl auf Leinwand,
Bayerische Staatsgemäldesammlungen, Neue Pinakothek, München**
Hans Makart, *The Falconer*, 1880, oil on canvas,
Bavarian State Painting Collections, Neue Pinakothek, Munich

**König Konrad der Junge bei der Falkenjagd,
Codex Manesse, um 1300–1340, Universitäts-
bibliothek Heidelberg, Heidelberg**
King Conrad the Younger hunting with a falcon,
from the *Codex Manesse*, around 1300–1340,
Heidelberg University Library, Heidelberg

Falconry glove

One type of glove which, like the metal gauntlet that complements a knight's armor, conjures up the European Middle Ages is the falconry glove. Falconry, in which trained birds of prey are used to hunt down animals, is part of a tradition that dates back thousands of years. It is thought to have originated in Asia as long as 3,500 years ago.[1] In Europe, falconry experienced its heyday in the High Middle Ages, when this prestigious form of hunting was the privilege of those of noble birth. The bird perched on a gloved hand became a status symbol in its own right during this period, and also featured in portraits of rulers.[2]

A falconry glove is essential for hunting. When the bird is not in the air, it rests on the falconer's hand. To protect this (usually the left) hand from the bird's sharp claws and beak, a particularly robust leather glove is required. This is often made of rolled buffalo or deerskin, which is reinforced or lined in several layers.[3] The shaft length of the single glove varies; most are equipped with a long cuff that covers half of the wearer's forearm and thus protects it. Current models often also feature a small ring for securing the bird with a long leash.

Nowadays, the falconry also plays an important role at airports to scare away flocks of birds.

---

[1] On the history of falconry, see, for example, Niesters 2012.

[2] Cf. Niesters 2012, p. 162. The spread of knowledge about falconry and its popularity can be traced back in particular to Kaiser Frederick II with his book *The Art of Falconry* penned in the mid-13th century. This was considered the most important treatise on falconry in European literature until modern times. Cf. ibid.

[3] See Latour 1947 V, p. 2650, and Loschek 1993, p. 84.

In einer Falknerei, um 1953, Frankreich
In a falconry, approx. 1953, France

Falke ruht auf einem Falkner-Handschuh, 2013, USA
Falcon resting on a falconer's glove, 2013, USA

Frans Floris, *Der Falkenjäger*, 1558, Öl auf Eichenholz, Herzog Anton Ulrich-Museum, Braunschweig
Frans Floris, *Falconer*, 1558, oil on oak, Herzog Anton Ulrich-Museum, Braunschweig

BLUETOOTH-HANDSCHUH, *Fashion Music Gloves,* **o. O., 2021/22/Polyester, Kunststoff, Metall/L: 22 cm, B: 13 cm, T: 2 cm/o. Nr.** BLUETOOTH GLOVE, *Fashion Music Gloves,* place unknown, 2021/22/Polyester, plastic, metal/L: 22 cm, W: 13 cm, D: 2 cm/No number

62

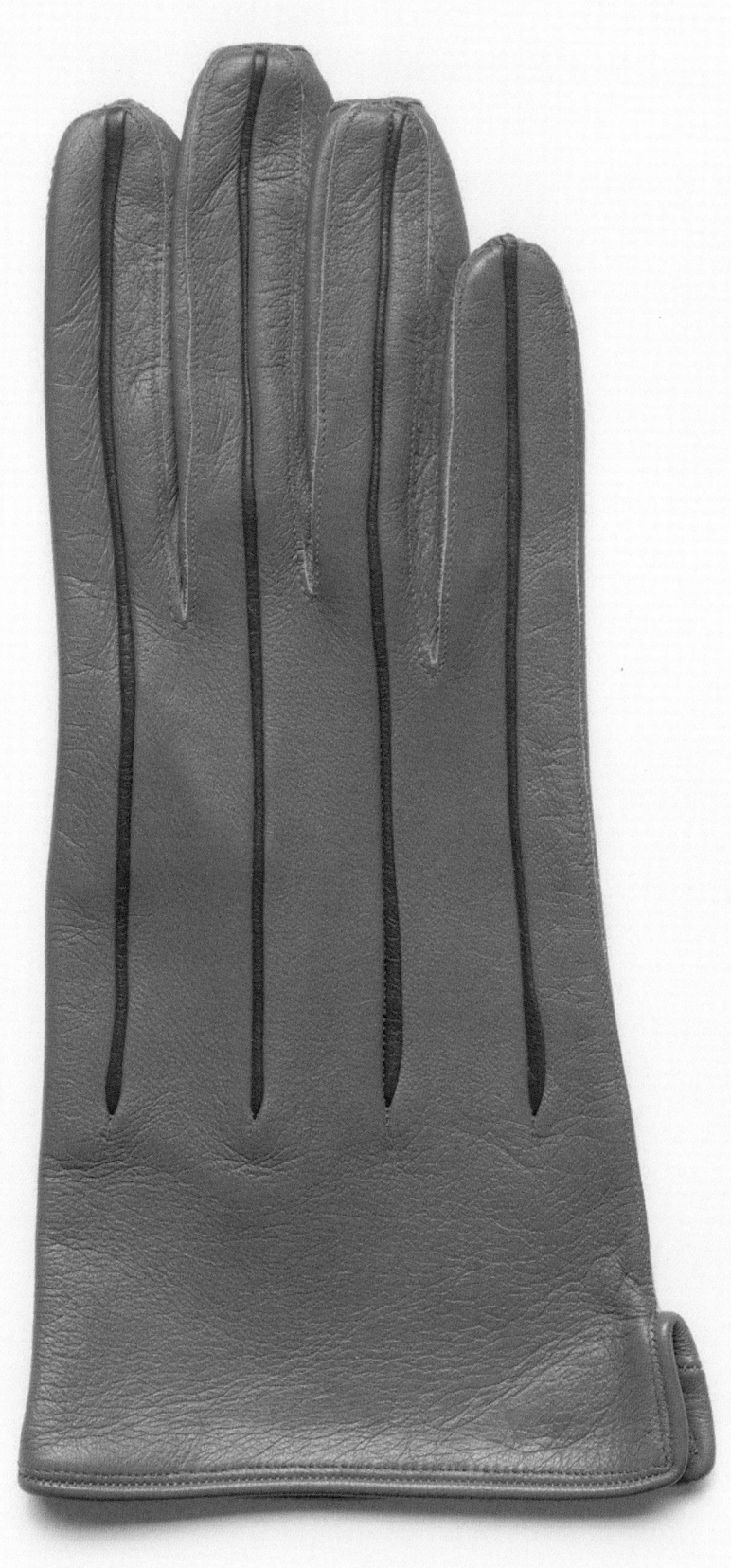

HANDSCHUH, Erzgebirge, DDR, **1970–1990**/Lammleder, Zierpaspeln/**L: 25 cm, B: 12 cm**/**Inv.-Nr. 15410**; **Provenienz: Schenkung Erzgebirgische Lederhandschuhe GmbH, Johanngeorgenstadt, 1991** GLOVE, Erzgebirge, East Germany, 1970–1990/Lambskin, decorative piping/L: 25 cm, W: 12 cm/Inv. no. 15410; provenance: donated by Erzgebirgische Lederhandschuhe GmbH, Johanngeorgenstadt, 1991

HANDSCHUHE, Chanel, Frankreich, 1991 / Schweinsvelours, Fell / L: 40 cm, B: 30 cm, T: 8 cm / Inv.-Nr. 21461; Provenienz: Ankauf von Vestiaire Collective, Paris, 2021 GLOVES, Chanel, France, 1991 / Pig suede, fur / L: 40 cm, W: 30 cm, D: 8 cm / Inv. no. 21461; provenance: purchased from Vestiaire Collective, Paris, 2021

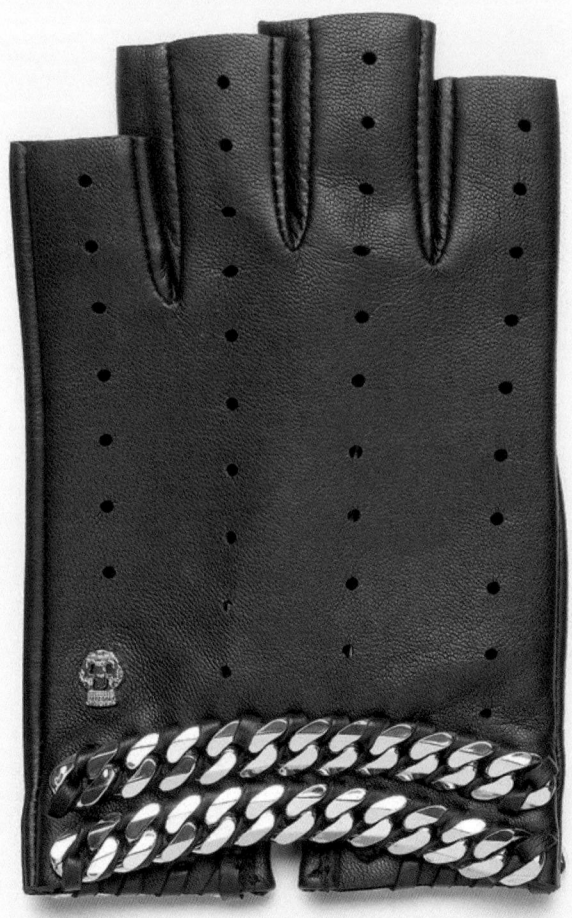

HALBFINGERHANDSCHUHE, *Tribute to Karl,* **ROECKL, Indien, 2022/**Nappaleder, Metall, Textil/L: 16 cm, B: 10 cm/Inv.-Nr. 21489; Provenienz: Schenkung der Roeckl Handschuhe & Accessoires GmbH & Co. KG, München, 2022 HALF-FINGER GLOVES, *Tribute to Karl,* ROECKL, India, 2022/ Nappa leather, metal, textile/L: 16 cm, W: 10 cm/Inv. no. 21489; provenance: donated by Roeckl Handschuhe & Accessoires GmbH & Co. KG, Munich, 2022

HALBHANDSCHUHE, Fa. M. & P. Händel, Grimma, 1908 / Schafleder, Tambourstickerei, Perlmutt / L: 21 cm, B: 7,5 cm / Inv.-Nr. T42; Provenienz: M. & P. Händel, Grimma, 1938 HALF GLOVES, M. & P. Händel company, Grimma, 1908 / Sheepskin, tambour embroidery, mother-of-pearl / L: 21 cm, W: 7.5 cm / Inv. no. T42; provenance: M. & P. Händel, Grimma, 1938

Liebespfand

Als Liebespfand ist der Handschuh vor allem aus dem Kontext des Minnediensts[1] im mittelalterlichen Europa bekannt.[2] Die hohe Minne, bei der es sich um eine Art Spiel handelte, verkörperte die tugendhaften Ideale der höfischen Kultur und prägte das Wertesystem der adeligen Gesellschaft. Der (Frauen-)Dienst des Ritters umfasste die Verehrung und edle Liebe zu einer höhergestellten, zumeist verheirateten Dame, deren Gunst es zu erlangen galt, indem ehrenvolle Taten vollbracht und ihr gewidmet wurden.[3] Als Zeichen der Zugewandtheit übergab die Dame dem Ritter persönliche Gegenstände wie ihren Handschuh oder ihr Taschentuch, die dieser dann bei Turnieren oder im Kampf am Helm oder Körper trug. Der Brauch setzte sich bis ins 17. Jahrhundert fort; so ist etwa bekannt, dass der Herzog von Cumberland, der Ritter von Königin Elisabeth I. von England, sich bei Turnieren in ihren Farben und mit ihrem Handschuh am Hut kleidete.[4]

Während das Werfen des (Fehde-)Handschuhs zu einem Zweikampf herausforderte, diente der Handschuhwurf einer Dame vor die Füße eines Ritters als Aufforderung zu Liebesbeweisen. Mit einer eindrucksvollen Geste wird eine Verbindung zwischen einer Hofdame und ihrem Verehrer in Friedrich Schillers *Der Handschuh* gelöst. In der bekannten Ballade lässt Kunigunde ihren Handschuh absichtlich in einen Raubkatzenzwinger fallen und fordert den Ritter Delorges auf, ihr diesen als Liebesbeweis zurückzubringen. Mutig steigt er in den Zwinger herab, holt den Handschuh zurück und wirft ihn ihr ins Gesicht mit den Worten: „Den Dank, Dame, begehr ich nicht!"[5]

---

[1] Der Minnedienst war integraler Bestandteil des höfischen Lebens und prägte das Wertesystem der adeligen, ritterlichen Gesellschaft. Literarisch fand dieser sich vor allem ab der zweiten Hälfte des 12. Jh. im Minnesang wieder.

[2] Neben dem Handschuh spielte etwa auch das Taschentuch als Minnegabe der Dame an den Verehrer eine wichtige Rolle. Vgl. Loschek 1999, S. 10. Keupp nennt darüber hinaus auch Broschen. Vgl. Keupp 2011, S. 109.

[3] Bekannt ist vor allem die autobiografische Erzählung von Ulrichs von Liechtenstein über seinen Frauendienst.

[4] Ebenso trug Herzog Christian von Braunschweig den Handschuh seiner Cousine Elisabeth Stuart. Vgl. Loschek 1993, S. 86.

[5] Schiller, *Der Handschuh*, zitiert nach Thalheim I 2005, S. 428.

Johann Heinrich Meyer, Illustration der achten Strophe von Friedrich Schillers Ballade *Der Handschuh*, „Und der Ritter, in schnellem Lauf, steigt hinab in den furchtbaren Zwinger mit festem Schritte, und aus der Ungeheuer Mitte nimmt er den Handschuh mit keckem Finger.", Klassik Stiftung Weimar, Weimar

Johann Heinrich Meyer, illustration of the 8th verse of Friedrich Schiller's ballad *The Glove*, "And the knight, in a moment, with dauntless tread, Jumps into the lists, nor seeks to linger, And, from out the midst of those monsters dread, Picks up the glove with a daring finger.", Klassik Stiftung Weimar, Weimar

Nicholas Hilliard, *George Clifford, 3. Earl of Cumberland*, um 1590, Aquarell auf Pergament, auf Holz aufgezogen, National Maritime Museum, London

Er trägt am Helm den Handschuh von Königin Elisabeth I.

Nicholas Hilliard, *George Clifford, 3rd Earl of Cumberland*, approx. 1590, watercolor on vellum laid on panel, National Maritime Museum, London

He wears the glove of Queen Elizabeth I on his helmet.

Love token

As a token of love, gloves are associated primarily with courtly love[1] in medieval Europe.[2] Courtly love, which was rather like a game, embodied the virtuous ideals of courtly culture or chivalry, and shaped the value system of noble society. The knight's service (to the lady) included the veneration and noble love of a higher-ranking, usually married woman, whose favor was to be gained through his performance of noble deeds and his dedicating them to her.[3] As a sign of esteem, the lady gave the knight personal items such as her glove or handkerchief, which the knight then wore on his helmet or body during tournaments or in battle. The custom continued into the 17th century, and it is known, for example, that the Duke of Cumberland, the knight of Queen Elizabeth I of England, dressed in her colors and wore her glove on his hat during tournaments.[4]

While throwing down a glove (in a feud) was a challenge to a duel, the throwing of a lady's glove at the feet of a knight served as a summons to prove love. An impressive gesture is used to break a connection between a court lady and her suitor in Friedrich Schiller's *Der Handschuh (The Glove)*. In the famous ballad, Kunigunde deliberately drops her glove among the big cats and asks the knight Delorges to return it to her as a proof of love. Courageously, he descends into the pit and retrieves the glove, but throws it in her face with the words, "I desire no such thanks from you, my Lady!"[5]

---

[1] Courtly love was an integral part of courtly life and shaped the value system of noble, chivalrous society. In literary terms, this was reflected in Minnesang, especially from the second half of the 12th century onward.

[2] In addition to the glove, the handkerchief also played an important role as a gift from the lady to her suitor. Cf. Loschek 1999, S. 10. Keupp also mentions brooches. Cf. Keupp 2011, p. 109.

[3] Best known is Ulrich von Liechtenstein's autobiographical account of his service to women.

[4] Likewise, Duke Christian of Brunswick wore the glove of his cousin Elizabeth Stuart. Cf. Loschek 1993, p. 86.

[5] Schiller, *The Glove*, quoted from Stokes 2005.

Mann hebt einen heruntergefallenen Handschuh einer Dame auf, 1864
Man picking up a glove a lady has dropped, 1864

Mittelalterliche Hochzeitsszene, bei der der Bräutigam einen Handschuh als Pfand übergibt
Medieval wedding scene where the groom hands over a glove as a pledge

Darstellung des Schweizer Minnesängers Wernher von Teufen in Begleitung einer Dame, *Codex Manesse*, um 1300–1340, Universitätsbibliothek Heidelberg, Heidelberg
Illustration of the Swiss minnesinger Wernher von Teufen accompanied by a lady, *Codex Manesse*, approx. 1300–1340, Heidelberg University Library, Heidelberg

HANDSCHUHE, Fa. Roger Faré, Paris, Frankreich, 2. Hälfte 20. Jh./Leder, Lederband, gehäkelt/L: 24,5 cm, B: 11 cm/Inv.-Nr. 16359; Provenienz: Nachlass von John Frederick Uihlein, Milwaukee, 1993 GLOVES, Roger Faré company, Paris, France, second half of 20th c./Leather, leather strap, crocheted/L: 24.5 cm, W: 11 cm/Inv. no. 16359; provenance: estate of John Frederick Uihlein, Milwaukee, 1993

MUFF FÜR KINDER, Europa, 1. Drittel 20. Jh. / Kaninchenfell, Textilfutter, Kordel / **H: 12 cm, B: 20 cm, T: 7 cm / Inv.-Nr. 20176**; Provenienz: Schenkung von Dagmar Währisch, Offenbach am Main, 2005 MUFF FOR CHILDREN, Europe, first third of 20th c. / Rabbit fur, textile lining, cord / H: 12 cm, W: 20 cm, D: 7 cm / Inv. no. 20176; provenance: donated by Dagmar Währisch, Offenbach/Main, 2005

FELLPFLEGEHANDSCHUH FÜR HAUSTIERE, NELADE, China, 2021/22 / Silikon, Kunststoffgewebe / L: 22,5 cm, B: 18,5 cm / o. Nr. PET GROOMING GLOVE, NELADE, China, 2021/22 / Silicone, plastic fabric / L: 22.5 cm, W: 18.5 cm / No number

BASEBALLHANDSCHUH, *The Pro*, Japan, vor 1983, und Baseball, Acorn, USA, 1994 / Handschuh: Leder, Rohhautschnürung, Schaumstoff, Nylonfaden, Metall / L: 29 cm, B: 21 cm, T: 15 cm / Inv.-Nr. 13154; **Provenienz: Ankauf aus Privatbesitz,** Frankfurt am Main, 1983; **BALL: Obermaterial:** Leder, Rohhautschnürung, Schaumstoff, Nylonfaden, Metall / L: 29 cm, B: 21 cm, T: 15 cm / Inv.-Nr. 13154; Leder, Garn; **Füllung:** Kork, Gummi, Wollgarn, Baumwollgarn / D: 23 cm / Inv.-Nr. 21486; **Provenienz: Alter Bestand** BASEBALL GLOVE, *The Pro*, Japan, before 1983, and baseball, Acorn, USA, 1994 / Glove: leather, rawhide lacing, foam, nylon thread, metal / L: 29 cm, W: 21 cm, D: 15 cm / Inv. no. 13154; provenance: purchased from private ownership, Frankfurt/Main, 1983; BALL: outer material: leather, yarn; filling: cork, rubber, wool yarn, cotton yarn / D: 23 cm / Inv. no. 21486; provenance: old stock

Sporthandschuhe

Heutzutage gehören Handschuhe zu einer Vielzahl von Sportausrüstungen. Bei einigen sportlichen und kämpferischen Betätigungen wie beispielsweise Reiten, Jagen, insbesondere mit Greifvögeln, oder Bogenschießen steht die Verwendung von Handschuhen in einer jahrhundertealten Tradition. Der Gebrauch eines Handschutzes beim Boxen lässt sich bis in die Antike zurückverfolgen. Werden bei Homer noch Lederriemen zum Umwickeln der Hände beschrieben, die die Boxer*innen bei den Faustkämpfen der Olympischen Spiele 688 v. Chr. trugen, dienten Handschuhe später nicht nur dem Schutz der Hände. Vielmehr wurden sie mit Schlagringen oder wie bei den römischen *Caesti* der Gladiatoren etwa mit Metallzacken versehen auch als Waffe eingesetzt.[1] Demgegenüber sind die Boxhandschuhe von heute dem sportlichen Charakter entsprechend schaumstoffgepolstert.[2] Ebenso für seine Sportart essentiell ist der Handschuh des Catchers beim Baseball.[3] Zunächst wurde barhändig gespielt, bevor in den 1870er Jahren erste Spieler*innen gewöhnliche Arbeitshandschuhe aus Leder, die sie teilweise aufpolsterten, trugen. Ein Handschuh, der als Schutz vor Verletzung und zugleich als Fanghilfe diente, kam erst in den 1920er Jahren auf und entwickelte sich mit der Zeit zu dem charakteristischen schalenförmigen Baseballhandschuh.[4]

Die weniger bekannten Schwimmhandschuhe verfügen über Einsätze zwischen den Fingern, die den Schwimmhäuten von Wasservögeln nachempfunden sind. Sie werden jetzt aus wasserabweisendem Textil oder Gummi hergestellt, während sie Ende des 19. Jahrhunderts noch aus Leinen gefertigt wurden,[5] und dienen dem verbesserten Antrieb im Wasser. Wie alle Sporthandschuhe wurden sie entwickelt, um die Sportler*innen zu schützen oder deren Leistung effizienter zu gestalten.

---

[1] Siehe dazu Neumayer 2020 und Green 2021, S. 15. Kampfhandschuhe, bei denen neben dem Schutz vor allem auch die Schlagkraft verbessert und die Hand mithilfe eines Handschuhs zur Waffe erweitert wurde, setzten sich in den mittelalterlichen Panzerhandschuhen fort und finden sich in abgeschwächter Form heute etwa bei Quarzsandhandschuhen wieder.

[2] Im 18. Jh. wurde Boxen vor allem in England wieder populär. Auch die Boxhandschuhe, wie wir sie kennen, gehen auf diese Zeit zurück. 1743 entwarf Jack Broughton die sog. *mufflers*, Handschuhe, die mit Schafswolle, Rosshaar oder Baumwolle gefüttert waren, um die Schläge der Boxenden abzudämpfen. Seit Ende des 19. Jh. gehört die Verwendung von Boxhandschuhen nach dem Regelwerk von Queensbury fest zu diesem Sport. Siehe dazu etwa Neumayer 2020 und Irish 2002.

[3] Beim Baseball werden mehrere Arten von Handschuhen verwendet; der ikonische Handschuh ist der des Catchers.

[4] Zunächst war das Tragen von Handschuhen verpönt und wurden als „unmännlich" aufgefasst, bis Ende des 19. Jh. der erste Baseballhandschuh auf den Markt kam und auch von Profis getragen wurde. Zum Ende des Jahrhunderts spielte jede*r Spieler*in im offiziellen Baseball mit einem Handschuh. Die zweite große Innovation stammte von Bill Doak, dessen Entwurf ein Ledergurtband zwischen dem Zeigefinger und dem Daumen als 'Ballfalle' vorsah. Die patentierte Erfindung gilt als Vorläufer aller moderner Baseballhandschuhe. Vgl. Stamp 2013 und Green 2021, S. 185 ff.

[5] Vgl. Kment 1890, S. 53.

Werbung für den Baseballhandschuh *The Snare*, 1947, USA, Macgregor Goldsmith Inc.
Baseball glove advert for *The Snare*, 1947, USA, Macgregor Goldsmith Inc.

Golfspielerin im Kostüm mit Hut und Handschuhen, *Journal des Dames et des Modes*, Costumes Parisiens, 1912
Golf player wearing a coat, skirt, hat, and gloves, *Journal des Dames et des Modes*, Costumes Parisiens, 1912

Kunstreiterin, Dompteuse und Zirkusdirektorin Thérèse Renz mit Handschuhen
Trick rider, animal tamer, and circus director Thérèse Renz with gloves

Sports gloves

Nowadays, gloves form part of the equipment for a large number of sports. In some traditional and combat sports, such as horseback riding, hunting (especially falconry), or archery, using gloves is part of a centuries-old tradition. The use of hand protection in boxing can be traced back to Classical Antiquity. While Homer describes leather straps to wrap the hands, as used by boxers in the fist fights of the Olympic Games in 688 BCE, gloves later served not only to protect the hands, but also as weapons with brass knuckles. Or, as with the *caesti* worn by the gladiators of Ancient Rome, with metal studs.[1] By contrast, the boxing gloves of today are foam-padded in keeping with the sporting nature of the combat.[2] Another glove essential to a sport is that of the catcher in baseball.[3] Initially, the game was played bare-handed, until the 1870s when the first players wore ordinary leather work gloves, which they sometimes padded. A glove that served both for protection against injury and as a catching aid did not appear until the 1920s, and over time evolved into the characteristic cupped baseball glove.[4]

The lesser-known swimming gloves feature inserts between the fingers that mimic the webbed feet of waterfowl. Originally made of linen at the end of the 19th century,[5] they are now produced from water-repellent textile or rubber and help to achieve better propulsion in the water. Like all sports gloves, they were developed to protect athletes or enhance their performance.

---

[1] See Neumayer 2020 and Green 2021, p. 15. Combat gloves, in which not only protection but above all striking power was improved and the hand became a weapon with the aid of a glove, continued in the metal gauntlets of the Middle Ages and can be found in an attenuated form today in quartz sand gloves, for example.

[2] In the 18th century boxing became popular again, especially in England. Boxing gloves as we know them also date back to this period. In 1743 Jack Broughton designed the so-called *mufflers*, gloves lined with sheep's wool, horsehair, or cotton to cushion the boxers' blows. Since the end of the 19th century, the use of boxing gloves has been an integral part of the sport, according to the Queensbury rules. See for example Neumayer 2020 and Irish 2002.

[3] Several types of gloves are used in baseball, with the most iconic being the catcher's glove.

[4] At first, the wearing of gloves was frowned upon and considered "unmanly" until the end of the 19th century, when the first baseball glove came on the market and was also worn by professionals. By the end of the century, every player in official baseball was wearing a glove. The second great innovation came from Bill Doak, whose design included a leather strap between the index finger and thumb as a "ball trap". The patented invention is considered the forerunner of all modern baseball gloves. Cf. Stamp 2013 and Green 2021, p. 185 ff.

[5] Cf. Kment 1890, p. 53.

Wintersport-Mode mit Fäustlingen für Frauen, 1930er Jahre, Deutschland
Winter sports fashion with mittens for women, 1930s, Germany

Faustkämpfer vom Quirinal, **Bronze, 330 bis 50 v. Chr., Museo Nazionale Romano, Rom**
Boxer of the Qurinal, bronze, 330 to 50 BCE, National Museum of Rome, Rome

Sir Donald George Bradman, 1920, Bromöldruck, Bassano Ltd, National Portrait Gallery, London
Sir Donald George Bradman, 1920, bromide print, Bassano Ltd, National Portrait Gallery, London

FAUSTHANDSCHUHE FÜR KINDER, *Nylon Mitts 3D*, BARTS, China, 2021/22 / Obermaterial und Futter: Polyester; Handfläche: Polyurethan / L: 19,5 cm, B: 9 cm, T: 6 cm / o. Nr. CHILD'S MITTENS, *Nylon Mitts 3D*, BARTS, China, 2021/22 / Outer material and lining: polyester; palm: polyurethane / L: 19.5 cm, W: 9 cm, D: 6 cm / No number

HANDSCHUH, vmtl. Deutschland, 1920er Jahre / Kalbleder, Fischleder / L: 25,5 cm, B: 12 cm / Inv.-Nr. 15138; Provenienz: Alter Bestand GLOVE, probably Germany, 1920s / Calfskin, fish leather / L: 25.5 cm, W: 12 cm / Inv. no. 15138; provenance: old stock

81

HANDSCHUHE, Hermès, Frankreich, 21. Jh./Seidenjersey, bedruckt/L: 34 cm, B: 11 cm/Inv.-Nr. 21466; Provenienz: Ankauf von Vestiaire Collective, Paris, 2021 GLOVES, Hermès, France, 21st c./Silk jersey, printed/L: 34 cm, W: 11 cm/Inv. no. 21466; provenance: purchased from Vestiaire Collective, Paris, 2021

HANDSCHUHE ZUM AUTOFAHREN, *Lugano*, ROECKL, Rumänien, 2022 / Peccaryleder, perforiert / L: 20 cm, B: 9 cm / Inv.-Nr. 21490; Provenienz: Schenkung der Roeckl Handschuhe & Accessoires GmbH & Co. KG, München, 2022 DRIVING GLOVES, *Lugano*, ROECKL, Romania, 2022 / Peccary leather, perforated / L: 20 cm, W: 9 cm / Inv. no. 21490; provenance: donated by Roeckl Handschuhe & Accessoires GmbH & Co. KG, Munich, 2022

Autofahrhandschuhe

„Was die Handschuhe betrifft – tragen Sie niemals Wollhandschuhe, denn Wolle rutscht auf der glatten Oberfläche des Lenkrads und verhindert, dass man einen festen Griff bekommt. Handschuhe aus gutem, weichem Ziegenleder, pelzgefüttert, ohne Verschluss und nur mit einem Daumen versehen, sind die idealen Handschuhe für das Fahren im Winter."[1]

Während heutige Autofahrhandschuhe zumeist aus Gründen des Lifestyles getragen werden, waren ihre robusten Vorgänger bei den frühen Automobilen zu Beginn des 20. Jahrhunderts unabdingbar. Die ersten Wagen verfügten weder über eine Windschutzscheibe noch über ein Verdeck; auch die Autoheizung kam erst in den 1930er Jahren auf. Neben Mantel, Brille, Schal und Mütze gehörten die Handschuhe zur Grundausstattung der Fahrenden.

Mit einer langen Stulpe versehen, die über die Ärmel des Mantels gezogen wurden, aus dickem Leder gefertigt und mit Wolle oder Fell gefüttert, schützten die Handschuhe vor Kälte sowie Zugluft und hielten Insekten ab.[2] Mit der Fortentwicklung der Automobile ging auch eine Veränderung im Handschuhdesign einher. Beheizbare Autos ließen ein ungefüttertes Modell mit kurzem Schaft und aus dünnem Leder gefertigt, das die Griffigkeit am Lenkrad verbesserte, populär werden. Perforierte und mit Entlüftungslöchern versehene Handschuhe verhinderten, dass die Hände schwitzten. Heute sind sie für die Fahrsicherheit nicht mehr notwendig.[3] Eine Ausnahme bildet der Motorsport, bei dem schwer entflammbare Handschuhe zum Einsatz kommen, die vor Hitze schützen und teilweise über einen Chipsensor in der Handfläche zur Überwachung des Blutdrucks der Fahrer*innen verfügen.[4]

---

[1] Levitt 1909, S. 27, übersetzt von der Autorin.

[2] Vgl. Green 2021, S. 188 und Stork 2019 I. Helle Handschuhe gehörten hingegen lange zur Berufskleidung von professionellen Chauffeur*innen. In Japan werden Baumwollhandschuhe zuweilen bis heute von Taxi-, Bus- und Zugfahrer*innen getragen. Ursprünglich dienten sie dazu, Handsignale der Fahrer*innen sichtbarer zu machen. Vgl. Green 2021, S. 189.

[3] Vor allem mit der Einführung von rutschfesten Lenkrädern und der Servolenkung, die die Kraft, die beim Lenken benötigt wurde, reduzierte, waren die Hauptaufgaben der Autofahrhandschuhe hinfällig geworden.

[4] Vgl. Green 2021, S. 188 f.

Ryan Gosling mit Autofahrhandschuhen im Film *Drive*, 2011
Ryan Gosling wearing driving gloves in the movie *Drive*, 2011

Ein Autofahrer zeigt ein verkehrsgerechtes Abbiegen mit einem weißen Handschuh an, 1927, Berlin
A motorist demonstrates how to correctly indicate he is turning, wearing a white glove, 1927, Berlin

Driving gloves

"Regarding gloves – never wear woollen gloves, as wool slips on the smooth surface of the steering-wheel and prevents one getting a firm grip. Gloves made of good, soft kid, fur-lined, without a fastening, and made with just a thumb, are the ideal gloves for winter driving."[1]

While today's driving gloves are generally worn as lifestyle accessories, their robust predecessors were essential in early automobiles at the beginning of the 20th century. The first cars had neither a windshield nor a soft top, nor was there any heating in cars until the 1930s. Along with a coat, goggles, scarf, and cap, gloves were part of a driver's basic equipment.

Fitted with a long cuff that could be pulled over the sleeves of the coat, made of thick leather, and lined with wool or fur, the gloves provided protection against the cold as well as drafts; in addition, they warded off insects.[2] As automobiles developed, the design of driving gloves changed too. Heated cars helped to popularize an unlined model in a short format made of thin leather to deliver an improved grip on the steering wheel. Perforated gloves with vent holes prevented hands from sweating. These days, gloves are no longer required for driving safety.[3] One exception, however, is in motorsports, where flame-retardant gloves are used that protect against heat and sometimes have a chip sensor in the palm to monitor the driver's blood pressure.[4]

---

[1] Levitt 1909, p. 27.

[2] Cf. Green 2021, p. 188, and Stork 2019 I. Light-colored gloves, on the other hand, have long been part of the standard attire for professional chauffeurs. In Japan, to this day cotton gloves are sometimes worn by cab, bus, and train drivers. Originally, they were used to make drivers' hand signals more visible. Cf. Green 2021, p. 189.

[3] Especially with the introduction of non-slip steering wheels and power steering, which reduces the power you need to apply in order to steer, the main tasks which car driving gloves were designed to handle have become outdated.

[4] Cf. Green 2021, p. 188 f.

Eine Autofahrerin zeigt mit einem Handzeichen an, dass sie rechts abbiegen will; sie trägt einen Handschuh mit einem eingebauten Spiegel, 1930er Jahre, Fotografie, Barnaby's Studios Ltd, London
A motorist uses a hand signal to indicate her intention to turn right; she wears a glove with an in-set mirror, 1930s, photograph, unattributed, for Barnaby's Studios Ltd, London

Julius Klinger, *Ausstellung moderner Verkehrsmittel*, 1909, Lithografie, Kunstbibliothek, Staatliche Museen, Berlin
Julius Klinger, *Exhibition of modern transporting*, 1909, lithograph, Art Library, National Museums, Berlin

Autofahrerinnen des Women's Royal Naval Service (Königlicher Marinedienst der Frauen, genannt Wrens) in Arbeitsuniform mit Handschuhen, 1918, London
Women drivers from Women's Royal Naval Service (the Wrens) in working uniform complete with gloves, 1918, London

HANDSCHUHE, Dries Van Noten, Italien, 2021 / Stretch-Jersey, bedruckt / L: 65 cm, B: 11 cm / Inv.-Nr. 21467; Provenienz: Ankauf von NET-A-PORTER, 2021 GLOVES, Dries Van Noten, Italy, 2021 / Stretch jersey, printed / L: 65 cm, W: 11 cm / Inv. no. 21467; provenance: purchased from NET-A-PORTER, 2021

HANDSCHUH, Erzgebirge, Deutschland, 1938–1942 / Ziegenleder, Stickerei / L: 26 cm, B: 11,5 cm / Inv.-Nr. 15396; Provenienz: Schenkung Erzgebirgische Lederhandschuhe GmbH, Johanngeorgenstadt, 1991
GLOVE, Erzgebirge, Germany, 1938–1942 / Goatskin, embroidery / L: 26 cm, W: 11.5 cm / Inv. no. 15396; provenance: donated by Erzgebirgische Lederhandschuhe GmbH, Johanngeorgenstadt, 1991

89

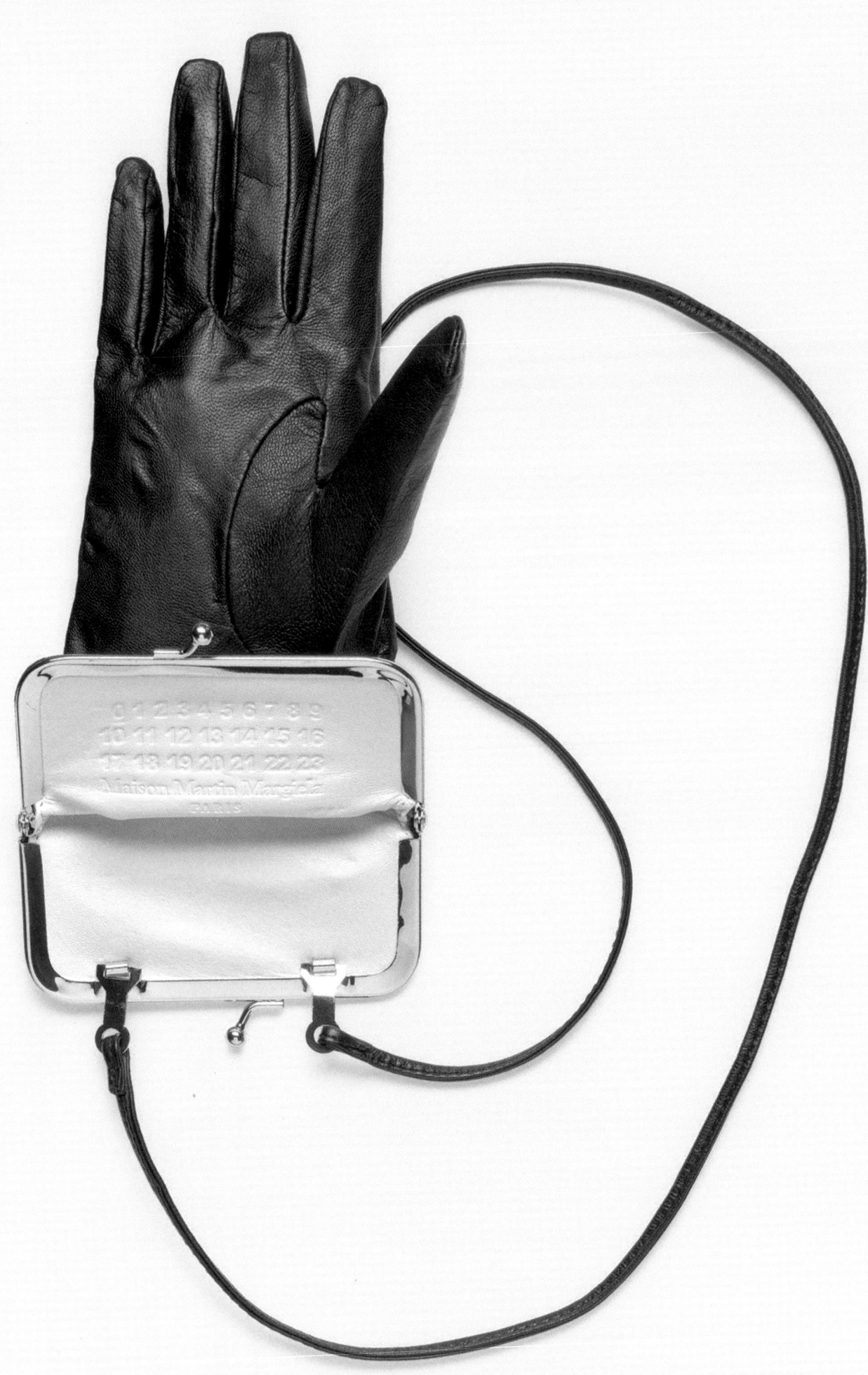

HANDSCHUH-GELDBÖRSE, Maison Martin Margiela und H&M, o. O., Frühling/Sommer 1999, Re-Edition 2012 / Leder, Metall / H: 27 cm, B: 10,5 cm, Tragriemen: B: 2,5 cm / Inv.-Nr.: 21457; Provenienz: Ankauf 2020 GLOVE PURSE, Maison Martin Margiela and H&M, place unknown, spring/summer 1999, re-edition 2012 / Leather, metal / H: 27 cm, W: 10.5 cm, strap: W: 2.5 cm / Inv. no. 21457; provenance: purchased 2020

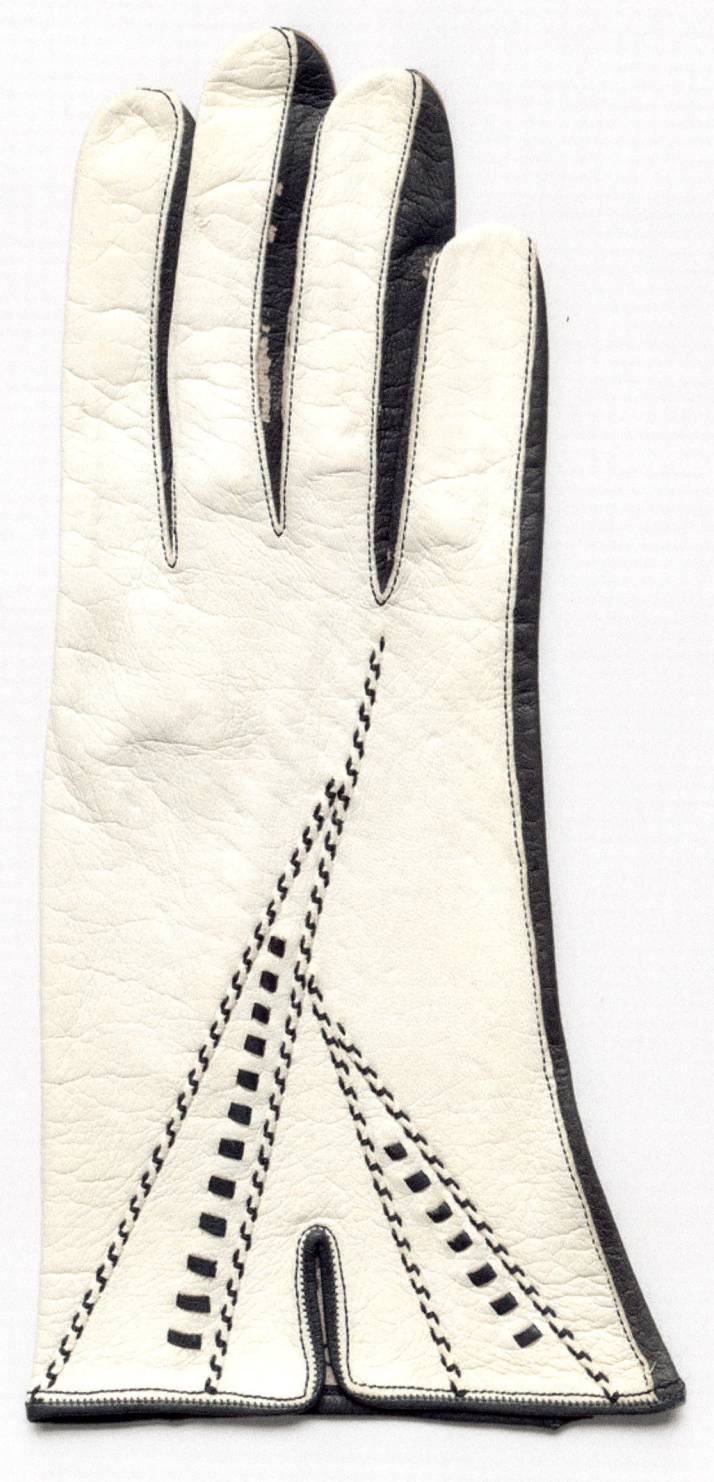

HANDSCHUH, Erzgebirge, Deutschland, 1938–1942/Ziegenleder, Ziernähte/L: 22,5 cm, B: 11 cm/Inv.-Nr. 15399; Provenienz: Schenkung Erzgebirgische Lederhandschuhe GmbH, Johanngeorgenstadt, 1991
GLOVE, Erzgebirge, Germany, 1938–1942/Goatskin, decorative stitching/L: 22.5 cm, W: 11 cm/Inv. no. 15399; provenance: donated by Erzgebirgische Lederhandschuhe GmbH, Johanngeorgenstadt, 1991

HANDSCHUHE, McDonald's, China, 2018/Synthetikgarn, gestrickt, bedruckt/L: 21,5 cm, B: 12,5 cm/Inv.-Nr. 21484; Provenienz: Ankauf 2020 GLOVES, McDonald's, China, 2018/Synthetic yarn, knitted, printed/L. 21.5 cm, W: 12.5 cm/Inv. no. 21484; provenance: purchased 2020

HANDSCHUHE, o. O., 2. Hälfte 20. Jh./Leder, Garn, gestrickt/L: 25 cm, B: 11,5 cm/Inv.-Nr. 16360; Provenienz: Nachlass von John Frederick Uihlein, Milwaukee, 1993 GLOVES, place unknown, second half of 20th c./Leather, yarn, knitted/L: 25 cm, W: 11.5 cm/Inv. no. 16360; provenance: estate of John Frederick Uihlein, Milwaukee, 1993

Das Handschuhfach

„[D]ie meisten Arbeiten am Auto (Tanken, etc., etc.) lassen sich genauso gut erledigen, wenn die Hände durch ein Paar Waschlederhandschuhe geschützt sind. Sie finden Platz für diese Handschuhe in der kleinen Schublade unter dem Sitz des Autos. Diese kleine Schublade ist das Geheimnis der zierlichen Autofahrerin."[1]

Dorothy Levitt, die erste britische Autorennfahrerin und Pionierin des Frauenautosports, gilt mit ihrer Empfehlung, Handschuhe nicht nur beim Autofahren zu tragen, sondern diese auch in der Schublade zu verwahren als Namensgeberin des Handschuhfachs.[2] Solche Schubladen und Kästen, zumeist unter dem Fahrersitz angebracht, dienten in den ersten Automobilen zur Unterbringung für verschiedene Ausrüstungsgegenstände. Mit der Verlagerung des Motors vom Wagenboden nach vorne schirmte fortan eine Trennwand die Fahrerkabine vom Motor ab; aus dieser wurde das Armaturenbrett entwickelt. Neben Schaltern und Anzeigen fand auch das Handschuhfach, zuerst als Aussparung, dann als Fach mit Deckel versehen, teilweise abschließbar, dort seinen Platz. Obschon seiner Zeit in einzelnen Wagen vorhanden, gehört es erst seit den 1930er Jahren zum Standard der Innenausstattung.[3] Seitdem wird es immer wieder neugestaltet und bietet für Verschiedenstes Stauraum.[4] Bereits bei Levitt wurden nicht nur Handschuhe in ihm aufgehoben:

„Was Sie darin verstauen, hängt von Ihrem Geschmack ab, aber ich rate Ihnen, die folgenden Gegenstände darin unterzubringen. Ein Paar saubere Handschuhe, ein zusätzliches Taschentuch, einen sauberen Schleier, eine Puderquaste (es sei denn, Sie verabscheuen sie), Haarnadeln und gewöhnliche Stecknadeln, einen Handspiegel – und manchmal sind Pralinen sehr beruhigend!"[5]

---

[1] Levitt 1909, S. 28, übersetzt von der Autorin.

[2] Vgl. Green 2021, S. 187 f. und Foresman 2018.

[3] Dem amerikanischen Automobilhersteller Packard wird die erste Aufbewahrungsbox in einem Auto um 1900 zugeschrieben. Erst in den Folgejahren fand das Handschuhfach seinen Platz im Armaturenbrett, Stork nennt den Pierce Arrow von 1915 des gleichnamigen Automobilherstellers als erstes Modell. Siehe dazu Foresman 2018 und Stork 2019 II. Auch Modelle von Mercedes sind Anfang der 1930er Jahre mit verschließbaren Handschuhfächern in den Preislisten erwähnt.

[4] So diente es etwa als Kühlfach oder zur Unterbringung des Duftflakons im Mercedes-Benz S-Klasse Coupé als Teil des automatischen Duftsystems AIR-BALANCE. Vgl. Mercedes Group 2014 und Stork 2019 II.

[5] Levitt 1909, S. 28 f., übersetzt von der Autorin.

This little drawer is the great secret, Schublade unter dem Fahrersitz, Abbildung aus Dorothy Levitts Buch *The Woman and the Car*, 1909
This little drawer is the great secret, drawer under the driver's seat, image from Dorothy Levitt's book *The Woman and the Car*, 1909

Handschuhfach eines Audi, 1935
Glove compartment in an Audi, 1935

The glove box

"[T]he majority of work on a car (filling tanks, &c. &c.) can be done just as well if one's hands are protected by a pair of wash-leather gloves. You will find room for these gloves in the little drawer under the seat of the car. This little drawer is the secret of the dainty motoriste."[1]

Dorothy Levitt, the first British female racing driver and a pioneer of women's motoring, is thought to have given the glove box its name with her recommendation that gloves should not only be worn when driving, but that they should also be stored in the in-car compartment.[2] These kinds of drawers and boxes, generally located under the driver's seat, were used in the first automobiles to store various items of equipment. With the relocation of the engine from the bottom of the car to the front, a partition was required to shield the driver's cabin from the engine, and this led to the development of the dashboard. The latter incorporated not only switches and gauges, but also the glove box – first as a recessed ledge, then as a closed compartment with a lid, which in some cases was lockable. At that time, it could be found only in certain cars: it has only been part of the standard interior fit-out since the 1930s.[3] It has meanwhile been redesigned on repeated occasions and offers storage space for a wide variety of things.[4] As early as in Levitt's time, it was used for more than just gloves:

"What you put in it depends upon your tastes, but the following articles are what I advise you to have in its recesses. A pair of clean gloves, an extra handkerchief, clean veil, powder-puff (unless you despise them), hair-pins and ordinary pins, a hand mirror – and some chocolates are very soothing, sometimes!"[5]

---

[1] Levitt 1909, p. 28.

[2] Cf. Green 2021, p. 187 f., and Foresman 2018.

[3] US automaker Packard is credited with the first storage box in a car around 1900. It was not until subsequent years that the glove box found its place in the dashboard; Stork cites the 1915 Pierce Arrow from the automaker of the same name as the first model. See Foresman 2018 and Stork 2019 II for details. Mercedes models with lockable glove compartments are also mentioned in price lists from the early 1930s.

[4] For example, it served as a cooling compartment or to house the fragrance bottle in the Mercedes-Benz S-Class Coupé as part of the AIR-BALANCE automatic fragrance system. Cf. Mercedes Group 2014 and Stork 2019 II.

[5] Levitt 1909, p. 28 f.

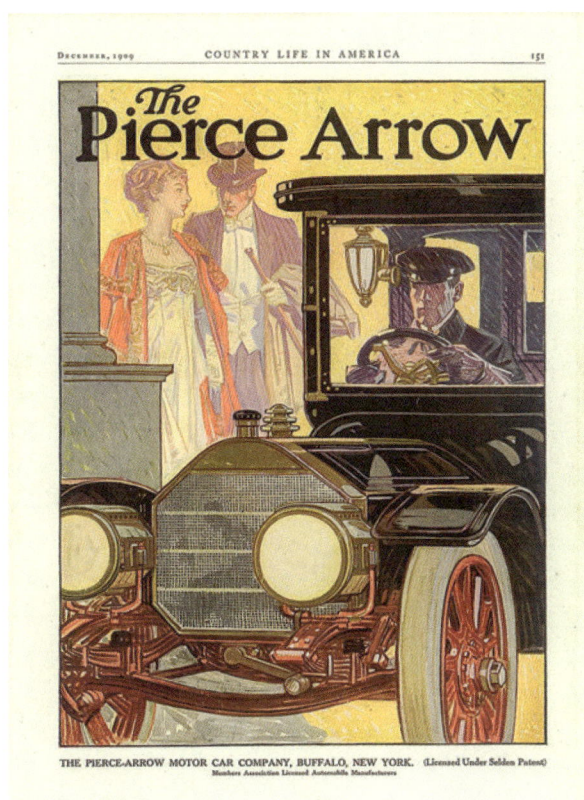

Werbung für *The Pierce-Arrow Motor Car Company*, *Country Life in America*, 1909
Advert for *The Pierce-Arrow Motor Car Company*, *Country Life in America*, 1909

Mercedes Typ 200 mit einer Aussparung im Armaturenbrett als Ablagemöglichkeit für Handschuhe, vor 1933
The Mercedes Type 200 boasted a cavity in the dashboard as a storage option for gloves, before 1933

Volkswagen, Armaturenbrett mit einem abschließbaren Handschuhfach, 1952
Volkswagen, dashboard with a lockable compartment for gloves, 1952

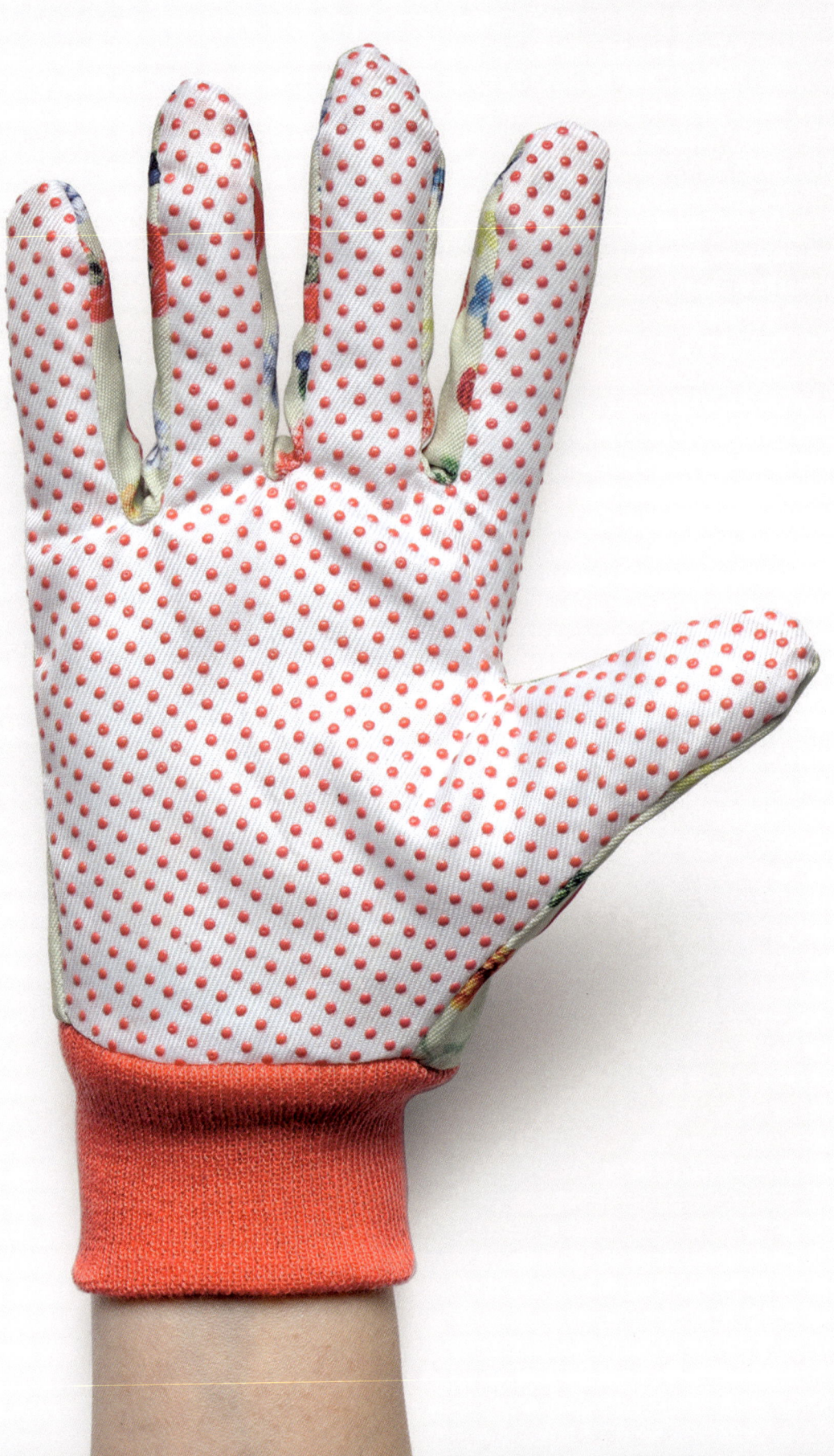

GARTENHANDSCHUH, Ober- und Unterhand, *Blatt und Blüte*, moses. Verlag, o. O., 2021/22 / Polyester / L: 23,3 cm, B: 10,5 cm / o. Nr. **GARDENING GLOVE**, upper and lower hand, *Leaf and Flower*, moses. Verlag, place unknown, 2021/22 / Polyester / L: 23.3 cm, W: 10.5 cm / No number

FAUSTHANDSCHUH, USA, o. J./Obermaterial: Bisonfell (Oberhand und Stulpe), Leder (Innenhand); Futter: Textil/L: 35 cm, B: 24,5 cm, T: 6 cm/Inv.-Nr. 13920; Provenienz: Ankauf durch den Förderkreis DLM von Robert Stolper, London, 1987 MITTEN, USA, date unknown/Outer material: bison hide (back and cuff), leather (palm); lining: textile/L: 35 cm, W: 24.5 cm, D: 6 cm/Inv. no. 13920; provenance: purchased by the Patrons DLM from Robert Stolper, London, 1987

HANDSCHUH-BRALETTE, *Florence Icy Green*, **T LABEL, Großbritannien, 2021/Dupionseide/H: 14 cm, B: 73 cm/Inv.-Nr. 21471; Provenienz: Ankauf von T LABEL, London, 2021** GLOVE BRALETTE, *Florence Icy Green*, T LABEL, United Kingdom, 2021/Dupion silk/H: 14 cm, W: 73 cm/Inv. no. 21471; provenance: purchased from T LABEL, London, 2021

FAUSTHANDSCHUHE, Christina Utsi, Lappland, Schweden, um 1975/Obermaterial: Rentierpelz, Filz; Futter: Textil/L: 29 cm, B: 14 cm, T: 13 cm/Inv.-Nr. 13286; Provenienz: Tausch mit der Bata Shoe Museum Foundation, Toronto, 1983 **MITTENS**, Christina Utsi, Lapland, Sweden, approx. 1975/Outer material: reindeer fur, felt; lining: textile/L: 29 cm, W: 14 cm, D: 13 cm/Inv. no. 13286; provenance: exchange with the Bata Shoe Museum Foundation, Toronto, 1983

HANDSCHUHE IM MINIATURFORMAT, ROECKL, München, 2022 / Garn, gestrickt / L: 6 cm, B: 4 cm / Leihgabe aus Privatbesitz MINIATURE GLOVES, ROECKL, Munich, 2020 / Yarn, knitted / L: 6 cm, W: 4 cm / Loan from private collection

Handschuhgrößen

Bis in das 19. Jahrhundert hinein fiel jedes Handschuhpaar, trotz Geschicklichkeit und handwerklichen Könnens der Handschuhmacher*innen, verschieden aus. Die Einführung von Handschuhgrößen geht auf Xavier Jouvin zurück, der über einen Zeitraum von fünf Jahren in einem Grenobler Krankenhaus Hände von Patient*innen studierte. Auf der Grundlage seiner Daten entwickelte er ein System von 320 Größen, für die er die Proportionen eines jeweils gutsitzenden Handschuhs an den verschiedenen anatomischen Gegebenheiten orientiert berechnete.[1] Die Etablierung von Konfektionsgrößen garantierte der Kundschaft fortan einen besseren Sitz sowie Tragekomfort und vereinfachte den Herstellungsprozess, mussten doch Maße nicht mehr individuell genommen werden.[2] Bis heute bildet eine Variation des Systems die Grundlage für Handschuhgrößen. Da diese nicht genormt sind, dienen die Größen eher als Richtwerte und können sich je nach Hersteller, Schnitt und Material unterscheiden.

Für die Ermittlung der Handschuhgröße wird ein Maßband an der breitesten Stelle der Hand, den Daumen ausgenommen, angesetzt, um den Handumfang zu messen.[3] Mithilfe einer Umrechnungstabelle kann die entsprechende Größe abgelesen werden. Liegen die Maße zwischen den Größen, empfiehlt es sich, für Lederhandschuhe auf die nächste halbe oder ganze Zahl abzurunden, da die Handschuhe eng anliegen sollen, und das Material sich mit dem Tragen noch dehnt.

Eher unbekannt dürfte sein, dass der Handschuh im mittelalterlichen Europa zuweilen auch als Hohlmaß diente. In Schweden soll etwa „dem Fremden, der durch den Wald geht, gestatte[t] [sein], seinen Handschuh bis zum Däumling mit Nüssen zu füllen"[4]. Andere Quellen weisen den Handschuh zu dieser Zeit als Gegenstand, der bei Wurfmaßen verwendet wurde, aus.[5]

---

[1] Jouvin berücksichtigte bei seiner Studie nicht nur die unterschiedlichen Längen und Handrückenbreiten, sondern auch Alter und Geschlecht seiner Proband*innen. Vgl. Green 2021, S. 59 f. und Redwood 2016, S. 33.

[2] Seither garantierten Pappschablonen der jeweiligen Größe identisch geschnittene Handschuhe. Eine weitere bedeutende Erfindung von Jouvins war die Entwicklung der *main-de-fer*, der sog. eisernen Hand, die für die serielle Produktion von Handschuhen revolutionär war. Auf der Grundlage der Handschuhgrößen wurden Ausstanzformen gefertigt, die sechs Lederstücke gleichzeitig zuschneiden konnten; eine weitere Form stanzte die Daumen. Seine 1838 patentierte Stanzpresse (Fentiermaschine) verhalf der Grenobler Handschuhproduktion zu einem ungeahnten Aufschwung. Siehe dazu Colonel und Dalmasso 2022, S. 21 f. sowie Latour 1947 III, S. 2631.

[3] Anstelle eines flexiblen Maßbands kann auch eine Schnur verwendet werden, deren Länge an einem Lineal bestimmt werden kann. Rechtshänder*innen messen die rechte, Linkshänder*innen die linke Hand. Häufig sind die Größen bei Herstellern traditionell nach dem Ursprung des Handwerks in französischem Zoll angegeben. Ein Zoll entspricht ca. 2,707 cm.

[4] Schwineköper 1937, S. 120 f.

[5] Schwineköper nennt verschiedene Beispiele, bei denen durch einen Handschuhwurf eine Strecke bzw. ein Längenmaß festgelegt wurde. Siehe dazu ebenda, S. 121.

Statue von Xavier Jouvin in Grenoble
Statue of Xavier Jouvin in Grenoble

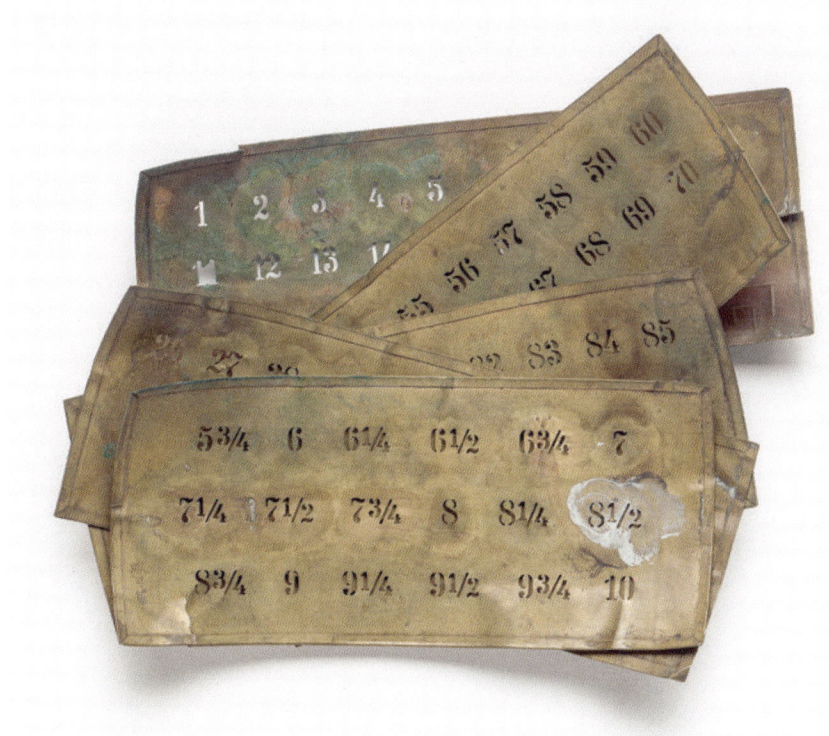

Schablonen zur Beschriftung von Konfektionsgrößen, 20. Jh., Deutsches Ledermuseum
Stencils for adding glove sizes, 20th c., Deutsches Ledermuseum

Ein Verkäufer zeigt einer Frau verschiedene Handschuhmodelle, Werbekarte der Handschuhmanufaktur Gant Perrin, 1903, Grenoble
A salesman shows a woman different glove models, advertising card for Perrin glovemakers, 1903, Grenoble

Glove sizes

Until the 19th century, despite the skill and craftsmanship of the glove makers, each pair of gloves was different. The introduction of glove sizes can be traced back to Xavier Jouvin, who studied patients' hands in a Grenoble hospital over a period of five years. Based on his data, he then developed a system of 320 sizes for which he calculated the proportions of a well-fitting glove based on various anatomical conditions.[1] From then on, the establishment of ready-to-wear sizes guaranteed customers a better fit and wearing comfort, but it also simplified the manufacturing process as measurements no longer had to be taken individually.[2] A variation of the system still forms the basis for glove sizes to this day. Since these are not standardized, the sizes serve more as guidelines and can differ depending on the manufacturer, cut, and material.

To determine the glove size, a tape measure is applied to the widest part of the hand, excluding the thumb, to measure its circumference.[3] A conversion table is then used to gauge the corresponding size. If the measurements are between the sizes, it is recommended to round down to the nearest half or whole number for leather gloves, as the gloves should fit snugly and the material stretches with wear.

It is perhaps little known that in medieval Europe the glove sometimes also served as a hollow measure. In Sweden, for example, a stranger walking through the forest was allowed to "fill his glove up to the thumb with nuts"[4]. Other sources indicate the glove at that time was an object used to ascertain throwing distances.[5]

---

[1] In his study, Jouvin took into account not only the different lengths and hand back widths, but also the age and gender of his test subjects. Cf. Green 2021, p. 59 f., and Redwood 2016, p. 33.

[2] Since then, cardboard templates of the respective size guaranteed identically cut gloves. Another important invention of Jouvin's was the development of the *main-de-fer*, the so-called iron hand, which was revolutionary for the serial production of gloves. Based on glove sizes, punching dies were made that could cut six pieces of leather at a time; another die punched the thumbs. His punch press (the Fentier machine), patented in 1838, gave Grenoble glove production an unforeseen boost. See Colonel and Dalmasso 2022, p. 21 f., and Latour 1947 III, p. 2631.

[3] Instead of a flexible measuring tape, a string can also be used, the length of which can be determined using a ruler. Right-handed people measure the right hand, left-handed people the left. Often, manufacturers traditionally measure sizes in French inches according to the origin of the craft. One inch is equal to approximately 2.707 cm.

[4] Schwineköper 1937, p. 120 f.

[5] Schwineköper cites various examples in which a distance or a measure of length was determined by throwing a glove. See ibid., p. 121.

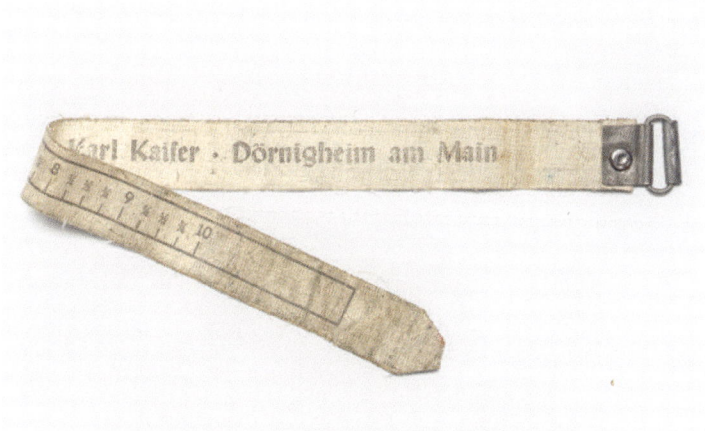

Bandmaß zur Ermittlung der Handschuhgröße aus der Lederhandschuhfabrik Karl Kaiser in Dörnigheim am Main, 20. Jh., Deutsches Ledermuseum
Tape measure used to identify glove size; from Lederhandschuhfabrik Karl Kaiser factory in Dörnigheim/Main, 20th c., Deutsches Ledermuseum

Eine Frau zieht ihre Handschuhe an, Prägung, Detail einer Handschuhtasche, um 1900, Deutsches Ledermuseum
A woman puts on her gloves, embossing, detail of a glove bag, approx. 1900, Deutsches Ledermuseum

Werbemotiv von ROECKL, um 1920
Advertising theme ROECKL, approx. 1920

DREIFINGERHANDSCHUHE, Evelyn Toomistu-Banani, Frankfurt am Main, 2010/12/Veloursleder, Goldfolie/L: 40 cm, B: 17,5 cm/Inv.-Nr. 21284; Provenienz: Schenkung von Evelyn Toomistu-Banani, Frankfurt am Main, 2015 THREE-FINGER GLOVES, Evelyn Toomistu-Banani, Frankfurt/Main, 2010/12/Suede, gold foil/L: 40 cm, W: 17.5 cm/Inv. no. 21284; provenance: donated by Evelyn Toomistu-Banani, Frankfurt/Main, 2015

KOSTÜMHANDSCHUH FÜR KINDER, Marvel Avengers Infinity Gauntlet, NUWIND, China, 2018/19/Kunststoff/L: 29 cm, B: 15 cm, T: 7 cm/o. Nr. CHILD'S COSTUME GLOVE, Marvel Avengers Infinity Gauntlet, NUWIND, China, 2018/19/Plastic/L: 29 cm, W: 15 cm, D: 7 cm/No number

FAUSTHANDSCHUH MIT ABZUGSFINGER FÜR DAS US-MILITÄR, Franklin Manufacturing Company, USA, 1951 / **Überhandschuh: Baumwolle, Leder, Metall; Innenhandschuh: Wolle, gestrickt** / Überhandschuh: **L: 36 cm, B: 19 cm, T: 3,5 cm,** Innenhandschuh: **L: 30 cm, B: 16,5 cm, T: 1,5 cm** / Inv.-Nr. **21479**; **Provenienz: Ankauf 2022** MITTEN WITH TRIGGER FINGER FOR THE US MILITARY, Franklin Manufacturing Company, USA, 1951 / Over-glove: cotton, leather, metal; Inner-glove: wool, knitted / Over-glove: L: 36 cm, W: 19 cm, D: 3.5 cm, Inner-glove: L: 30 cm, W: 16.5 cm, D: 1.5 cm / Inv. no. 21479; provenance: purchased 2022

HANDSCHUHTASCHE, Coburg, Anfang 20. Jh./Leder, Lederschnitt, Textilfutter/H: 30,5 cm, B: 11 cm, T: 3 cm/Inv.-Nr. 21485; Provenienz: Schenkung von Prof. Dr. Günther Gademann, Magdeburg, 2022, aus dem Nachlass von Brigitte Krieg (1921–2009), Überlingen GLOVE BAG, Coburg, early 20th c./Leather, leather cut, textile lining/H: 30.5 cm, W: 11 cm, D: 3 cm/Inv. no. 21485; provenance: donated by Prof. Dr. Günther Gademann, Magdeburg, 2022, from the estate of Brigitte Krieg (1921–2009), Überlingen

Handschuhzubehör

Im 19. Jahrhundert erlebten Handschuhe insbesondere aufgrund verbesserter Fertigungsmöglichkeiten eine Hochzeit.[1] Für eine breitere Gesellschaftsschicht erschwinglich, waren sie in der Frauen- wie auch Männergarderobe allgegenwärtig. Mit der hohen Nachfrage an dieses Accessoire stieg zudem der Bedarf an Zubehör.

Die zu der Zeit modischen Glacéhandschuhe sollten wie eine zweite Haut sitzen. Zum Anziehen der enggeschnittenen Modelle bediente man sich eines Dehners, um die Handschuhe vor dem Überstreifen zu weiten. Die Anziehhilfe war aus Holz, in höheren Preisklassen aus Elfenbein und Silber gearbeitet.

„Es ist nicht zulässig, Glacé-Handschuhe im Geschäft anzuprobieren. Fragen Sie nach dem Kauf eines Paares nach dem Handschuhdehner (der in allen guten Geschäften zur Bequemlichkeit der Kunden bereitgehalten wird) und spannen Sie dann die Handschuhe darauf, es sei denn, Sie haben einen Handschuhdehner zu Hause. Dies erleichtert das Anziehen der Handschuhe, wenn Sie sie anziehen. Handschuhdehner sind in den Geschäften erhältlich oder sollten es sein. Sie werden so manchen neuen Handschuh vor dem Zerreißen bewahren."[2]

Ein ebenso unabdingbares Hilfsmittel war der Knöpfer oder auch Knopfhaken. Am Ende des Griffs mit einem kleinen Haken oder einer Schlaufe ausgestattet, erleichterte er das Verschließen der zierlichen Metall- oder Perlmuttknöpfchen an den Arminnenseiten der langen Damenhandschuhe.[3]

Mit eigens zur Aufbewahrung hergestellten, verschließbaren Handschuhkästen und -schatullen wurde der Wert des Kleidungsstücks betont. Während einfachere Varianten aus Pappe und beschichtetem Papier gefertigt waren, bestand der Korpus der luxuriöseren Modelle aus Leder oder Holz, oft reich verziert und im Inneren mit Samt oder Seide ausgekleidet. Häufig waren sie mit einer kleinen Plakette versehen, um die zumeist massenproduzierten Behältnisse mit einer Gravur der Initialen der Besitzer*innen individualisieren zu können.

---

[1] Im Zuge der Industrialisierung wurden Maschinen entwickelt, die die Handschuhherstellung erleichterten und beschleunigten, etwa eine Maschine, die Handschuhe glättete und faltete, sowie Maschinen zum Anbringen von Knöpfen. Die Handschuhfertigung erreichte in diesem Jahrhundert ihren Höhepunkt. Siehe dazu Green 2021, S. 64 und S. 95.

[2] Eliza Leslie's *The Ladies Guide to True Politeness and Perfect Manners*, 1864 zitiert nach Green 2021, S. 101, übersetzt von der Autorin.

[3] Siehe zu den verschiedenen Knöpfhilfen auch Collins 1945, S. 73. Solche Knöpfer wurden ebenso als Schließhilfe für die ab der zweiten Hälfte des 19. Jh. populär gewordenen Knöpfchenstiefel in der Damenmode verwendet.

Werbung für das 20-jährige Jubiläum der französischen Handschuhmanufaktur Le Gant Neyret, 1926, Frankreich
Advert for the 20th anniversary of glove manufactory Le Gant Neyret, 1926, France

Abbildung aus dem französischen Magazin *FEMINA*, die das Anziehen von Glacéhandschuhen unter Einsatz eines Handschuhdehners veranschaulicht, 1905, Frankreich
Illustration from the French magazine *FEMINA*, illustrating the donning of glacé gloves with the use of a glove stretcher, 1905, France

Handschuhkasten, 1887, Europa, Deutsches Ledermuseum
Glove case, 1887, Europe, Deutsches Ledermuseum

Glove accessories

During the 19th century, improved manufacturing methods, in particular, led to a heyday in the wearing of gloves.[1] Affordable to the broader social classes, they were ubiquitous in both women's and men's wardrobes. As the demand for gloves grew, so did the need for accessories to go with them.

The glacé gloves that were fashionable at the time were designed to fit like a second skin. A stretching tool was required for these tight-fitting models to widen them before they were slipped on. This dressing aid was made of wood, with more expensive versions available in ivory and silver.

"It is not admissible to try on kid gloves in store. After buying a pair, ask for the glove-strechter (which they keep in all good shops, for the convenience of customers) and then stretch the gloves upon it, unless you have a glove-stretcher at home. This will render them easy to put on when you take them into wear. Glove-stretchers are to be bought at the variety stores; or ought to be. The will save many a new glove from tearing."[2]

An equally indispensable tool was the button hook. Equipped with a small hook or loop at the end of the handle, the tool made it easier to fasten the delicate metal or mother-of-pearl buttons on the inside of the arms of long ladies' gloves.[3]

Lockable glove boxes and caskets made specifically for storage underscore the value such garments could have. While simpler variants were made of cardboard and coated paper, the body of the more luxurious models was made of leather or wood, often richly decorated, and lined inside with velvet or silk. They were often equipped with a small plaque so that the mostly mass-produced containers could be personalized with an engraving of the owner's initials.

---

[1] In the course of industrialization, machines were developed that facilitated and accelerated glove production, such as a machine that smoothed and folded gloves and machines for attaching buttons. Glove manufacturing reached its peak during that century. See Green 2021, p. 64 and p. 95.

[2] Eliza Leslie's *The Ladies Guide to True Politeness and Perfect Manners* 1864, quoted from Green 2021, p. 101.

[3] See also Collins 1945, p. 73, on the various buttoning aids. Such buttons were also used as closing aids for the buttoned boots that became popular in women's fashion from the second half of the 19th century.

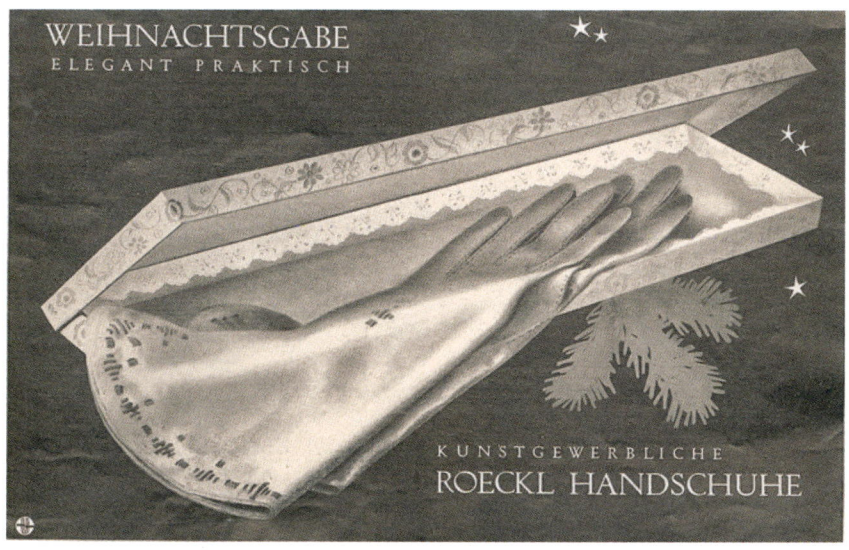

Anzeige für ROECKL Handschuhe, 1936
Advert for ROECKL Gloves, 1936

Weihnachtskarte von ROECKL, um 1910
Christmas card ROECKL, approx. 1910

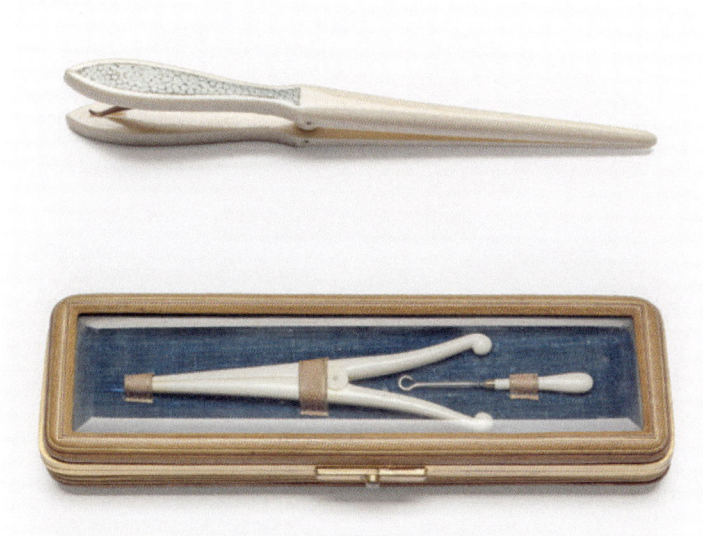

Handschuhdehner aus Elfenbein mit Rochenleder bezogen, 1920/30, Frankreich, Deutsches Ledermuseum und Handschuhkasten mit Handschuhdehner und Knöpfer, 2. Hälfte 19. Jh., Europa, Deutsches Ledermuseum
Glove stretcher made of ivory covered with stingray leather, 1920/30, France, Deutsches Ledermuseum and glove case with glove stretcher and button hook, second half of 19th c., Europe, Deutsches Ledermuseum

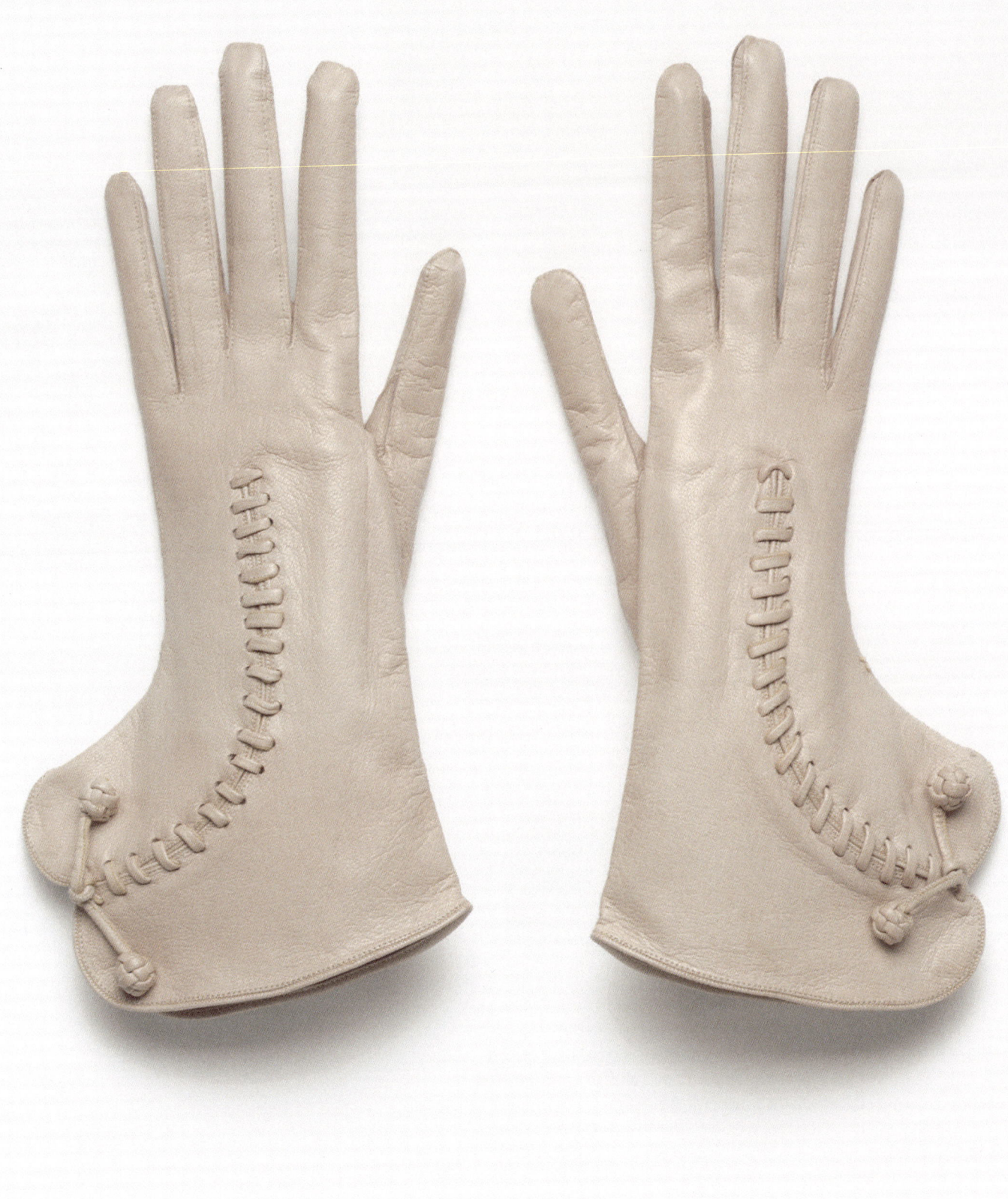

HANDSCHUHE, Luick & Pirmann, Deutschland, 1930er Jahre/Ziegenleder/L: 29 cm, B: 15 cm/Inv.-Nr. T46; Provenienz: Luick & Pirmann, Esslingen, 1938 GLOVES, Luick & Pirmann, Germany, 1930s/Goatskin/L: 29 cm, W: 15 cm/Inv. no. T46; provenance: Luick & Pirmann, Esslingen, 1938

HANDSCHUH ZUM MOTORRADFAHREN, Deutschland, 1920/30er Jahre/Obermaterial: Leder, Metall; Futter: Wollplüsch, Leder/L: 30 cm, B: 17 cm/Inv.-Nr. 18800; Provenienz: Schenkung von Rosemarie Bell, Frankfurt am Main, 1999 GLOVE FOR MOTORCYCLE RIDING, Germany, 1920s/30s/Outer material: leather, metal; lining: wool plush, leather/L: 30 cm, W: 17 cm/Inv. no. 18800; provenance: donated by Rosemarie Bell, Frankfurt/Main, 1999

SCHWIMMHANDSCHUH, Speeron, o. O., 2021/22 / Gummi / L: 23,0 cm, B: 20,5 cm / o. Nr. SWIMMING GLOVE, Speeron, place unknown, 2021/22 / Rubber / L: 23.0 cm, W: 20.5 cm / No number

HANDSCHUHE, *PARIS parfumé*, THOMASINE, Ungarn, 2021/22 / Obermaterial: Lammleder, parfümiert; Futter: Seide / L: 29 cm, B: 10 cm / Inv.-Nr. 21482; Provenienz: Ankauf von THOMASINE, Paris, 2022
GLOVES, *PARIS parfumé*, THOMASINE, Hungary, 2021/22 / Outer material: lambskin, perfumed; lining: silk / L: 29 cm, W: 10 cm / Inv. no. 21482; provenance: purchased from THOMASINE, Paris, 2022

Parfümierte Handschuhe

Im 16. und 17. Jahrhundert erfreuten sich parfümierte Handschuhe großer Beliebtheit bei der gesellschaftlichen Elite in Europa.[1] Als modischer Luxusartikel wurden sie von Frauen und Männern gleichermaßen getragen. Düfte aus pflanzlichen und tierischen Essenzen überspielten sowohl den oft starken Geruch des gegerbten Leders als auch unangenehme Körpergerüche der Träger*innen. Darüber hinaus wurde den duftenden Handschuhen eine desinfizierende Wirkung zugesprochen, die vor der Ansteckung mit Seuchen schützen sollte, deren Erreger in schlechter Luft und Übelgerüchen vermutet wurden.[2]

Zahlreiche Rezepte für Handschuhparfums sind überliefert; gemein ist ihnen die Kombination von intensiv riechenden Inhaltsstoffen wie Amber, Moschus, Zibet, Jasmin, Nelken, Orangenblüten, Rosenwasser und Muskatnuss, die erfrischend und belebend wirken sollten.[3] Zunächst parfümierten die professionellen Handschuhmacher*innen ihre Accessoires, sodann kamen Bücher wie *The English Huswife* von 1623 mit Rezepturen für den Hausgebrauch heraus.[4] Die Handschuhe wurden verschiedenen Prozeduren unterzogen, bei denen sie entweder durch das Baden und Bestreichen mit flüssigen Duftmischungen oder durch die gemeinsame Aufbewahrung mit Riechsäckchen den gewünschten Geruch annahmen.[5] Mit der kosmetischen Verwendung von Parfums ging die Nachfrage an den parfümierten Accessoires allerdings zurück. Heute führen nur wenige die jahrhundertealte Tradition fort, eine von ihnen ist Thomasine Barnekow, die mehrere Modelle ihrer Kollektion in verschiedenen Duftkompositionen anbietet.[6]

---

[1] Das Tragen von parfümierten Handschuhen ist aus Spanien, Italien, England und Frankreich bekannt, wo sich die Mode vor allem durch die Ankunft von Caterina de Medici nach ihrer Heirat mit Heinrich II. 1533 verbreitete. Siehe dazu und zur Bedeutung der französischen Stadt Grasse als Zentrum für parfümierte Handschuhe Redwood 2016, 27 ff. Für den deutschsprachigen Raum siehe Kment 1890, S. 43 f.

[2] Vgl. Collins 1945, S. 15 f. und Green 2021, S. 50 sowie Redwood 2016, S. 28.

[3] Siehe dazu Collins 1945, S. 27 ff., Green 2021, S. 51 und Latour 1947 V, S. 2645.

[4] Siehe Markham 1623, S. 142 f.

[5] Latour und Redwood beschreiben verschiedene Vorgehensweisen bei der Parfümierung von Handschuhen. Siehe Latour 1947 V, S. 2645 und Redwood 2016, S. 28.

[6] Vereinzelt legen Handschuhfirmen Sondereditionen auf. Aus einer Kooperation zwischen dem französischen Parfumhersteller Guerlain mit dem Luxushandschuhhersteller Agnelle 2015 ging etwa anlässlich des 50-jährigen Jubiläums des Dufts *Habit Rouge* eine limitierte Edition parfümierter, schwarzer Lammlederhandschuhe für Herren hervor. Vgl. Green 2021, S. 53.

Nicolas II. de Larmessin, *Habit de Parfumeur*, **Fantasiekostüm eines Parfümeurs mit Attributen seines Gewerbes, Serie** *Les Costumes Grotesques: Habits des métiers et professions*, **1695, Kupferstich, Paris**

Nicolas II de Larmessin, *Habit de Parfumeur*, fantasy costume of a perfumer with attributes of his trade, series *Les Costumes Grotesques: Habits des métiers et professions*, 1695, copper engraving and etching, Paris

Werbekarte für Parfum und Handschuhe, um 1925, Frankreich

Advertising card for perfume and gloves, approx. 1925, France

Perfumed gloves

In the 16th and 17th centuries, perfumed gloves enjoyed great popularity among the social elite in Europe.[1] As fashionable luxury items, they were worn by women and men alike. Fragrances made from plant and animal essences masked both the often-strong smell of the tanned leather and wearers' unpleasant body odors. In addition, the scented gloves were said to have a disinfecting effect, which was supposed to protect against infection with plagues, the pathogens of which were thought to be carried in bad air and bad smells.[2]

Numerous recipes for glove perfumes have survived, with a common feature being the combination of heady-smelling ingredients such as amber, musk, civet, jasmine, cloves, orange blossom, rose water, and nutmeg, which were supposed to have a refreshing and invigorating effect.[3] Initially, professional glove makers perfumed their accessories, then books such as *The English Huswife* of 1623 came out with recipes for home use.[4] The gloves were subjected to various procedures in which they acquired the desired odor either through bathing and brushing with liquid scent mixtures or storage together with scent sachets.[5] With the cosmetic use of perfumes, however, demand for the perfumed accessories declined. Today, only a few continue the centuries-old tradition. One such person is Thomasine Barnekow, who offers several models from her collection in various fragrance compositions.[6]

---

[1] The wearing of perfumed gloves is known from Spain, Italy, England, and France, where the fashion spread especially through the arrival of Catherine de Medici after her marriage to Henry II in 1533. On this and the importance of the French town of Grasse as a center for perfumed gloves, see Redwood 2016, 27 ff. For the German-speaking world, see Kment 1890, p. 43 f.

[2] Cf. Collins 1945, p. 15 f., and Green 2021, p. 50, as well as Redwood 2016, p. 28.

[3] See Collins 1945, p. 27 ff., Green 2021, p. 51, and Latour 1947 V, p. 2645.

[4] See Markham 1623, p. 142 f.

[5] Latour and Redwood describe various procedures for perfuming gloves. See Latour 1947 V, p. 2645, and Redwood 2016, p. 28.

[6] Occasionally, glove companies launch special editions. A cooperation in 2015, for example, between the French perfume manufacturer Guerlain and luxury glovemaker Agnelle resulted in a limited-edition perfumed black lambskin glove for men to mark the 50th anniversary of the *Habit Rouge* fragrance. See Green 2021, p. 53.

Portrait Katharina von Medici, 16. Jh.
Portrait Caterina de Medici, 16th c.

Andre Wilquin, Werbeplakat für Handschuhe, Parfum, Spitzen und Strümpfe, 1934, Frankreich
Andre Wilquin, advertising poster for gloves, perfume, lace, and stockings, 1934, France

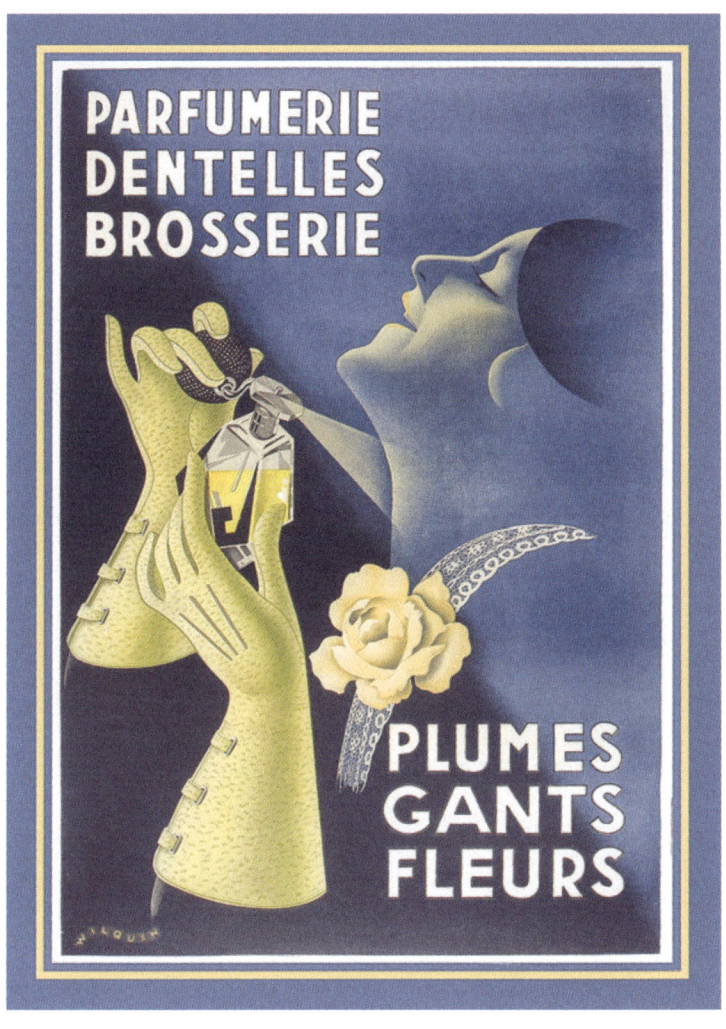

Andre Wilquin, Werbeplakat für Galanteriewaren, 1920er Jahre, Frankreich
Andre Wilquin, advertising poster for fashion accessories including gloves, 1920s, France

HANDSCHUH, Brehme & Siegel, Arnstadt, 1920er Jahre / Oberhand: Fischleder; Innenhand: Ziegenleder / L: 24,5 cm, B: 11 cm / Inv.-Nr. T8; Provenienz: Brehme & Siegel, Arnstadt, 1937 GLOVE, Brehme & Siegel, Arnstadt, 1920s / Back: fish leather; palm: goatskin / L: 24.5 cm, W: 11 cm / Inv. no. T8; provenance: Brehme & Siegel, Arnstadt, 1937

HANDSCHUHE MIT UMSCHLAGSTULPEN, Fa. Maurice Vallet, Paris, Frankreich, 1910/20er Jahre/Leder, Seidenrips, Tambourstickerei/L: 22,5 cm, B: 8 cm/Inv.-Nr. 21478: Provenienz: Ankauf über 1stDIBS, 2022 GLOVES WITH ENVELOPE CUFFS, Maurice Vallet company, Paris, France, 1910s/20s / Leather, silk rips, tambour embroidery/L: 22.5 cm, W: 8 cm/Inv. no. 21478; provenance: purchased via 1stDibs, 2022

HANDSCHUH, Ober- und Unterhand, England, 17. Jh./Elchleder/L: 45,5 cm, B: 26 cm, T: 4 cm/Inv.-Nr. 4958; Provenienz: Ankauf von John Hunt, London, 1935 GLOVE, upper and lower hand, England, 17th c./ Elk leather / L: 45.5 cm, W: 26 cm, D: 4 cm/Inv. no. 4958; provenance: purchased from John Hunt, London, 1935

HANDSCHUHE, Saint Laurent Rive Gauche, Frankreich, 1980er Jahre/Obermaterial: Ziegenvelours, Schmuckstein-Imitationen aus Kunststoff; Futter: Seide/L: 32 cm, B: 11 cm/Inv.-Nr. 21464; Provenienz: Ankauf über 1stDIBS, 2021 GLOVES, Saint Laurent Rive Gauche, France, 1980s/Outer material: goat suede, imitation gemstones made of synthetic material; lining: silk/L: 32 cm, W: 11 cm/Inv. no. 21464; provenance: purchased via 1stDibs, 2021

128

MUFF, HANS SCHWARZ, Frankfurt am Main, 2021/22/Bluefrost-Fuchs, Lammnappa, Metall/H: 30 cm, B: 28 cm, T: 21 cm/Leihgabe von Hans Schwarz, Frankfurt am Main MUFF, HANS SCHWARZ, Frankfurt/Main, 2021/22/Blue frost fox, lamb nappa, metal/H: 30 cm, W: 28 cm, D: 21 cm/On loan from Hans Schwarz, Frankfurt/Main

Der Muff

In der europäischen Mode des 16. Jahrhunderts kam der Muff, ein röhrenförmiges Moderequisit, in das die Hände zum Wärmen gesteckt werden, als luxuriöse Alternative zu Handschuhen auf.[1] Das zumeist aus Pelz gefertigte Accessoire wurde zunächst von Männern und Frauen der privilegierten Gesellschaftsschicht gleichermaßen getragen, bevor es Ende des 18. Jahrhunderts zum femininen Kleidungsstück avancierte. Wie Handschuhe und Fächer ist der Muff ein Mittel der Koketterie und ist aufgrund der taktil-sinnlichen Beschaffenheit des Pelzes und dem Hineinführen der entblößten Hände erotisch konnotiert.

Über die Jahrhunderte hinweg diente er nicht nur als praktisches Kleidungsstück für kalte Winter, sondern vielmehr auch als prestigeträchtiges Standeszeichen.[2] Material, Dekor und Größe variierten im Wandel der Moden; zeitweise soll er so voluminös gewesen sein, dass in ihm kleine Schoßhündchen Platz fanden.[3] Stets auf die Garderobe der Damen abgestimmt, wurden die gefütterten Muffe der Oberschicht aus weichen Pelzen, feinen Samtstoffen und im ausgehenden 19. Jahrhundert mit Federn und Fellen exotischer Tiere gefertigt. Eine häufig eingearbeitete Innentasche bot Platz für ein Taschentuch oder kleine Habseligkeiten. Im Muff getragene Handwärmer, die etwa ein heißes Kohlestück beherbergten, hielten die Hände zusätzlich warm.[4] Neuinterpretiert kehren Muffe regelmäßig in den Winterkollektionen großer Modehäuser zurück auf die Laufstege.

---

[1] Der Begriff Muff leitet sich vom lateinischen *muffula* für Pelzhandschuhe und dem Französischen *moufle*, heute *manchon* ab. Vgl. Loschek 1993, S. 302. Die Herkunft des Muffs ist hingegen nicht eindeutig geklärt. Es könnte sein, dass er sich aus der Muffe, einer trichterförmigen Erweiterung am Ärmelende von Wams und Kleid entwickelt hat. Diese wurden bis in das letzte Drittel des 14. Jh. getragen. Wurden die Hände zusammengeführt, entstand eine Art Muff. Vgl. Loschek 1993, S. 198.

[2] Als Alternative zu den Muffen trugen einfache Bürger*innen im 17. und 18. Jh. zusammengelegte Decken, in der Form einem Muff gleichend, als Kälteschutz. Vgl. Loschek 2011, S. 384.

[3] Vgl. Loschek 1993, S. 198. Da die funktionell bedingte Form des Muffs keine Abweichungen in der Formgebung zuließ, änderten sich vor allem die Größe und die verwendeten Pelzarten. Vgl. Bayerische Versicherungskammer 1979, S. 38.

[4] Vgl. Loschek 1993, S. 198 f.

Wenzel Hollar, *Fünf Muffe*, 1645, Radierung, Staatliche Kunsthalle Karlsruhe, Karlsruhe
Wenzel Hollar, *A Muff in Five Views*, 1645, etching, Staatliche Kunsthalle Karlsruhe, Karlsruhe

Elisabeth Vigee-Lebrun, *Portrait von Madame Mole Reymond*, 1786, Öl auf Tafel, Louvre, Paris
Elisabeth Vigee-Lebrun, *Portrait of Madame Mole Reymond*, 1786, oil on panel, Louvre, Paris

Kostüme aus Paris, Milchbäuerin und Ritter von Saint-Louis unter Ludwig XIV., 2. Hälfte 17. Jh., Radierung koloriert
Special attire from Paris, milkmaid and knight of Saint-Louis under Louis XIV, second half of 17th c., colored etching

The muff

In 16th century European fashion, the muff, a tubular fashion prop into which the hands are tucked for warmth, emerged as a luxurious alternative to gloves.[1] Generally made of fur, the accessory was initially worn by both men and women of the privileged social class before becoming a feminine garment in the late 18th century. Like gloves and fans, the muff is a means of coquetry and has erotic connotations due to the tactile-sensual nature of the fur and the insertion of the bare hands.

Over the centuries, it served not only as a practical piece of clothing for cold winters, but more as a prestigious sign of status.[2] Material, decoration, and size varied with the changing fashions; at times it is said to have been so voluminous that it could even hold small lapdogs.[3] Always coordinated with the colors of ladies' wardrobe, the lined muffs of the upper class were made of soft furs, fine velvets and, in the late 19th century, with the feathers and skins of exotic animals. A frequently incorporated inner pocket provided space for a handkerchief or small belongings. Hand warmers held within the muff, which might have contained a hot piece of coal, for example, helped to keep hands even warmer.[4] Reinterpreted muffs are regularly found back on the catwalks in the winter collections of major fashion houses.

---

[1] The term muff is derived from the Latin *muffula* for fur gloves and the French *moufle*, now *manchon*. Cf. Loschek 1993, p. 302. On the other hand, the origin of the muff is not clearly understood. It could be that it developed from the muffle, a funnel-shaped extension at the end of the sleeves of a doublet and dress. These were worn until the last third of the 14th century. If the hands were brought together, a kind of muff was created. Cf. Loschek 1993, p. 198.

[2] As an alternative to a muff, ordinary citizens in the 17th and 18th centuries used folded blankets, similar in shape to a muff, as protection against the cold. Cf. Loschek 2011, p. 384.

[3] Cf. Loschek 1993, p. 198. Since the muff's functionally determined shape did not permit any deviations in design, it was primarily the size and the types of fur used that changed. Cf. Bayerische Versicherungskammer 1979, p. 38.

[4] Cf. Loschek 1993, p. 198 f.

Plakat des Luxuswarenunternehmens Bally, Nr. 40, 1950, Schönenwerd, Schweiz, Deutsches Ledermuseum
Advertising poster by luxury brand Bally, No. 40, Schönenwerd, Switzerland, 1950, Deutsches Ledermuseum

James Sayers, *Sir Charles Turner*, 1782, Radierung, National Portrait Gallery, London
James Sayers, *Sir Charles Turner*, 1782, etching, National Portrait Gallery, London

Im 19. Jh. gehörten Muffe sowohl zur eleganten Damen- wie auch Kindergarderobe, *Journal des Dames et des Modes*, Costumes Parisiens, 1837
In the 19th c., muffs were a must in an elegant lady's wardrobe or even in children's wardrobes, *Journal des Dames et des Modes*, Costumes Parisiens, 1837

HYGIENEHANDSCHUH, *Pinky Gloves,* o. O., 2021 / Kunststoff, Karton / Handschuh: L: 27 cm, B: 24,5 cm, Verpackung: H: 2,7 cm, B: 11,9 cm, T: 7,3 cm / o. Nr. **HYGIENE GLOVE,** *Pinky Gloves,* place unknown, 2021 / Plastic, cardboard / Glove: L: 27 cm, W: 24.5 cm, packaging: H: 2.7 cm, W: 11.9 cm, D: 7.3 cm / No number

HALBHANDSCHUHE, Deutschland, 19. Jh./Strickspitze, Borte aus Stickspitze/L: 33 cm, B: 10,5 cm/Inv.-Nr. 8776; Provenienz: Ankauf von Frau Merck, Offenbach am Main, 1942 HALF GLOVES, Germany, 19th c./Knitted lace, border of embroidered lace/L: 33 cm, W: 10.5 cm/Inv. no. 8776; provenance: purchased from Ms. Merck, Offenbach/Main, 1942

FAUSTHANDSCHUHE, Northwest Territories, Kanada, um 1940/Karibupelz/L: 23 cm, B: 11 cm, T: 6 cm/Inv.-Nr. 14738; Provenienz: Ankauf mit Mitteln der Stiftung der Städtischen Sparkasse Offenbach am Main von Alika Webber, Kanada, 1989/90 MITTENS, Northwest Territories, Canada, approx. 1940/Caribou fur/L: 23 cm, W: 11 cm, D: 6 cm/Inv. no. 14738; provenance: purchased with funds from the Foundation of the Städtische Sparkasse Offenbach am Main from Alika Webber, Canada, 1989/90

FAUSTHANDSCHUHE, VEB Erzgebirgische Lederhandschuhwerke Johanngeorgenstadt, Erzgebirge, DDR, 1984 / Obermaterial: Lammleder; Futter: Lammwebpelz / Pink: L: 24,5 cm, B: 10,5 cm / Inv.-Nr. 15412 / Blau: L: 24 cm, B: 10,5 cm / Inv.-Nr. 15413; Provenienz: Beide Schenkung Erzgebirgische Lederhandschuhe GmbH, Johanngeorgenstadt, 1991 MITTENS, VEB Erzgebirgische Lederhandschuhwerke Johanngeorgenstadt, Erzgebirge, East Germany, 1984 / Outer material: lambskin; lining: lambskin fur / Pink: L: 24,5 cm, W: 10.5 cm / Inv. no. 15412 / Blue: L: 24 cm, W: 10.5 cm / Inv. no. 15413; provenance: both donated by Erzgebirgische Lederhandschuhe GmbH, Johanngeorgenstadt, 1991

HANDSCHUHE, Europa, Ende 19./Anfang 20. Jh./Leder, Metall/L: 29 cm, B: 8 cm/Inv.-Nr. 21477; Provenienz: Alter Bestand **GLOVES**, Europe, late 19th/early 20th c./Leather, metal/L: 29 cm, W: 8 cm/Inv. no. 21477; provenance: old stock

BALLSPENDEN, vmtl. Wien, um 1900 / Glacéleder / L: 5,9 cm / Inv.-Nr. 18414; Provenienz: Schenkung von Ingeborg Steinacker, Frankfurt am Main, 1997 BALL DONATIONS, probably Vienna, approx. 1900 / glacé leather / L: 5.9 cm / Inv. no. 18414; provenance: donated by Ingeborg Steinacker, Frankfurt/Main, 1997

Etikette

„Tanzen Sie nie ohne Handschuhe. Dies ist eine zwingende Regel"; „Handschuhe sollten von Damen in der Kirche und an öffentlichen Vergnügungsstätten getragen werden. Ziehen Sie sie nicht aus, um die Hand zu schütteln." und „Im Haus [...] gilt die Regel, dass [ein Gentleman] einer Dame nicht die behandschuhte Hand reichen darf."[1]

Über die Jahrhunderte hinweg entwickelte sich aus den höfischen Sitten eine elaborierte Etikette des Handschuhtragens,[2] die ihren Höhepunkt in den bürgerlichen Konventionen des 19. Jahrhunderts fand. Komplexe geschlechtsspezifische und kontextabhängige Regeln schrieben das adäquate Tragen von Handschuhen vor.[3] Diese mündeten in zahlreiche Ratgeber, die ihre Leser*innen vorbildliches Benehmen lehrten. Bei der Wahl der Handbekleidung wurde nach Anlässen und Tageszeiten differenziert, die jeweils unterschiedliche Lederarten, Schnitte oder Farben verlangten.[4] Um dem Regelwerk nachzukommen, wechselte die vornehme Gesellschaft die Handschuhe mehrmals täglich;[5] ein Gentleman um 1840 verwendete bestenfalls sechs Paar:

„Renntierhandschuhe [sic], um am Morgen seinen Jagdwagen zu führen, chamoislederne bei der Fuchsjagd, Biberhandschuhe bei der Rückkehr im Tilbury, Chevreauhandschuhe bei der Promenade im Hydepark, in Begleitung einer Dame oder bei Visiten, hellgelbe beim Dinner und mit Seide bestickte Canepinhandschuhe zum Ball oder zur Soirée."[6]

Bis in das letzte Jahrhundert hinein waren Handschuhe selbstverständlicher Bestandteil der Damen- und Herrengarderobe. In den 1950er Jahren galt eine Frau etwa nur mit Handschuhen als anständig gekleidet, die Accessoires – Hut, Handtasche, Schirm und Handschuhe – wurden farblich aufeinander abgestimmt.[7] Zeitschriften gaben Auskunft über den Handschuh-Knigge und sprachen Empfehlungen zur angemessenen Handschuhwahl aus.

---

[1] Auszüge aus Cecil B. Hartley: *The Gentlemen's Book of Etiquette and Manual of Politeness* von 1860 und Samuel Wells: *How to Behave: A Pocket Manual of Republican Etiquette, and Guide to Correct Personal Habits, Embracing an Exposition of the Principles of Good Manners* von 1887, zitiert nach Green 2021, S. 108, übersetzt von der Autorin.

[2] Ab dem 15. Jh. entstand eine komplexe Etikette, die das Tragen und Nichttragen vorschrieb. So gab es etwa Regeln für das Empfangen von Besuch oder für das Tanzen. Das Gegenübertreten einer sozial höhergestellten Person verlangte das Ausziehen der Handschuhe, anderenfalls wurde es als Affront aufgefasst. Siehe hierzu Loschek 1993, S. 85, Kment 1890, S. 37 sowie Schwineköper 1937, S. 125 ff. Unzählige Schriften hielten diese Regeln fest, die sich teilweise widersprachen und mit der Zeit immer wieder veränderten. Siehe auch Latour 1947 IV, S. 2636 ff.

[3] Nicht nur der Besitz von Handschuhen, sondern auch das Beherrschen der Etikette fungierte als Distinktionsmerkmal zu dieser Zeit. Ebenso mussten die Handschuhe in einem tadellosen Zustand sein, da über diesen Rückschlüsse auf die moralischen Werte und den Charakter der Träger*innen gezogen wurden. Siehe zur sozialen Bedeutung des Kleidungsstücks im 19. Jh. Green 2021, S. 95 ff. sowie 105.

[4] Green bietet einen sehr guten Überblick über die vielfältigen und komplexen Vorschriften. Siehe dazu ebenda, S. 94–113.

[5] Bereits im 18. Jh. wechselte eine Dame mehrmals am Tag ihre Handbekleidung für verschiedene Aktivitäten; bei höfischen Veranstaltungen wurde etwa das Tragen von *Mitaines* erwartet. Vgl. Loschek 1993, S. 88.

[6] Comte d'Orsay, zitiert nach Latour 1947 IV, S. 2641.

[7] Vgl. Loschek 1993, S. 92.

Auguste Renoir, *Der Tanz in der Stadt*, 1883, Öl auf Leinwand, Musée d'Orsay, Paris
Auguste Renoir, *The Dance in the City*, 1883, oil on canvas, Musée d'Orsay, Paris

Plakat des Luxuswarenunternehmens Bally, Nr. 608, 1961, Schönenwerd, Schweiz, Deutsches Ledermuseum
Advertising poster by luxury brand Bally, No. 608, 1961, Schönenwerd, Switzerland, Deutsches Ledermuseum

Die Accessoires sind perfekt aufeinander abgestimmt, 1950er Jahre, England
Perfectly coordinated accessories, 1950s, England

Etiquette

"Never dance without gloves. This is an imperative rule"; "Gloves should be worn by ladies in church, and in places of public amusement. Do not take them off to shake hands" and "In the house [...] the rule is imperative, [a gentleman] must not offer a lady a gloved hand."[1]

Over the centuries, courtly mores evolved into an elaborate etiquette of glove wearing,[2] which culminated in the bourgeois conventions of the 19th century. Complex gender-specific and context-dependent rules prescribed the appropriate wearing of gloves,[3] resulting in numerous books providing advice to their readers on the correct, exemplary behavior. The choice of handwear differed according to the occasion and time of day, with each requiring different types of leather, cuts, or colors.[4] To comply with the rules, distinguished society changed gloves several times a day;[5] a gentleman in around 1840 would ideally use six pairs:

"Reindeer gloves to lead his hunting carriage in the morning, chamois leather ones for foxhunting, beaver gloves when returning in the tilbury, chevreau gloves for a promenade in Hyde Park, in the company of a lady, or on visits, bright yellow ones at dinner, and silk-embroidered canepin gloves to a ball or soirée."[6]

Until well into the 20th century, gloves were an integral part of women's and men's wardrobes. In the 1950s, for example, a woman was considered properly dressed only when wearing gloves, and her accessories – hat, handbag, umbrella, and gloves – were all color-coordinated.[7] Magazines provided information on glove etiquette and made recommendations on the appropriate choice of gloves.

---

[1] Excerpts from Cecil B. Hartley: *The Gentlemen's Book of Etiquette and Manual of Politeness* from 1860 and Samuel Wells: *How to Behave: A Pocket Manual of Republican Etiquette, and Guide to Correct Personal Habits, Embracing an Exposition of the Principles of Good Manners* from 1887, quoted from Green 2021, p. 108.

[2] From the 15th century, a complex etiquette emerged, prescribing what to wear and what not to wear. For example, there were rules for receiving visitors or for dancing. Stepping before a socially superior person required the removal of gloves, otherwise it was considered an affront. See Loschek 1993, p. 85, Kment 1890, p. 37, and Schwineköper 1937, p. 125 ff. Countless writings recorded these rules, some of which contradicted each other and changed again and again over time. See also Latour 1947 IV, p. 2636 ff.

[3] Not only the possession of gloves, but also the mastery of etiquette functioned as a mark of distinction at that time. The gloves also had to be in impeccable condition, as from this people would draw conclusions about the moral values and character of the wearer. On the social significance of the garment in the 19th century, see Green 2021, pp. 95–97 and 105.

[4] Green provides a very good overview of the diverse and complex regulations. See ibid., pp. 94–113.

[5] As early as the 18th century, a lady changed her handwear several times a day for various activities; at courtly events, for example, the wearing of *mitaines* was expected. Cf. Loschek 1993, p. 88.

[6] Comte d'Orsay, quoted from Latour 1947 IV, p. 2641.

[7] Cf. Loschek 1993, p. 92.

Plakat des Luxuswarenunternehmens Bally, Schönenwerd, Schweiz, Deutsches Ledermuseum
Advertising poster by luxury brand Bally, Schönenwerd, Switzerland, Deutsches Ledermuseum

Modisch gekleidete Gentlemen, *Journal des Dames et des Modes*, Costumes Parisiens, 1832
Fashionably dressed gentlemen, *Journal des Dames et des Modes*, Costumes Parisiens, 1832

EISHOCKEYHANDSCHUH, Fa. Walther A. Fischer, Neustadt an der Orla, DDR, um 1965 / Leder, Textilfutter, gepolstert / L: 35 cm, B: 18,5 cm, T: 8 cm / Inv.-Nr. 21472; Provenienz: Ankauf von Gert Fischer und Ines Schuberg, Königs Wusterhausen, 2021 ICE HOCKEY GLOVE, Walther A. Fischer company, Neustadt an der Orla, East Germany, approx. 1965 / Leather, textile lining, padded / L: 35 cm, W: 18.5 cm, D: 8 cm / Inv. no. 21472; provenance: purchased from Gert Fischer and Ines Schuberg, Königs Wusterhausen, 2021

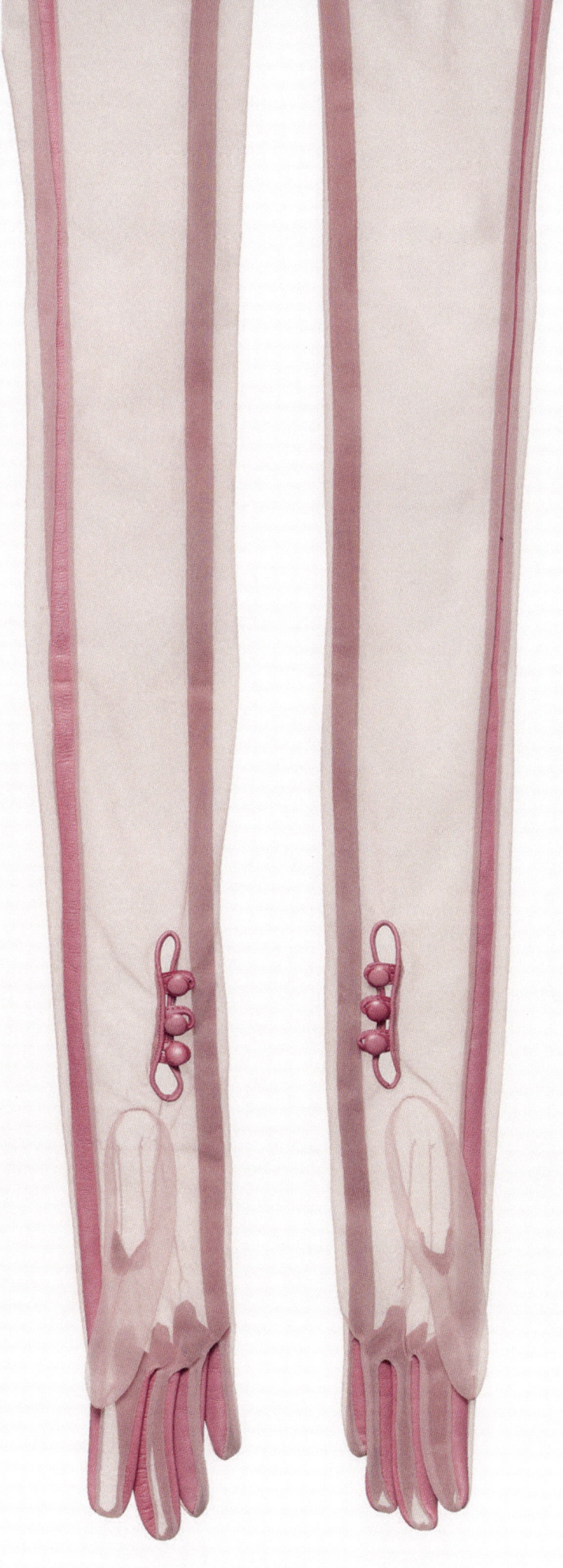

HANDSCHUHE, Marc Jacobs für Louis Vuitton in Kollaboration mit Richard Prince, Frankreich, 2008/Tüll, Lammleder/L: 75 cm, B: 12 cm/Inv.-Nr. 21460; Provenienz: Ankauf von Vestiaire Collective, Paris, 2020 GLOVES, Marc Jacobs for Louis Vuitton in collaboration with Richard Prince, France, 2008/Tulle, lambskin/L: 75 cm, W: 12 cm/Inv. no. 21460; provenance: purchased from Vestiaire Collective, Paris, 2020

HANDSCHUHE, vmtl. Deutschland, 1830er Jahre/Baumwollgarn, eingestrickte Glasperlen/L: 26 cm, B: 14 cm/Inv.-Nr. 11142; Provenienz: Schenkung von Dr. Johannes Jantzen, Bad Homburg, 1961 GLOVES, probably Germany, 1830s/Cotton yarn, knitted-in glass beads/L: 26 cm, W: 14 cm/Inv. no. 11142; provenance: donated by Dr. Johannes Jantzen, Bad Homburg, 1961

146

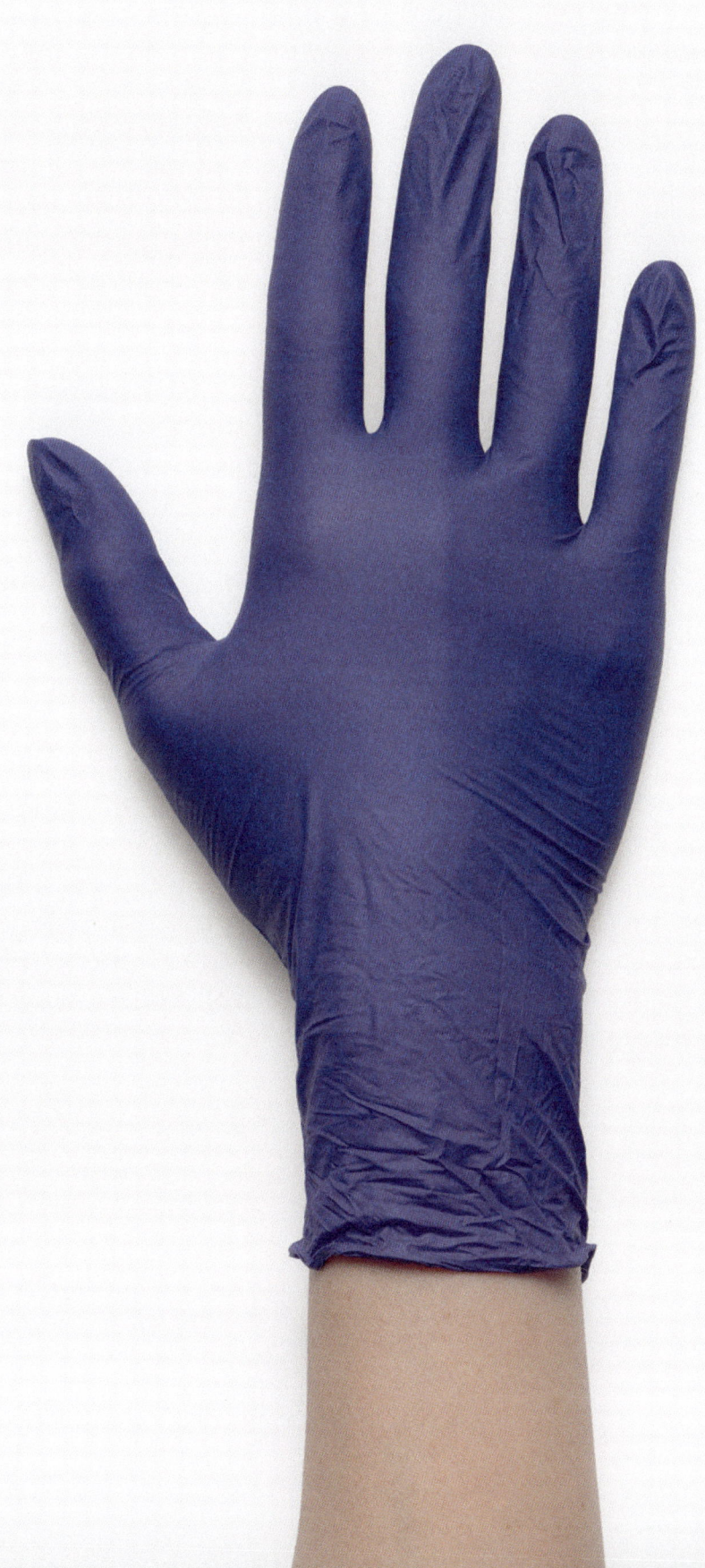

EINWEGHANDSCHUH, BINGOLD, Vietnam, 2021/22 / Nitrilkautschuk / L: 24 cm, B: 11 cm / o. Nr. DISPOSABLE GLOVE, BINGOLD, Vietnam, 2021/22 / Nitrile rubber / L: 24 cm, W: 11 cm / No number

Einmalhandschuhe

Den größten Markt und den höchsten Bedarf an Handschuhen bilden Einmalhandschuhe aus Gummi und Latex, die vor allem aus hygienischen Gründen verwendet werden. Die impermeablen Handschuhe schützen sowohl die Tragenden vor äußeren Einflüssen als auch das Gegenüber oder Gegenstände, die sie berühren, vor den Mikroorganismen auf der Haut.

Nach einmaligem Gebrauch werden die Handschuhe entsorgt. Massenproduziert seit den 1960er Jahren, steigt im Zuge der globalen Covid-19 Pandemie die Nachfrage stetig und liegt bei mehreren Billionen Handschuhen im Jahr.[1] Im medizinischen Bereich finden vor allem dünne, elastische Handschuhe aus Latex oder Nitril Anwendung, um Übertragungen von Infektionen vorzubeugen.[2]

Zunächst wurden in der Medizin Handschuhe aus Textilien wie Zwirn, Seide oder Leinen sowie auch aus Leder und tierischem Darm oder Blase gefertigt. Im 18. Jahrhundert kamen solche etwa in der Gynäkologie als Schutzmaßnahme für die Mediziner*innen zum Einsatz.[3] In den 1880er Jahren wurden Gummihandschuhe[4] für das chirurgische Personal aus dermatologischen Gründen eingeführt, sodann hielten sie als steriler Schutz für Patient*innen sowie Behandelnde Einzug in die OP-Säle.[5] Heute sind sie im Gesundheitswesen allgegenwärtig.

In anderen Sektoren sind Einweghandschuhe aus Vinyl oder Polyethylen (PE) gebräuchlich. Für den hygienischen Umgang mit Lebensmitteln etwa zur Entnahme von Backwaren in den Supermärkten oder auch an Tankstellen, als Dieselhandschuhe bezeichnet, werden PE-Handschuhe benutzt. Im Haushalt finden hingegen eher robustere Gummihandschuhe für den Mehrfachgebrauch, vor allem zum Schutz der Hände vor Reinigungsmitteln, Verwendung. Der Versuch, mit *Pinky Gloves* Einmalhandschuhe als Hygieneartikel für Frauen zu etablieren, bewährte sich allerdings nicht.[6]

---

[1] Siehe dazu Redwood 2016, S. 56 und Green 2021, S. 183. Auf das durch die Pandemie geförderte Sicherheitsbedürfnis haben etwa Handschuhfirmen wie Echo Design und Rhanders reagiert, die waschbare und auch antibakterielle Handschuhe auf den Markt brachten und somit auch auf die Müllproblematik von Einmalhandschuhen reagierten. Den Müll dokumentierte etwa der Fotograf Dan Giannopoulos mit seiner Serie *Virus*.

[2] Darüber hinaus fungieren sie auch als psychologische Grenze und signalisieren den professionellen Charakter des intimen Kontakts zwischen Patient*innen und Ärzt*innen. Vgl. Green 2021, S. 183.

[3] Vgl. Ebstein 1927 und 1926 sowie Wittmann 2018.

[4] Charles Goodyears Erfindung der Vulkanisation im Jahr 1839 eröffnete auch für die Handschuhherstellung neue Möglichkeiten.

[5] Vgl. Green 2021, S. 77 f. sowie Redwood 2016, S. 58. Die Einführung von Gummihandschuhen geht auf den amerikanischen Chirurgen William Stewart Halsted zurück, der der Erzählung nach zunächst Gummihandschuhe für seine im OP arbeitende Freundin anfertigen ließ, um ihre Hände vor aggressiven Desinfektionsmitteln zu schützen. Vgl. Redwood 2016, S. 58. Im deutschsprachigen Raum fanden sie laut Ebstein ebenfalls Ende des 19. Jh. Anwendung. Vgl. Ebstein 1926, S. 343.

[6] Der Hygieneartikel, der in dem Fernsehformat *Höhle der Löwen* gepitcht wurde, erregte vor allem in den Sozialen Medien große Aufmerksamkeit und erntete viel Kritik als antifeministisches Produkt und Mittel zur Tabuisierung der Menstruation. Die Produktion der Handschuhe wurde in Folge der anhaltenden Kritik eingestellt.

Werbung für Haushaltshandschuhe der Fa. Ansell Rubber Gloves, *The Australian Women's Weekly*, 1950, Australien
Advertising for kitchen gloves made by Ansell Rubber Gloves, *The Australian Women's Weekly*, 1950, Australia

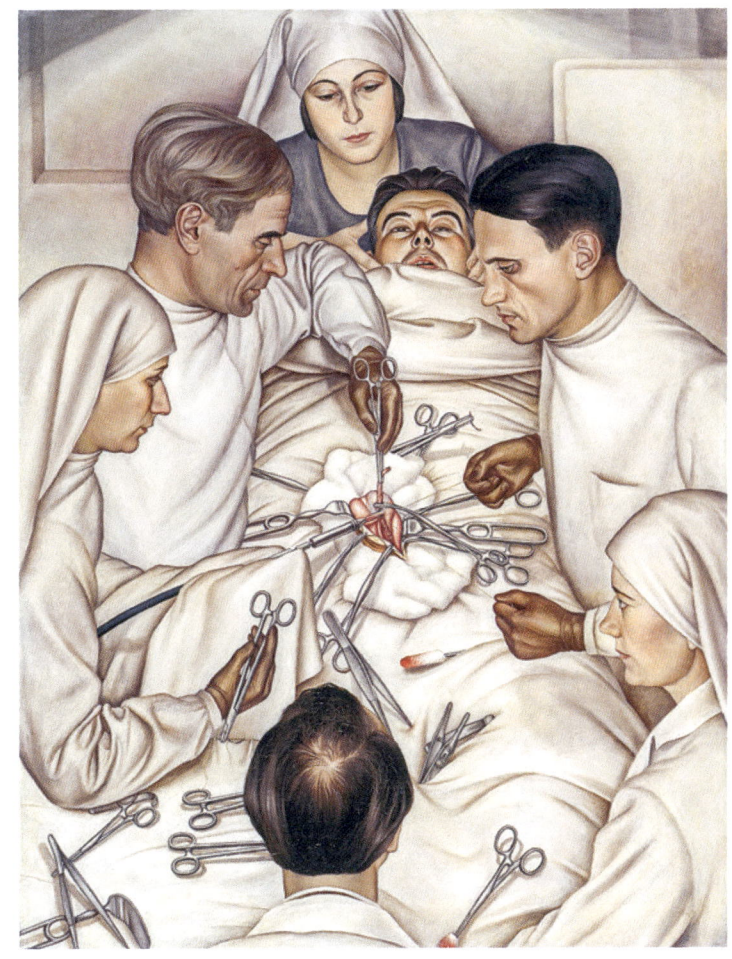

Christian Schad, *Operation*, 1929, Öl auf Leinwand, Städtische Galerie im Lenbachhaus und Kunstbau München, München
Christian Schad, *Operation*, 1929, oil on canvas, Städtische Galerie im Lenbachhaus und Kunstbau München, Munich

Herstellung von PVC-Handschuhen in Rugao, China
PVC gloves manufacturing in Rugao, China

Disposable gloves

Today, the largest market and the greatest demand for gloves is for disposable rubber and latex gloves, which are used mainly for hygiene purposes. The impermeable gloves protect both the wearer against external influences and the counterpart or the objects they touch against microorganisms on the skin.

After a single use, the gloves are thrown away. Mass-produced since the 1960s, they are in rising demand in the wake of the global Covid-19 pandemic and number several trillion each year.[1] In the medical sector, thin, elastic gloves made of latex or nitrile are used mainly to prevent the transmission of infections.[2]

Initially, medical gloves were made of textiles such as yarn, silk, or linen, as well as leather, animal intestines, or bladder. In the 18th century, such gloves were used in gynecology, for example, as a protective measure for doctors.[3] In the 1880s, rubber gloves[4] were introduced for surgical staff for dermatological reasons and then found their way into operating theaters as sterile protection for patients as well as those treating them.[5] These days, they are ubiquitous in the healthcare sector.

In other sectors, disposable gloves made of vinyl or polyethylene (PE) are common. PE gloves are used, for example, for hygienic food handling, for picking out bakery products in supermarkets, or even at gas stations, where they are known as diesel gloves. In households, meanwhile, more robust rubber gloves are used for various purposes, especially to protect the hands against cleaning agents. The attempt to establish disposable gloves as a hygiene article for women with *Pinky Gloves*, however, did not prove successful.[6]

---

[1] See Redwood 2016, p. 56, and Green 2021, p. 183. Glove companies such as Echo Design and Rhanders responded to the need for safety arising from the pandemic by launching washable and antibacterial gloves, and thus also responded to the problem of waste caused by disposable gloves. The photographer Dan Giannopoulos documented the waste with his series *Virus*.

[2] In addition, they also function as a psychological boundary and signal the professional character of the intimate contact between patients and doctors. Cf. Green 2021, p. 183.

[3] Cf. Ebstein 1927 and 1926, and Wittmann 2018.

[4] Charles Goodyear's invention of vulcanization in 1839 also opened up new possibilities for glove manufacture.

[5] Cf. Green 2021, p. 77 f., and Redwood 2016, p. 58. The introduction of rubber gloves can be traced back to the American surgeon William Stewart Halsted, who, or so the legend goes, initially had rubber gloves made for his girlfriend working in the operating room in order to protect her hands against aggressive disinfectants. Cf. Redwood 2016, p. 58. According to Ebstein, they were likewise in use in German-speaking countries at the end of the 19th century. Cf. Ebstein 1926, p. 343.

[6] The hygiene product, which was pitched in the TV format *Höhle der Löwen* (the German version of *Dragons' Den*), attracted a lot of attention, especially on social media, and earned much criticism as an anti-feminist product and a means of making menstruation taboo. Production of the gloves was discontinued as a result of the ongoing criticism.

Sarah Jessica Parker in ihrer Rolle als Carrie Bradshaw in *And Just Like That* …, mit Gummihandschuhen, die ihre Hände vor Zigarettengeruch schützen sollen, 2021
Sarah Jessica Parker in her role as Carrie Bradshaw in *And Just Like That* …, wearing rubber gloves intended to protect her hands against the odor of cigarettes, 2021

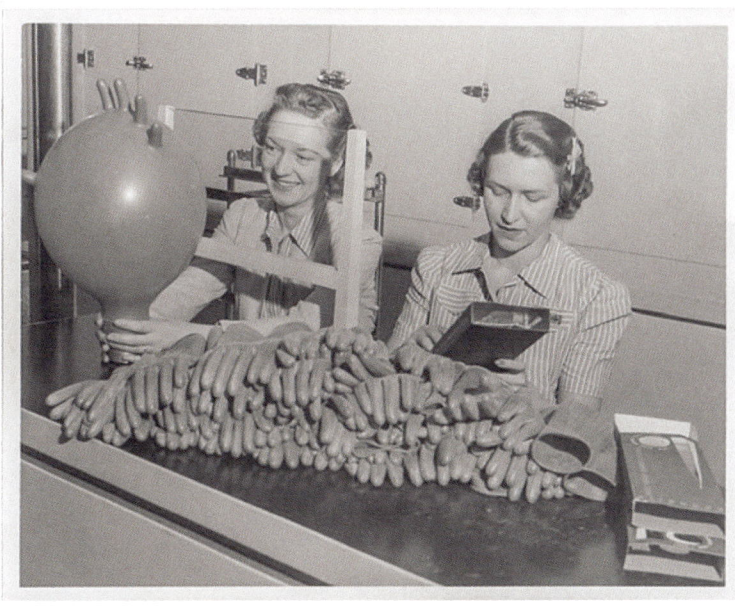

Frauen testen und verpacken Latexhandschuhe, New Yorker Weltausstellung, 1939/40
Women testing and packaging latex gloves, New York World's Fair, 1939/40

Chirurgischer Gummihandschuh, frühes 20. Jh., über ein Band am Handgelenk konnte der weite Handschuh angepasst werden, USA
Rubber surgeon's glove, early 20th c., the wide glove could be adjusted by a strap on the wrist, USA

PAARHANDSCHUHE, *Glovers*, Franziska Holzmann für Radius Design, Deutschland, 2021/22/Thermo-Fleece/L: 28 cm, B: 32 cm, T: 2,5 cm/o. Nr. COUPLE GLOVES, *Glovers*, Franziska Holzmann for Radius Design, Germany, 2021/22/Thermal fleece/L: 28 cm, W: 32 cm, D: 2.5 cm/No number

BONDAGE-HANDSCHUH, BDSMAGE, China, 2021/22 / Obermaterial: folienbeschichtetes Spaltleder, Metall; Futter: Textil, gepolstert / L: 27,5 cm, B: 16 cm, T: 5 cm / o. Nr.
BONDAGE GLOVE, BDSMAGE, China, 2021/22 / Outer material: foil-coated split leather, metal; lining: textile, padded / L: 27.5 cm, W: 16 cm, D: 5 cm / No number

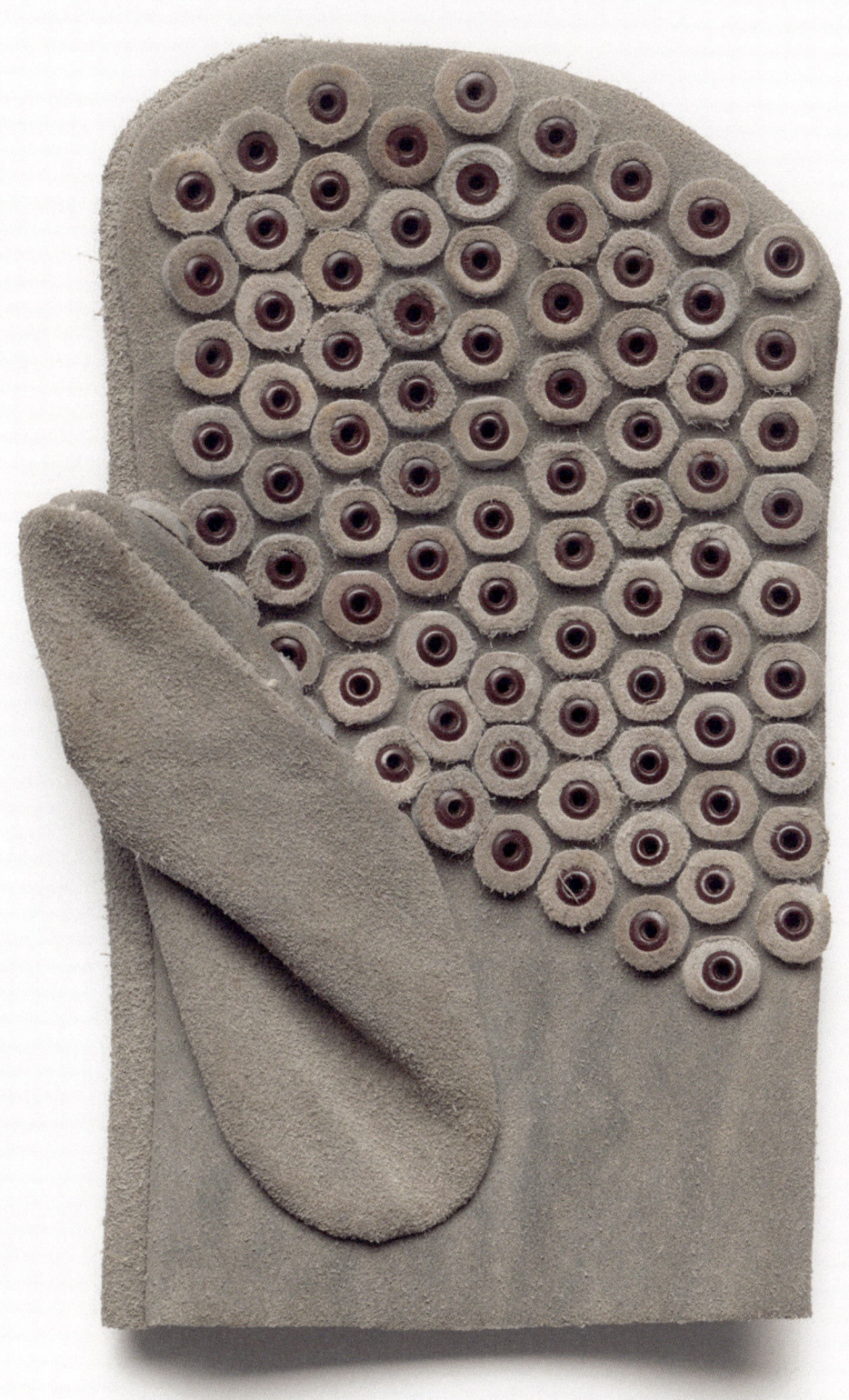

ARBEITSHANDSCHUH, Fa. Johann Duttiné, Mühlheim am Main, um 1960 / Rauleder, perforiert, Metall / L: 23 cm, B: 14 cm / Inv.-Nr. 20192; Provenienz: Schenkung von Madeleine Duttiné, Offenbach am Main, 2006 WORK GLOVE, Johann Duttiné company, Mühlheim/Main, approx. 1960 / Suede, perforated, metal / L: 23 cm, W: 14 cm / Inv. no. 20192; provenance: donated by Madeleine Duttiné, Offenbach/Main, 2006

Schutz- und Arbeitshandschuhe

„Nur Laertes fand er [Odysseus] im schöngeordneten Fruchthain.
Um ein Bäumchen die Erd' auflockern. Ein schmutziger Leibrock
Deckt' ihn, geflickt und grob; und seine Schenkel umhüllten
Gegen die ritzenden Dornen geflickte Stiefeln [sic] von Stierhaut;
Und Handschuhe die Hände der Disteln wegen; die Scheitel
Eine Kappe von Ziegenfell: so traurte [sic] sein Vater."[1]

Die Verwendung von Handschuhen als Schutz- und Arbeitsmittel lässt sich bis in die Antike zurückverfolgen.[2] **Dienten Gartenhandschuhe, wie im Epos** *Odyssee* **beschrieben, als Schutz vor Verletzungen durch Dornen, erweitern aktuelle Modelle darüber hinaus die Funktionalität der Handschuhe, wenn sie mit Krallen an den Fingerkuppen zum Auflockern der Erde ausgestattet sind.**[3]

Neuere Technologien und Materialien finden vor allem im Arbeitshandschuhmarkt Eingang. Für spezielle Anforderungen entwickelte Handschuhe schützen die Hände vor Chemikalien, Hochspannung oder extremen Temperaturen, ohne die nötige Fingerfertigkeit der Träger*innen bei den auszuübenden Tätigkeiten einzuschränken. Andere aus rostfreiem Stahl gefertigte Handschuhe bieten Schutz vor Schnitten und Klingen; Arbeitshandschuhe mit einer PU-Beschichtung eine bessere Griffsicherheit.

Innovative Erfindungen vereinfachen Arbeitsschritte, indem Abläufe effizienter gestaltet werden. So steigert der Handschuhscanner von *ProGlove*, **der vor allem in Logistikunternehmen zum Einsatz kommt, zusätzlich die Produktivität.**[4] **Auch die Bandbreite von Haushaltshandschuhen wird kontinuierlich erweitert. Geschirrspülhandschuhe mit Silikonnoppen auf der Handfläche versprechen etwa einen besseren Reinigungserfolg, ohne empfindliche Oberflächen zu zerkratzen, und machen Spülschwämme überflüssig. Die Fellpflege von Hunden und Katzen soll durch Bürstenhandschuhe, die den Vierbeiner gleichzeitig massieren, erleichtert werden.**

---

[1] Homer, Odyssee, 24. Gesange, Vers 225–230, zitiert nach Voß 1890.

[2] Handschuhe fungierten sowohl als schützendes Hilfsmittel bei Feldarbeiten wie der Flachsbearbeitung oder beim Weinanbau als auch beim Speisen mit den Fingern als Hitzeschutz. Siehe dazu Loschek 1993, S. 83 und Kment 1890, S. 4 ff.

[3] Eine weitere Produktsparte bilden Gartenhandschuhe, die durch spezielle synthetische Gewebe einen besonderen UV-Schutz bieten und vor Hautalterungen schützen sollen. Handschuhe dienten bereits im 18. Jh. als Sonnenschutz, um das Bräunen zu vermeiden und somit die Zugehörigkeit zu höheren Kreisen der Gesellschaft zu demonstrieren. Sonnengebräunte Haut verwies auf Arbeiten im Freiem. Darüber hinaus galt ein *weißer* Hautton lange als weibliches Schönheitsideal.

[4] Ein an einem Handschuh angebrachter Barcode-Scanner erleichtert die Arbeit bei Logistikumschlagplätzen. Mitarbeiter*innen müssen nicht mehr vom Gabelstapler absteigen, um Paletten zu scannen oder um Lagerorte zu erfassen, sondern können alle relevanten Informationen, wie mit dem Artikel zu verfahren ist, über das Scannen in einer Entfernung von bis zu zehn Metern abrufen und sich über ein kleines Display anzeigen lassen.

Arbeiten am Brennofen in den Southern Potteries, 1933, Tennessee
Working at a kiln in the Southern Potteries, 1933, Tennessee

Plakat *Schütze Deine Hände*, Großhandels- und Lagerei-Berufsgenossenschaft, 1960er Jahre
Poster *Protect Your Hands* issued by the German Wholesalers and Warehousing Trade Association, 1960s

Handschuhscanner von *ProGlove*, Workaround GmbH, München
Wearable barcode scanner from *ProGlove*, Workaround GmbH, Munich

Protective and work gloves

"…he [Odysseus] found his father alone in the well-constructed vineyard,
digging around a plant, in a filthy tunic,
patched and shabby, and round his shins he'd fastened
stitched leggings of oxhide, to stop him getting scratched,
with gloves on his hands against the thorns, and above them
on his head a goatskin cap – all fostering his sorrow."[1]

The use of gloves for protection and work can be traced back to Classical Antiquity.[2] While gardening gloves, as described in the epic *Odyssey*, served as protection against injuries from thorns, current models also extend the functionality of the gloves when they are equipped with claws on the fingertips for loosening the soil.[3]

Newer technologies and materials are finding their way onto the market for work gloves, in particular. Gloves developed for special requirements protect the hands from chemicals, high voltage, or extreme temperatures without restricting the dexterity required of the wearer for the activities to be performed. Other gloves made of stainless steel afford protection against cuts and blades, or a PU coating on work gloves provides a better grip.

Innovative inventions simplify work steps by making processes more efficient. The glove scanner from *ProGlove*, for example, which is used primarily in logistics companies, also helps to boost productivity.[4] The range of household gloves is likewise continuously being expanded. Dishwashing gloves with silicone nubs on the palm, for example, promise better cleaning results without scratching sensitive surfaces, rendering dishwashing sponges superfluous. Meanwhile, the grooming of dogs and cats can be made easier by brush gloves that simultaneously massage the four-legged friend.

---

[1] Homer, Odyssey, book 24, lines 225–230, quoted from Green 2018.

[2] Gloves functioned both as a protective aid for field work, such as working flax or cultivating vines, and as heat protection for eating with the fingers. See Loschek 1993, p. 83, and Kment 1890, p. 4 ff.

[3] Another product line is gardening gloves that offer particular UV protection thanks to special synthetic fabrics and are designed to protect against skin aging. Gloves were already used in the 18th century as sun protection to prevent tanning and thus demonstrate membership of higher circles of society. Sun-tanned skin indicated work outdoors. Meanwhile, a *white* skin tone was long considered the female ideal of beauty.

[4] A barcode scanner attached to a glove facilitates work at logistics handling points. Employees no longer have to get off the forklift to scan pallets or record storage locations. Instead, they can call up all the relevant information on how to handle the item by scanning it at a distance of up to ten meters and thus display it on a small screen.

Kunz von Rosenheim bei der Falkenbeize in einem Kornfeld, vor ihm eine Schnitterin mit Handschuhen, *Codex Manesse*, um 1300–1340, Universitätsbibliothek Heidelberg, Heidelberg
Kunz von Rosenheim enjoying falconry in a field of corn, in front of him a reaper wearing gloves, *Codex Manesse*, approx. 1300–1340, Heidelberg University Library, Heidelberg

Édouard Manet, *Jeanne (Spring)*, 1881, Öl auf Leinwand, The J. Paul Getty Museum, Los Angeles
Édouard Manet, *Jeanne (Spring)*, 1881, oil on canvas, The J. Paul Getty Museum, Los Angeles

Hanns Hubmann, Verkehrspolizist in Uniform mit Handschuhen, 1946
Hanns Hubmann, traffic policeman in uniform with gloves, 1946

HANDSCHUH, VEB Erzgebirgische Lederhandschuhwerke Johanngeorgenstadt, Erzgebirge, DDR, 1980/90 / Lammleder, perforiert / L: 25 cm, B: 12 cm / Inv.-Nr. 15414; Provenienz: Schenkung Erzgebirgische Lederhandschuhe GmbH, Johanngeorgenstadt, 1991 GLOVE, VEB Erzgebirgische Lederhandschuhwerke Johanngeorgenstadt, Erzgebirge, East Germany, 1980/90 / Lambskin, perforated / L: 25 cm, W: 12 cm / Inv. no. 15414; provenance: donated by Erzgebirgische Lederhandschuhe GmbH, Johanngeorgenstadt, 1991

FAUSTHANDSCHUHE FÜR BABYS, PICKAPOOH, Deutschland, 2021/22/Bio-Merinoschurwolle, Seide/L: 14 cm, B: 7 cm, T: 3 cm/o. Nr. MITTENS FOR BABIES, PICKAPOOH, Germany, 2021/22/Organic merino wool, silk/L: 14 cm, W: 7 cm, D: 3 cm/No number

FAUSTHANDSCHUHE FÜR KINDER, Finnland, vor 1925 / Obermaterial: Rentierpelz, Filz; Futter: Textil / L: 16,5 cm, B: 9 cm, T: 2,5 cm / Inv.-Nr. 1933; Provenienz: Ankauf von Julius Konietzko, Hamburg, 1925
MITTENS FOR CHILDREN, Finland, before 1925 / Outer material: reindeer fur, felt; lining: textile / L: 16.5 cm, W: 9 cm, D: 2.5 cm / Inv. no. 1933; provenance: purchased from Julius Konietzko, Hamburg, 1925

HANDSCHUHE, Fendi, Italien, 21. Jh./Obermaterial: Kalbfell, bedruckt mit Leopardenmuster, Veloursleder, Metall; Futter: Textil/L: 21,5 cm, B: 9,5 cm/Inv.-Nr. 21462; Provenienz: Ankauf von Vestiaire Collective, Paris, 2021 GLOVES, Fendi, Italy, 21st c./Outer material: calfskin, printed with leopard pattern, suede, metal; lining: textile/L: 21.5 cm, W: 9.5 cm/Inv. no. 21462; provenance: purchased from Vestiaire Collective, Paris, 2021

EINWEGHANDSCHUHE, *TouchNTuff*, Ansell, Thailand, 2021/22/Nitril/L: 29,5 cm, B: 11 cm/o. Nr. **DISPOSABLE GLOVES,** *TouchNTuff*, Ansell, Thailand, 2021/22/Nitrile/L: 29,5 cm, W: 11 cm/No number

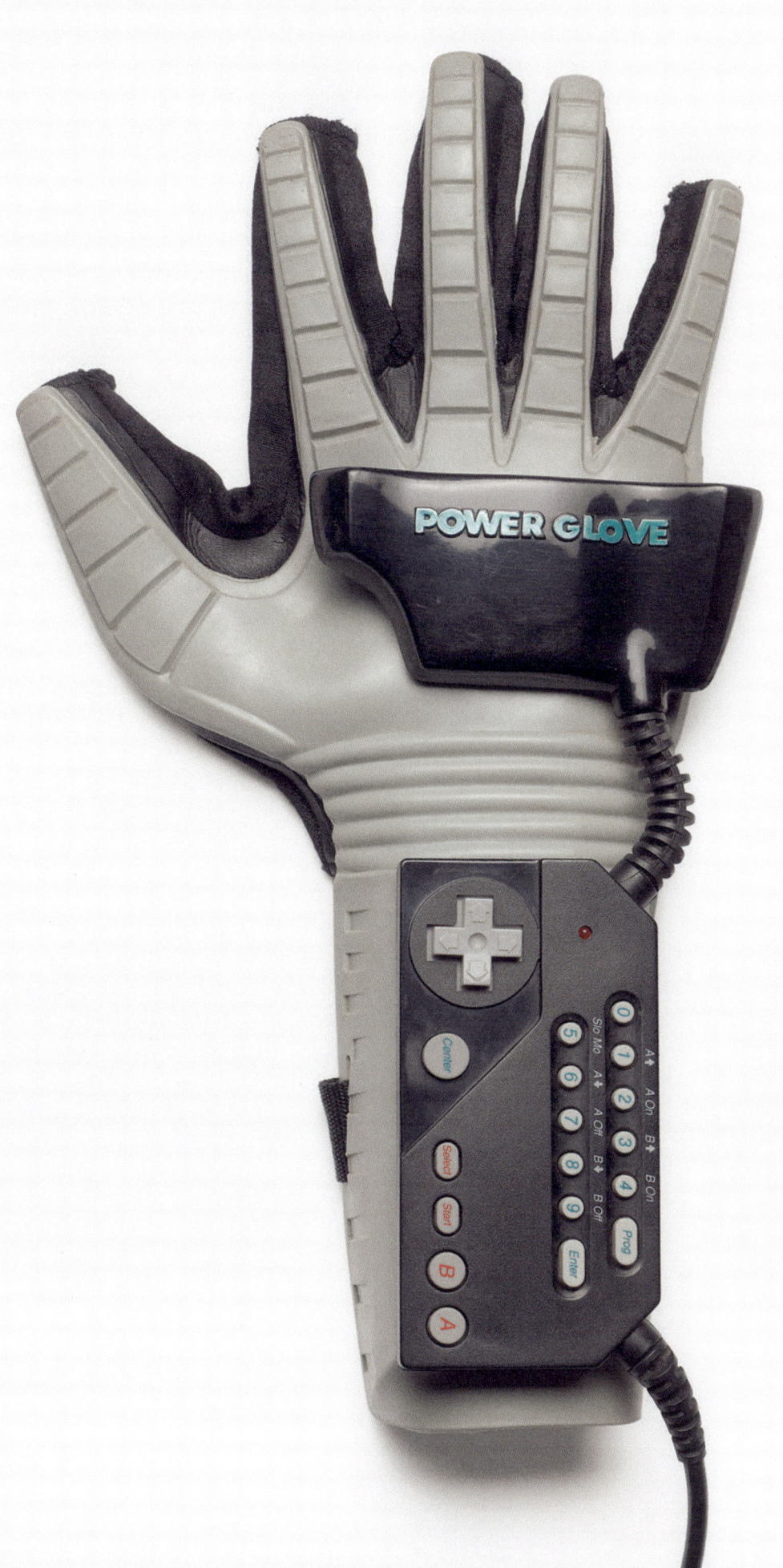

POWER GLOVE FÜR DIE SPIELKONSOLE NINTENDO ENTERTAINMENT SYSTEM, Mattel, Kalifornien, USA, 1989/Kunststoff, Textil, Metall/L: 35 cm, B: 18 cm, T: 7 cm/Leihgabe des Digital Retro Park Offenbach am Main POWER GLOVE FOR THE NINTENDO ENTERTAINMENT SYSTEM GAME CONSOLE, Mattel, California, USA, 1989/Plastic, textile, metal/L: 35 cm, W: 18 cm, D: 7 cm/On loan from Digital Retro Park Offenbach/Main

High-Tech Handschuhe

In den letzten Jahrzehnten haben technische Entwicklungen auch das Handschuhdesign beeinflusst. Mittlerweile gibt es immer mehr Handschuhe, die auch mit High-Tech-Elementen versehen sind. Nicht alle können die in sie gesetzten Erwartungen erfüllen; manche bleiben eher konzeptionell wie der, Ende der 1980er Jahre auf den Markt gebrachte *Power Glove* für Nintendo. Der von dem Spielzeughersteller Mattel gebaute Controller sollte über Gesten des rechten Arms der Träger*innen gesteuert werden. In der Praxis stellte sich die erste VR-Steuerungshilfe für Videospiele allerdings als zu kompliziert und ungenau heraus; dennoch erlangte der *Power Glove* Kultstatus.[1]

Mit der Etablierung des Smartphones und seiner Bedienung via Touchpad mussten neue Lösungen gefunden werden, wollte man das Mobiltelefon auch bei kalten Temperaturen nutzen, ohne die Handschuhe auszuziehen. Handschuhe mit in einer oder mehreren Fingerkuppen eingenähten, leitfähigen Silbergarnen erlauben die Bedienung. Darüber hinaus sind einige Modelle mit einer Bluetooth-Funktion zum Telefonieren ausgestattet. Anrufe können über Knöpfe am Handschuh entgegengenommen werden; die Hand formt mit Daumen, in dem ein Lautsprecher integriert ist, und kleinem Finger, in dem ein Mikrofon verbaut ist, einen Hörer.

Die ursprüngliche Funktion von Handschuhen als Kälteschutz wird durch innovative, zusätzlich beheizbare Outdoorhandschuhe erweitert. In ihnen enthaltene elektrische Heizelemente, die über Akkus betrieben werden, können über verschiedene Heizstufen Temperaturen von bis zu 65 Grad erreichen. Um im Straßenverkehr die Sichtbarkeit zu erhöhen, sind andere Modelle zum Fahrrad- und Motorradfahren mit LED-Lichtern ausgestattet, die auch als Blinker verwendet werden können, um den Richtungswechsel der Fahrer*innen anzuzeigen.

---

[1] Auch wenn die Produktion des Handschuh-Controllers nach einem Jahr wieder eingestellt wurde, avancierte der *Power Glove* zu einer Gaming-Ikone, der 2017 ein Film gewidmet wurde. Siehe auch Green 2021, S. 196. Die Umsetzung der Idee, sich bei Videospielen via Gestensteuerung im virtuellen Raum zu bewegen, gelang Nintendo schlussendlich 2006 mit der Konsole *Wii*. Vgl. Heinz Nixdorf MuseumsForum 2021.

Werbeplakat für den *Power Glove*, 1989
Advertising poster for the *Power Glove*, 1989

Eine junge Frau zeigt ihren Handschuh, in dem sich eine Armbanduhr befindet, 1933, Barnaby's Studios Ltd, London
A young woman shows off her glove, which has an integrated wristwatch, 1933, Barnaby's Studios Ltd, London

High-tech gloves

In recent decades, glove design has also been influenced by technological developments, and there is now an increasing number of gloves that also feature high-tech elements. Not all of them can live up to the expectations placed on them, and some remain rather conceptual, such as the *Power Glove* for Nintendo, which was launched in the late 1980s. Built by toy manufacturer Mattel, this controller was designed to be operated through the movements of the wearer's right arm. In practice, however, what represented the first VR control aid for video games turned out to be too complicated and imprecise. The *Power Glove* managed to achieve cult status all the same.[1]

With the emergence of the smartphone and its operation via touchpad, new solutions had to be found if people were to use their cell phones in cold temperatures without taking off their gloves. Gloves with conductive silver yarns sewn into one or more fingertips allow you to use the touchscreen, while some models are even equipped with a Bluetooth function for making phone calls. Calls can be answered via buttons on the glove: the hand forms a handset with the thumb, in which a speaker is integrated, and the little finger, which incorporates a microphone.

The original function of gloves as protection against the cold has been expanded to include innovative outdoor gloves that can be heated up. Electric heating elements contained in them, powered by rechargeable batteries, can be set to various heat levels with temperatures of up to 65 degrees. To increase visibility in road traffic, other models for cycling and motorcycling are equipped with LED lights that can also be used as turn signals to indicate the rider's change of direction.

---

[1] Even though production of the glove controller was discontinued after one year, the *Power Glove* became a gaming icon and a film was dedicated to it in 2017. See also Green 2021, p. 196. The idea of moving around in the virtual space of video games via gesture control was finally realized by Nintendo in 2006 with the *Wii* console. Cf. Heinz Nixdorf MuseumsForum 2021.

Werbemotiv von ROECKL, 1970er Jahre
Advertising theme ROECKL, 1970s

PANZERÄRMEL (KOTE), Japan, vmtl. 18./19. Jh./Seidendamast, Eisenblech, Kettengeflecht, Hirschleder, Seide, Leinengewebe/L: 76 cm, B: 17 cm, T: 11 cm/Inv.-Nr. 4524; Provenienz: Schenkung von Umlauff, Hamburg, 1933 ARMORED SLEEVE (KOTE), Japan, probably 18th/19th c./Silk damask, iron sheet, chain mesh, buckskin, silk, linen fabric/L: 76 cm, W: 17 cm, D: 11 cm/Inv. no. 4524; provenance: donated by Umlauff, Hamburg, 1933

HANDSCHUH, Ober- und Unterhand, VEB Erzgebirgische Lederhandschuhwerke Johanngeorgenstadt, Erzgebirge, DDR, 1985 / Lammleder, perforiert / L: 23,5 cm, B: 10,5 cm / Inv.-Nr. 15405; Provenienz: **Schenkung Erzgebirgische Lederhandschuhe GmbH, Johanngeorgenstadt, 1991** GLOVE, upper and lower hand, VEB Erzgebirgische Lederhandschuhwerke Johanngeorgenstadt, Erzgebirge, East Germany, 1985 / Lambskin, perforated / L: 23.5 cm, W: 10.5 cm / Inv. no. 15405; provenance: donated by Erzgebirgische Lederhandschuhe GmbH, Johanngeorgenstadt, 1991

HAUSHALTSHANDSCHUHE, tattooed *Love/Hate*, Sumitomo Rubber Industries für TRUEGLOVE, Malaysia, 2020/21 / Nitril, bedruckt / L: 27,5 cm, B: 11,5 cm / o. Nr. HOUSEHOLD GLOVES, tattooed *Love/Hate*, Sumitomo Rubber Industries for TRUEGLOVE, Malaysia, 2020/21 / Nitrile, printed / L: 27.5 cm, W: 11.5 cm / No number

HANDSCHUHE, Prada, Italien, 2017 / Obermaterial: Lammleder, Glasperlenstickerei; Futter: Seide / L: 30,5 cm, B: 13 cm / Inv.-Nr. 21463; Provenienz: Ankauf von Vestiaire Collective, Paris, 2021 GLOVES, Prada, Italy, 2017 / Outer material: lambskin, glass bead embroidery; lining: silk / L: 30.5 cm, W: 13 cm / Inv. no. 21463; provenance: purchased from Vestiaire Collective, Paris, 2021

Objekt der Begierde

„Wär ich der Handschuh doch auf dieser Hand Und [sic] küsste diese Wange!"[1] Romeos Ausruf drückt den Wunsch aus, zum einen Julias Wange zum anderen ihrer Hand nah sein zu wollen. Zwischen Hand und Hülle besteht schon immer, insbesondere beim enganliegenden Fingerhandschuh, ein intimes Verhältnis. Früh erfuhr die behandschuhte Hand eine erotische Konnotation.[2] Beim Flirten und bei der Kontaktaufnahme zwischen den Geschlechtern diente der Handschuh als Mittel der Koketterie. So signalisierte etwa eine Dame mit dem absichtlichen Fallenlassen des Handschuhs eine Aufforderung zur Konversation, andere Gesten zeigten eine Liebesbekundung oder den Wunsch nach einem Kuss an.[3]

Im 19. Jahrhundert avancierte der Handschuh zum erotisch gelesenen weiblichen Accessoire und somit zum Objekt männlichen Begehrens mit hoher Symbolkraft und Fetischcharakter.[4] In Literatur und bildender Kunst fungierte er regelmäßig als Sinnbild für leidenschaftliche Liebe und Hingabe.[5] Wollte Romeo noch selbst Handschuh sein, wünschten Andere sich den Besitz der Handbekleidung der Angebeteten: „Der Handschuh war das, was er am meisten von einer Frau begehrte, er war die Form und der Abdruck ihrer Hand, ein Gegenstand, der etwas vom Leben ihrer Finger bewahrte."[6] Max Klinger widmete dem sinnlich aufgeladenen Accessoire den Radierungszyklus *Ein Handschuh*. In Traumsequenzen dient ein von einer unbekannten Frau abhandengekommener Handschuh als Projektionsfläche für ambivalente Emotionen wie Sehnsucht, Verlangen, aber auch Angst und Verzweiflung.

Das Bild des Handschuhs als intimes und verführerisches Kleidungstück setzt sich bis in die Gegenwart fort und findet vor allem in Werbung und Film Widerhall.[7]

---

[1] Shakespeare, *Romeo und Julia*, II. Aufzug, 2. Szene, zitiert nach Schlegel 2021, S. 42.

[2] Die Identifikation des Manns mit dem Handschuh, der die Frau umschließt, wird etwa für die Zeit der Renaissance von Stallybrass und Jones aufgezeigt. Vgl. Stallybrass und Jones 2001, S. 128.

[3] Siehe dazu Green 2021, S. 144.

[4] Dem Handschuh werden in verschiedenen Kontexten unterschiedliche Wirkungsmacht und Bedeutungen zugeschrieben, die ihm nicht als primäre Eigenschaften zukommen. Mit seiner Verweisfunktion, wie etwa anhand des Königshandschuhs gezeigt, kann er die Anwesenheit des Abwesenden bezeichnen. Siehe S. 40 in dieser Publikation. Damit ist der Handschuh auch ein geeignetes Objekt des sexuellen Fetischismus. Vgl. Kilchmann 2010, S. 280. Je geringer der eigentliche Nutzwert des Handschuhs etwa als Einzelstück ist, desto besser eignet er sich als Fetisch bzw. als Projektionsfläche semantischer Beladungen. Vgl. Göhlsdorf 2015, S. 280.

[5] Handschuhpaare wurden häufig als Liebessymbol verwendet. In der Moderne diente entsprechend der Paarmetapher der einzelne, nutzlos gewordene Handschuh auch als Symbol für Einsamkeit bzw. Abwesenheit von Liebe. Siehe dazu Green 2021, S. 171 ff. Die Identifikation von Handschuh und Frau zeigte sich bereits in der mittelalterlichen Praxis des Liebespfands, bei der die Minnedame dem Ritter ein intimes Kleidungsstück schenkte. Siehe dazu S. 68 in dieser Publikation. Siehe zu Beispielen aus Kunst und Literatur Kilchmann 2010, S. 280 f. und ausführlich bei Green 2021, S. 161–173.

[6] Edmond de Goncourt: *Chérie*, 1884, zitiert nach Green 2021, S. 161, übersetzt von der Autorin.

[7] Ebenso spielt der Handschuh bei Fetischen als sexuelle Präferenz und bei sexuellen Praktiken eine Rolle. Dies kann das Tragen, An- und Ausziehen des Kleidungstücks betreffen, aber auch bestimmte Materialien, aus denen die Handschuhe gefertigt sind, wie etwa enge Latexhandschuhe oder weiche Pelzhandschuhe, sowie spezielle Modelle, die für bestimmte Rollenspiele oder Praktiken wie Bondage verwendet werden, bei denen durch die Handschuhe die Bewegungsfreiheit der Hände eingeschränkt wird.

Carolus Duran, *Die Dame mit dem Handschuh*, 1869, Öl auf Leinwand, Musée d'Orsay, Paris
Carolus Duran, *The Lady with the Glove*, 1869, oil on canvas, Musée d'Orsay, Paris

Rudolf Roessler, *Liebesglück*, 1888, Farblithografie
Rudolf Roessler, *Lover's bliss*, 1888, color lithograph

„Es schlägt neun Uhr, den anderen Handschuh werde ich Ihnen in Ihrer Wohnung anziehen müssen", Ernst Heilemann, *Neunuhr-Ladenschluß*, *Simplicissimus* Jg. 5, 1900
"It's close to Nine o'clock, I'll have to help you put on the other glove in your apartment", Ernst Heilemann, *Neunuhr-Ladenschluß*, *Simplicissimus*, vol. 5, 1900

Object of desire

"O, that I were a glove upon that hand, That I might touch that cheek!"[1] Romeo's exclamation expresses the desire to be close to both Juliet's cheek and her hand. There has always been an intimate relationship between the hand and the garment that covers it, especially with a close-fitting glove. Early on, the gloved hand acquired an erotic connotation.[2] During flirting and in the initiation of contact between the sexes, the glove served as a means of coquetry. By deliberately dropping the glove, for example, a lady signaled an invitation to strike up a conversation, while other gestures indicated an expression of love or a desire for a kiss.[3]

In the 19th century, the glove advanced to become a women's accessory with erotic connotations, and thus an object of male desire with high symbolic power and a somewhat fetishist character.[4] In literature and the visual arts, it regularly functioned as a symbol of passionate love and devotion.[5] While Romeo wanted to be that very glove, others desired to possess the handwear of their beloveds: "The glove was the thing he most desired from a woman, it was the mold and imprint of her hand, an object that preserved some of the life of her fingers."[6] Max Klinger dedicated the etching cycle *Der Handschuh (Paraphrase on the Finding of a Glove)* to this sensually charged accessory. Meanwhile, in dream sequences a glove lost by an unknown woman serves as a projection surface for ambivalent emotions such as longing and desire, but also fear and despair.

The image of the glove as an intimate and seductive piece of clothing continues into the present day and is echoed especially in advertising and film.[7]

---

[1] Shakespeare's *Romeo and Juliet*, Act II, Scene 2, quoted from Green 2021, p. 163.

[2] The man's identification with the glove that encases the woman is demonstrated by Stallybrass and Jones for the Renaissance period, for example. Cf. Stallybrass and Jones 2001, p. 128.

[3] See Green 2021, p. 144.

[4] In various contexts, the glove is ascribed different powers of action and meanings that are not attributed to it as primary properties. With its referential function, as shown for example by the King's Glove, it can signify the presence of the absent. See p. 42 in this publication. Thus, the glove is also a suitable object of sexual fetishism. Cf. Kilchmann 2010, p. 280. The lower the actual utility value of the glove, for instance as a single piece, the more suitable it is as a fetish or as a projection surface for a semantic inference. Cf. Göhlsdorf 2015, p. 280.

[5] Pairs of gloves were often used as a symbol of love. In modern times, in accordance with the couple metaphor, the single glove that had become useless also served as a symbol for loneliness or the absence of love. On this, see Green 2021, p. 171 ff. The identification of the glove with the woman was already evident in the medieval practice of the love token, in which the lady would give the knight an intimate garment. See p. 70 in this publication. For examples from art and literature see Kilchmann 2010, p. 280 f., and in detail in Green 2021, pp. 161–173.

[6] Edmond de Goncourt: *Chérie*, 1884, quoted from Green 2021, p. 161.

[7] Likewise, the glove plays a role in fetishes as a sexual preference and in sexual practices. This can concern the wearing, putting on, and taking off of the garment, but also certain materials from which the gloves are made, such as tight latex gloves or soft fur gloves, as well as special models used for certain role-playing games or practices such as bondage, where the gloves restrict the hands' freedom of movement.

Max Klinger, *Handlung* (Paraphrase über den Fund eines Handschuhs, Opus VI, Blatt 2), 1881, Staatliche Kunsthalle Karlsruhe, Karlsruhe
Max Klinger, *Act* (plate 2 from Paraphrase on the Finding of a Glove, Opus VI), 1881, Staatliche Kunsthalle Karlsruhe, Karlsruhe

Max Klinger, *Ruhe* (Paraphrase über den Fund eines Handschuhs, Opus VI, Blatt 8), 1881, Staatliche Kunsthalle Karlsruhe, Karlsruhe
Max Klinger, *Repose* (plate 8 from Paraphrase on the Finding of a Glove, Opus VI), 1881, Staatliche Kunsthalle Karlsruhe, Karlsruhe

Weihnachtskarte von ROECKL, um 1910
Christmas card ROECKL, approx. 1910

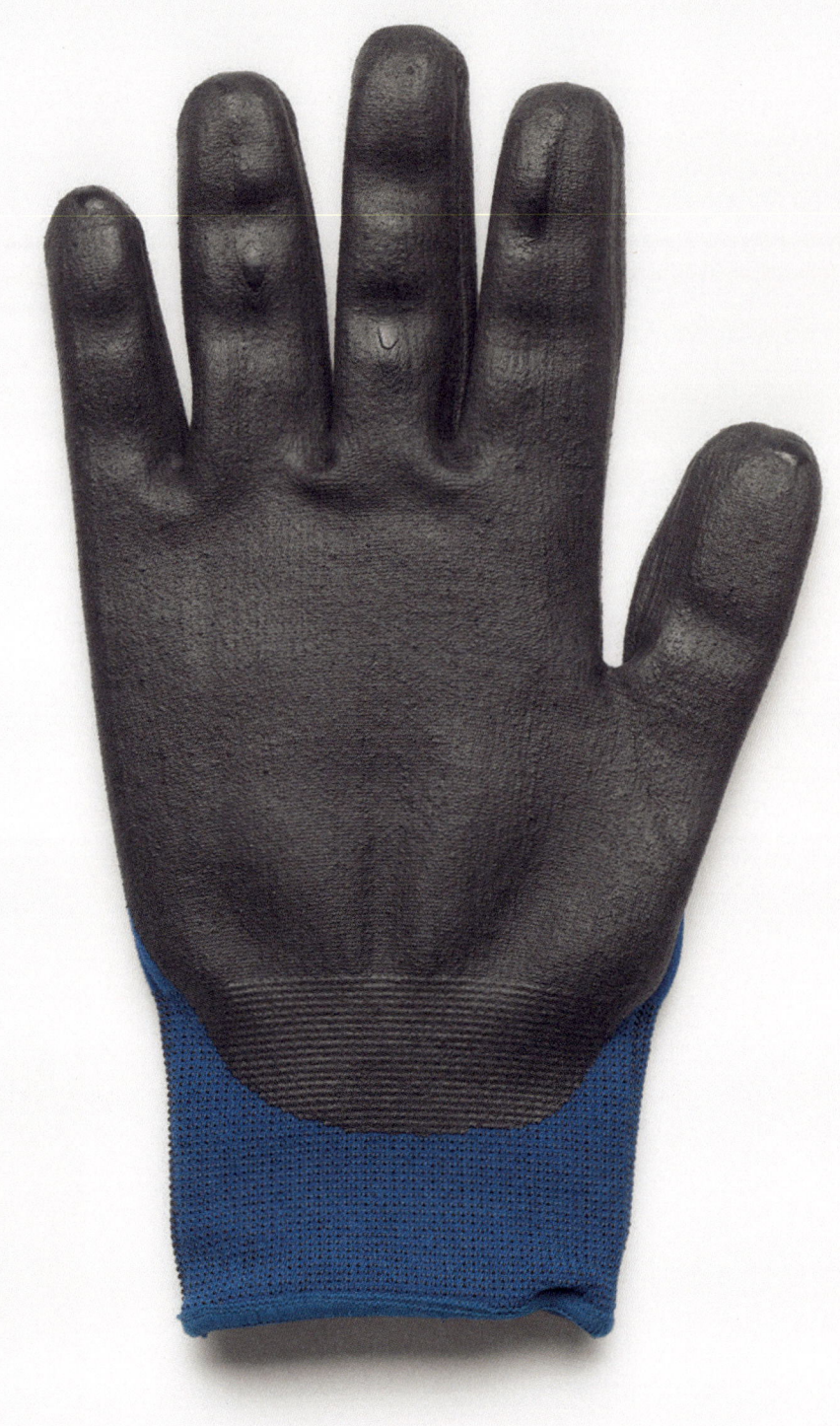

SCHUTZHANDSCHUH, *phynomic wet*, UVEX SAFETY Gloves, Deutschland, 2020/21 / Obermaterial: Polyamid, Elastan, Strickbündchen; Beschichtung: Aqua-Polymer-Schaum / L: 23,5 cm, B: 14 cm / o. Nr.
PROTECTIVE GLOVE, *phynomic wet*, UVEX SAFETY Gloves, Germany, 2020/21 / Outer material: polyamide, elastane, knitted cuff; coating: aqua polymer foam / L: 23.5 cm, W: 14 cm / No number

HANDSCHUH, Nordamerika, Ende 19. Jh. / Obermaterial: Leder, Glasperlenstickerei; Futter (Stulpen): Baumwolle / L: 37 cm, B: 22 cm / Inv.-Nr. 9266; Provenienz: Ankauf von Christof Drexel, München, 1949
GLOVE, North America, late 19th c. / Outer material: leather, glass bead embroidery; lining (cuffs): cotton / L: 37 cm, W: 22 cm / Inv. no. 9266; provenance: purchased from Christof Drexel, Munich, 1949

181

HANDSCHUH, *Rays Oz Green*, T LABEL, Großbritannien, 2021 / Nylon-Tüll / L: 58 cm, B: 32 cm / Inv.-Nr. 21468; Provenienz: Ankauf von T LABEL, London, 2021 GLOVE, *Rays Oz Green*, T LABEL, United Kingdom, 2021 / Nylon tulle / L: 58 cm, W: 32 cm / Inv. no. 21468; provenance: purchased from T LABEL, London, 2021

JUMBO MAUS HANDSCHUH, ORLOB Karneval, China, 2021/22 / Polyester, gefüttert, wattiert / L: 26 cm, B: 23,5 cm, T: 7 cm / o. Nr. **JUMBO MOUSE GLOVE, ORLOB carnival, China, 2021/22 / Polyester, lined, padded /** L: 26 cm, W: 23.5 cm, D: 7 cm / No number

Markenzeichen

„Ich fand einen Handschuh cool ... zwei Handschuhe zu tragen erschien mir so gewöhnlich."[1], antworte der King of Pop, als er auf sein ikonisches Accessoire angesprochen wurde. Michael Jackson trug den weißen mit Strasssteinen besetzten Handschuh zum ersten Mal während eines Fernsehauftritts zur Perfomance von *Billie Jean* anlässlich des 25-jährigen Jubiläums des Plattenlabels Motown im Jahr 1983. An diesem Abend feierte auch sein berühmter Moonwalk Premiere.[2] Beide sollten unverkennbare Markenzeichen des Popstars bleiben.[3]

Ebenso markant wirken die weißen Handschuhe der frühen Zeichentrickfiguren, die weniger auf eine modische Entscheidung als vielmehr auf animationstechnische Gründe zurückgehen. Charaktere wie Mickey Mouse stammen noch aus dem Zeitalter der Schwarz-Weiß-Trickfilme, in denen die Figuren zumeist dunkel gezeichnet waren.[4] Kontrastierende Handschuhe erleichterten das Erkennen von Gesten, da sie sich vom restlichen Körper abhoben. Ebenso sollte Mickey Mouse durch die Handschuhe für die Zuschauer*innen menschlicher wirken, auch wenn er nur vier Finger bekam.[5] Nach Einführung des Farbfilms behielten die Charaktere ihre Handschuhe an, die längst zu ihrem Erkennungszeichen geworden waren.[6]

Auch für Karl Lagerfeld war das Nichttragen von Handschuhen kaum vorstellbar: „Ich komme mir ohne Handschuhe auch tatsächlich nackt vor."[7] Lederne Halbfingerhandschuhe gehörten ebenso wie die zu einem Pferdeschwanz gebundenen Haare und eine dunkle Sonnenbrille zu dem charakteristischen Erscheinungsbild des Designers.

Die Handschuhe von bekannten Persönlichkeiten erzielen bei Auktionen mitunter hohe Preise, die die Fans bereit sind, für die ikonischen Kleidungsstücke ihrer Idole zu bezahlen. So wurde etwa ein Handschuh Michael Jacksons für 350.000 US Dollar, die Boxhandschuhe von Muhammad Ali sogar für 836.500 US Dollar verkauft.[8]

---

[1] Michael Jackson, zitiert nach Marsden 2016.

[2] Vgl. Babayigit 2010.

[3] Fans von Michael Jackson lokalisierten im *White-Glove-Tracking-Projekt* den weißen Handschuh in der Filmaufnahme der Motown-Show und nutzen die Daten für effektvolle Videos. Kultstatus erreichte dabei das Video *Giant White Glove*, in dem Jacksons überdimensionierte Hand wie die einer Comicfigur wirkt. Vgl. ebenda.

[4] Mickey Mouse trug zum ersten Mal in *The Opry* 1929 seine weißen Handschuhe. Zuvor waren seine Hände nur als schwarze Kreise dargestellt worden. Die „Toon-Handschuhe" sind an den Händen vieler Zeichentrickfiguren, nicht nur von Disney, üblich.

So trägt etwa auch Bugs Bunny oder Tom von *Tom und Jerry* weiße Handschuhe. Vgl. Burkett 2022.

[5] „Wir wollten nicht, dass er Maushände hat, weil er menschlicher sein sollte. Also gaben wir ihm Handschuhe." Walt Disney, zitiert nach Green 2021, S. 128, übersetzt von der Autorin.

[6] Der einzige Disney-Charakter, der seine Handschuhe endgültig ablegte, war Pinocchio, der bei seiner Metamorphose von der Holzpuppe zum Menschen anstelle der Handschuhe Hände erhielt. Siehe dazu auch Burkett 2022.

[7] Karl Lagerfeld, zitiert nach Prüfer 2014.

[8] Muhammad Ali trug die Handschuhe bei dem legendären Kampf gegen Sonny Liston. Sie wechselten 2014 die*den Besitzer*in. Bei dem 2009 versteigerten Handschuh von Michael Jackson handelte es sich um den eingangs beschriebenen von 1983. Vgl. Green 2021, S. 141.

Audrey Hepburn in ihrer Rolle als Holly Golightly im Film *Frühstück bei Tiffany*, **mit langen Handschuhen, Diadem und Zigarettenspitze, 1961**
Audrey Hepburn in her role as Holly Golightly in the film *Breakfast at Tiffany's*, with long gloves, a diadem and a cigarette holder, 1961

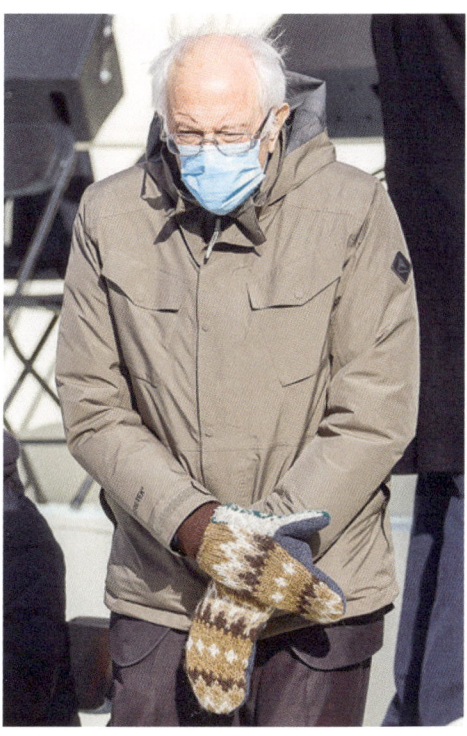

Bernie Sanders mit seinen ikonischen Fäustlingen bei der Amtseinführung von Joe Biden zum Präsidenten der Vereinigten Staaten von Amerika, 2021
Bernie Sanders with his iconic mittens at the inauguration of Joe Biden as president of the United States of America, 2021

Michael Jacksons Handschuh der Victory Tour, Versteigerung durch Julien's Auctions, 2010, USA
Michael Jackson's glove from the Victory Tour, on sale at Julien's Auctions, 2010, USA

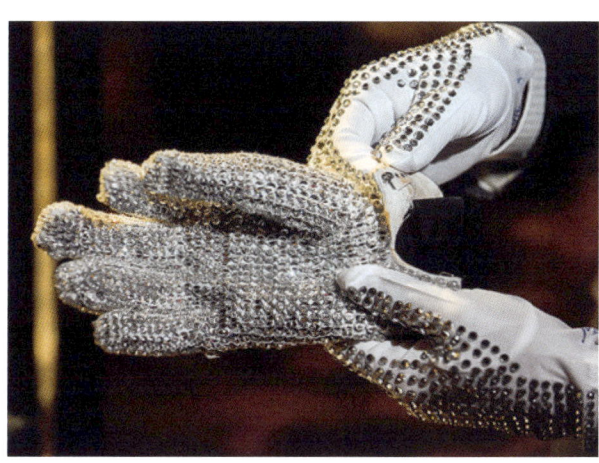

Trademark

"I felt that one glove was cool…wearing two gloves seemed so ordinary."[1], replied the King of Pop when asked about his iconic accessory. Michael Jackson wore the white glove studded with rhinestones for the first time during a television appearance for the performance of *Billie Jean* on the 25th anniversary of the Motown label in 1983. That was the night he premiered his famous moonwalk,[2] and both were to remain among the pop star's unmistakable trademarks.[3]

Equally distinctive are the white gloves worn by early cartoon characters, which are not so much a fashion decision as a requirement of animation technology. Characters like Mickey Mouse still date from the age of black-and-white animated films, in which the characters were mostly drawn in dark colors.[4] Contrasting gloves made it easier to recognize gestures because they stood out from the rest of the body. Likewise, the gloves were intended to make Mickey Mouse seem more human to viewers, even though he was given only three fingers and a thumb.[5] After the introduction of color film, the characters kept their gloves, which had long since become their recognizable trademark.[6]

For Karl Lagerfeld, too, not wearing gloves was almost unthinkable: "I actually feel naked without gloves."[7] Leather half-finger gloves were as much a part of the designer's characteristic appearance as hair tied in a ponytail and dark sunglasses.

The gloves of famous personalities sometimes fetch high prices at auctions, since fans are willing to shell out for the iconic pieces of clothing worn by their idols. One of Michael Jackson's gloves, for example, sold for 350,000 US dollars, while Muhammad Ali's boxing gloves went for as much as 836,500 US dollars.[8]

---

[1] Michael Jackson, quoted from Marsden 2016.

[2] Cf. Babayigit 2010.

[3] In the *White Glove Tracking Project*, fans of Michael Jackson located the white glove in the film recording of the Motown show and used the data for special-effect videos. The video *Giant White Glove*, in which Jackson's oversized hand looks like that of a comic figure, achieved cult status. Cf. ibid.

[4] Mickey Mouse wore his white gloves for the first time in *The Opry House* in 1929. Before that, his hands had only been depicted as black circles. "Toon gloves" are common on the hands of many cartoon characters, not only from Disney. Bugs Bunny, for example, and Tom from *Tom and Jerry* also wear white gloves. Cf. Burkett 2022.

[5] "We didn't want him to have mouse hands, because he was supposed to be more human. So we gave him gloves." Walt Disney, quoted from Green 2021, p. 128.

[6] The only Disney character to finally discard his gloves was Pinocchio, who received hands instead of gloves during his metamorphosis from wooden puppet to human. See also Burkett 2022.

[7] Karl Lagerfeld, quoted from Prüfer 2014.

[8] Muhammad Ali wore the gloves in the legendary fight against Sonny Liston, and they were auctioned in 2014. The Michael Jackson glove auctioned in 2009 was the 1983 glove described at the beginning of this article. Cf. Green 2021, p. 141.

Minnie und Mickey Mouse mit weißen Handschuhen in der Serie *Mickey Mouse*, Disney Channel
Minnie and Mickey Mouse, each with white gloves, in the *Mickey Mouse* series, Disney Channel

Karl Lagerfeld mit silberfarbenen Halbfingerhandschuhen bei der Ausstellungseröffnung *One Man Show*, 2006, Berlin
Karl Lagerfeld with silver half-finger gloves at the exhibition opening *One Man Show*, 2006, Berlin

HANDSCHUHE, Hope Brothers, England, 20. Jh./Kalbleder, teilweise geprägt und durchbrochen/L: 31 cm, B: 15 cm/Inv.-Nr. 16292; Provenienz: Ankauf von Robert Stolper, Bath, 1993 GLOVES, Hope Brothers, United Kingdom, 20th c./Calfskin, partly embossed and pierced/L: 31 cm, W: 15 cm/Inv. no. 16292; provenance: purchased from Robert Stolper, Bath, 1993

BOXHANDSCHUHE VON MAX SCHMELING, Deutschland, um 1970/Rindleder, Baumwollfutter, Wattierung, textile Bindebänder, Kunststoff, signiert/L: 30 cm, B: 18 cm, T: 13,5 cm/Inv.-Nr. 21035; **Provenienz: Ankauf durch den Förderkreis DLM, 2008** MAX SCHMELING BOXING GLOVES, Germany, approx. 1970/Cowhide, cotton lining, padding, textile laces, plastic, signed/L: 30 cm, W: 18 cm, D: 13.5 cm/Inv. no. 21035; provenance: purchased by the Patrons DLM, 2008

HANDSCHUH-TASCHE, Maison Martin Margiela und H&M, Bulgarien, Herbst/Winter 2007/08, Re-Edition 2012/Leder, Metall/Tasche: H: 15,5 cm, B: 32 cm, T: 3,5 cm; Tragriemen: L: 50 cm, B: 8 cm/Inv.-Nr. 21465; Provenienz: Ankauf von Vintage Berlin, 2021 GLOVE BAG, Maison Martin Margiela and H&M, Bulgaria, fall/winter 2007/08, re-edition 2012/Leather, metal/Bag: H: 15.5 cm, W: 32 cm, D: 3.5 cm; carrying strap: L: 50 cm, W: 8 cm/Inv. no. 21465; provenance: purchased from Vintage Berlin, 2021

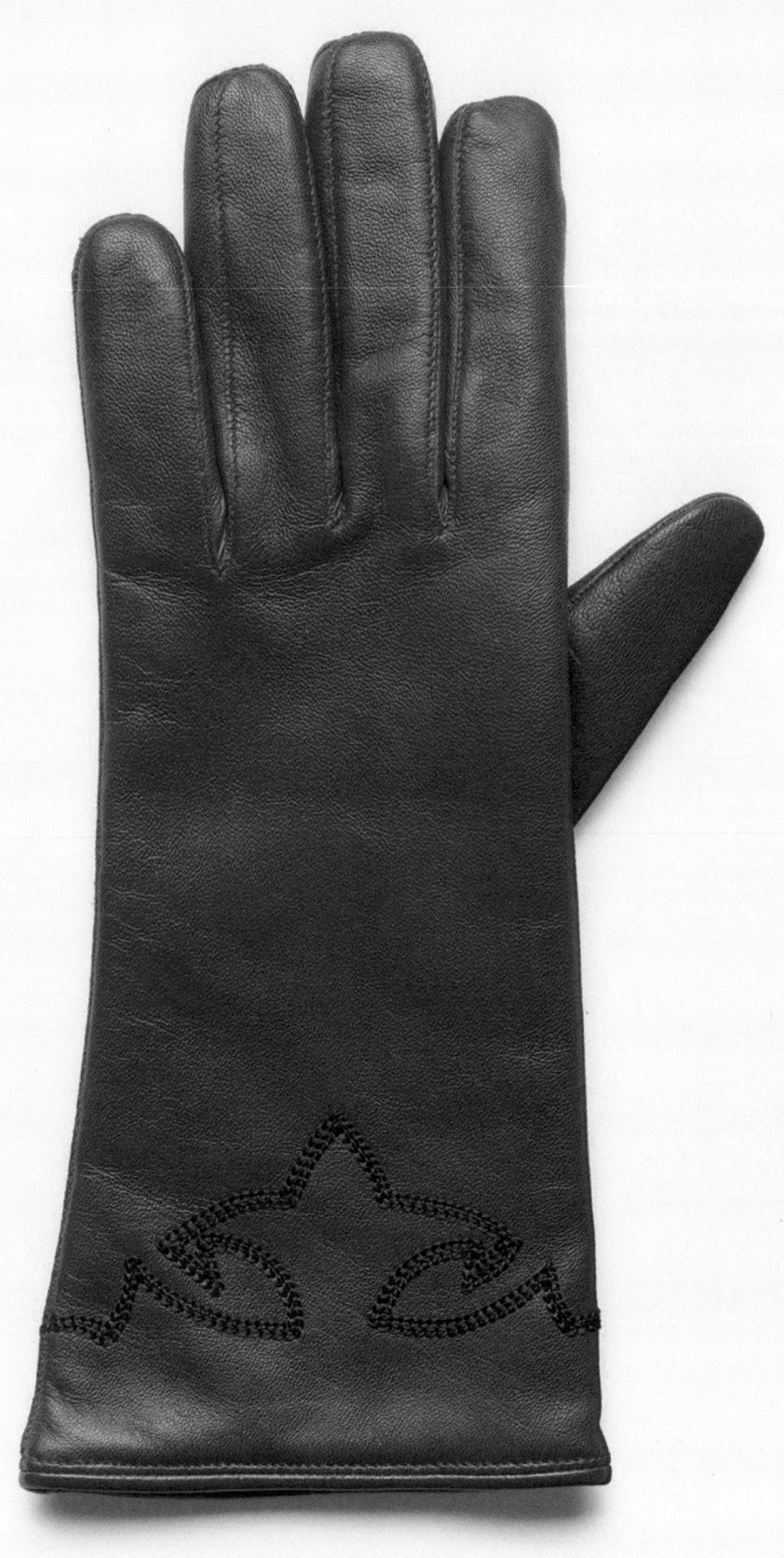

HANDSCHUH, VEB Erzgebirgische Lederhandschuhwerke Johanngeorgenstadt, Erzgebirge, DDR, 1980/90/Obermaterial: Lammleder, Stickerei; Futter: Strickstoff/L: 25 cm, B: 10,5 cm/Inv.-Nr. 15419; **Provenienz: Schenkung** Erzgebirgische Lederhandschuhe GmbH, Johanngeorgenstadt, 1991 GLOVE, VEB Erzgebirgische Lederhandschuhwerke Johanngeorgenstadt, Erzgebirge, East Germany, 1980/90/Outer material: lambskin, embroidery; lining: knitted fabric/L: 25 cm, W: 10.5 cm/Inv. no. 15419; provenance: donated by Erzgebirgische Lederhandschuhe GmbH, Johanngeorgenstadt, 1991

TOPFHANDSCHUHE, Belmalia, China, 2021/22/Silikon/L: 9,5 cm, B: 11 cm, H: 8 cm/o. Nr. OVEN GLOVES, Belmalia, China, 2021/22/Silicone/L: 9.5 cm, W: 11 cm, H: 8 cm/No number

Die Herstellung von Lederhandschuhen

Die manuelle Fertigung eines Lederhandschuhs ist Präzisionsarbeit mit einer langjährigen Tradition und lässt sich bis in das europäische Mittelalter, durch Zünfte, die zu dieser Zeit entstanden, zurückverfolgen.[1] Heute beherrschen nur noch Wenige die alte Handwerkskunst – seit 2011 ist in Deutschland der Beruf der Handschuhmacher*in kein anerkannter Ausbildungsberuf mehr.[2]

Lederhandschuhe variierten zwar über Jahrhunderte hinweg je nach Moden bei der Länge des Schafts, der Weite der Stulpen, der Art des Leders oder der Dekorationen, die Herstellungsweise blieb jedoch die gleiche: Jeder Handschuh wurde einzeln, mit einer Schere aus sorgfältig ausgewähltem Leder zugeschnitten und von Hand mit Nadel und Faden genäht.[3] Bis ins 19. Jahrhundert hinein blieb dieser Fertigungsprozess nahezu unverändert.[4]

Bahnbrechende Errungenschaften wie die Erfindung der Stanzpresse (Fentiermaschine) in den 1830er Jahren und die Einführung von Nähmaschinen Mitte des Jahrhunderts revolutionierten die Handschuhherstellung nachhaltig.[5] Weitere Neuerungen wie Vorrichtungen zum Dehnen und Bügeln der Handschuhe folgten in der zweiten Hälfte des 19. Jahrhunderts.[6] Die Mechanisierung vereinfachte die Arbeitsschritte des Zuschneidens und Nähens, vor allem erlaubte sie aber die Produktion einer höheren Stückzahl. In den Herstellungsprozess integriert, erleichtert sie Handschuhmacher*innen ihre Arbeit bis heute.

Um aus einem Stück Leder, in der Fachsprache auch Fell genannt, einen gut sitzenden Handschuh zu fertigen, bedarf es zahlreicher Arbeitsschritte.[7] Zu Beginn wird das Fell im Hinblick auf Qualität, Stärke, Farbe und Dehnbarkeit kontrolliert und ausgewählt.[8] Um das Material besser verarbeiten zu können, wird es kurze Zeit in feuchte Tücher eingeschlagen, die es elastischer machen. Falls das Fell keine einheitliche Dicke aufweist, muss es in einem nächsten Schritt maschinell oder von Hand dolliert, das heißt angeglichen werden.[9] Vor dem Zuschneiden wird das angefeuchtete Fell in Breite und Länge ausgereckt. Dafür wird es von den Handschuhmacher*innen mehrfach kräftig über eine Tischkante gezogen, um das Material zu dehnen. Das Bestreichen mit Talkumpuder macht etwaige Unebenheiten sichtbar, die später beim Schneiden berücksichtigt werden können. Für den Zuschnitt werden mit dem Zollstab die Maße der Handflächen mit den vier Fingern und der Daumen einzeln auf dem Fell ausgemessen und markiert. Das Depsieren, das Zerlegen des Fells in viereckige Stücke, erfolgt

---

[1] Als Berufsverbände vertraten die Zünfte die Interessen der Handschuhmacher*innen. Bis zur Mechanisierung des Gewerbes regulierten sie Handwerk und Ausbildung und sicherten somit die Qualität der Produkte. Aus England sind erste Zünfte im 10. Jh. bekannt. Vgl. Green 2021, S. 45 und Redwood 2016, S. 14 ff. Während Handwerker*innen in Frankreich sich etwa früh auf die Handschuhfertigung spezialisierten, stellten in Deutschland Beutler*innen und Säckler*innen Handschuhe lange Zeit als Nebenprodukt her. Vgl. Latour 1947 II, S. 2615. In Deutschland schufen vor allem die emigrierten Hugenotten im 17. Jh., die Wissen und Können der Glacéhandschuhfertigung aus Frankreich mitbrachten, die Grundlage des Handschuhgewerbes, das seine Blütezeit im 19. Jh. hatte; noch heute sind viele französische Fachausdrücke erhalten. Vgl. Latour 1947 II, S. 2621 ff. Siehe für traditionsreiche Zentren der europäischen Handschuhproduktion ebenda, S. 2615–2626.

[2] Vgl. Schleufe 2014.

[3] Zu Herstellungstechniken von textilen, etwa aus Leinen genähten sowie zu gestrickten Handschuhen siehe Cumming 1982, S. 17 ff. sowie Collins 1945, S. 112–124.

[4] Handschuhe wurden bereits vor der Industrialisierung in geschlechtsspezifischer Arbeitsteilung hergestellt. Das Bearbeiten der Rohfelle und der Zuschnitt wurde von Männern ausgeführt, Näharbeiten wie das Verzieren und das Zusammennähen von Frauen, zumeist in Heimarbeit, sodann auch in Fabriken. Siehe dazu auch Green 2021, S. 68 f.

[5] Verschiedene Neuerungen zu Beginn des Jahrhunderts erleichterten einzelne Arbeitsschritte wie etwa die Kammnähmaschine von James Winter, auch *Handschuh-Esel* genannt. Bei dieser handelte es sich um einen Holzständer mit einer Zahnklemme, um ebenmäßige Nähte zu erhalten. Vgl. Green 2021, S. 57 und Latour 1947 III, 2631. Zur Fentiermaschine von Jouvin siehe ebenda sowie S. 104 in dieser Publikation.

[6] Vgl. Redwood 2016, S. 64.

[7] Bei dem hier beschriebenen Vorgehen handelt es sich um eine vereinfachte Darstellung des

194

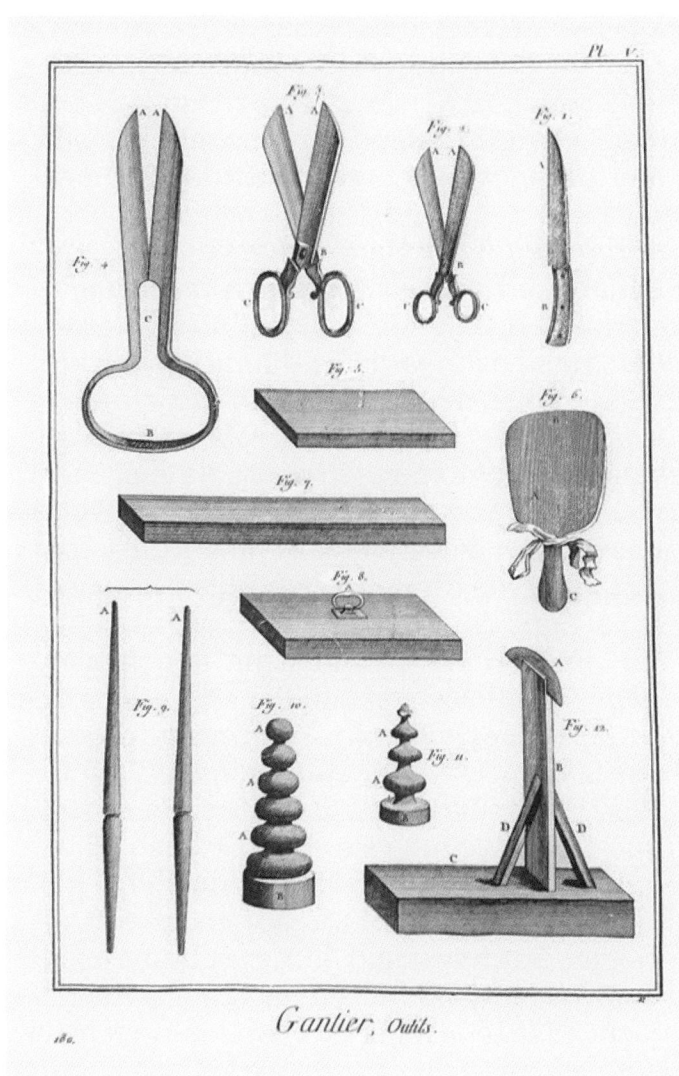

Handwerkszeug der Handschuhmacher*innen, Scheren und Messer (oben), Marmorplatten und Dolliermesser (Mitte) und Renformierhölzer und Spindeln zum Weiten der Finger (unten), *Encyclopédie* **von d'Alembert und Diderot 1751–1788, Deutsches Ledermuseum**
Hand tools used by glove makers, scissors and knives (above), marble slabs and scarping knives (middle) and stretching rods and spindles to expand the fingers (below), *Encyclopédie* by d'Alembert and Diderot 1751–1788, Deutsches Ledermuseum,

Schere, Fa. Carl Drohmann, Stuttgart, 1. Hälfte 20. Jh., Deutsches Ledermuseum
Scissors, Carl Drohmann Company, Stuttgart, first half of the 20th c., Deutsches Ledermuseum

Ausrecken und Zuschneiden der Felle, in einer Handschuhmanufaktur in Witney, 1930er Jahre
Stretching and cutting the skins, in a glove factory in Witney, 1930s

mit der Schere. Anschließend werden die Ränder der Fellrohlinge geglättet. Danach werden die Rohlinge, die Etavillons, erneut über die Tischkante vom Handgelenk zu den Fingerspitzen in die Länge gezogen und gedehnt, bevor sie auf eine Schnittschablone aus Pappe gearbeitet werden. Dies geschieht sowohl mit den Daumen- als auch Handflächenstücken.

Seine eigentliche Form erhält der Handschuh im nächsten Arbeitsschritt. Das Fentieren erfolgt mit der Stanzpresse und handförmigen Ausstechformen, den Kalibern. Auf diese Weise werden die Handflächen mit den Fingern, die Daumen und die schmalen, länglichen Seitenteile, die sogenannten Schichtel, die zwischen die Finger eingesetzt werden, ausgestanzt.[10] Einige Modelle erhalten zusätzlich rautenförmige Zwickel, die zwischen die Schichteln an den Fingerwurzeln angebracht werden. Bevor die Einzelteile der Handschuhe miteinander vernäht werden, erfolgt das Verzieren der Lederstücke wie etwa das Anbringen von Ziernähten, Raffungen, Stickereien oder Perforierungen auf der Oberhand. Anschließend werden die Handschuhteile mit verschiedenen Nahtarten, etwa mit Stepp- oder Laschnaht, mit der Maschine oder von Hand zusammengenäht.[11] Letzte Schritte umfassen bei gefütterten Handschuhen das Einziehen des Innenfutters, das Säumen, das Anbringen von Knöpfen oder anderen Verschlüssen. Um die Handschuhe in Form zu bringen, werden sie auf elektrisch erhitzbare Metallhände zum Bügeln, dem Dressieren, gezogen.[12]

Diese traditionelle Methode wird für Einzel- und Serienfertigungen von wenigen kleinen Betrieben und größeren Unternehmen wie Dents in England oder Roeckl in München nach wie vor angewendet. Handschuhmacher*innen in eigenen Manufakturen bieten darüber hinaus vor allem Maßanfertigungen an und können auch im Design auf die individuellen Gestaltungswünsche ihrer Kundschaft oder auf anatomische Gegebenheiten eingehen.

Herstellungsprozesses. Für eine ausführliche Beschreibung siehe etwa Toomistu-Banani 2011, S. 105–115 sowie Collins 1945, S. 102–111.

[8] Während heute verarbeitungsfertige Felle beim Händler gekauft werden, gerbten und färbten Handschuhmacher*innen die Rohfelle lange Zeit selbst bzw. hatten eigene Gerbereien, in denen nach Bedarf gearbeitet wurde. Siehe Latour 1947 III, S. 2627 f. sowie S. 2632–2635 und Redwood 2016, S. 21–26. Die gängigsten Lederarten in der Handschuhfertigung stammen von Ziege, Schaf, Rind, Schwein und Hirsch. Je nach Gerbmethode und Zurichtung werden sie als Nappa-, Glacé-, Mocha-, Velours- oder Sämischleder verwendet. Siehe dazu auch Collins 1945, S. 86 ff. sowie Toomistu-Banani 2011, S. 115 ff.

[9] Heutzutage erfolgt dies in der Regel maschinell und bereits vor dem Einkauf. In der Vergangenheit wurde das Dollieren mit Hilfe eines breitschneidigen Messers, mit dem das auf einer Marmorplatte ausgebreitete und ausgezogene Fell auf der Fleischseite abgeschabt wurde, von Hand ausgeübt. Vgl. Latour 1947 III, S. 2628 f. Beide Arbeitsmittel sind auf den bekannten Stichen der *Encyclopédie* von d'Alembert und Diderot abgebildet.

[10] Vor der Einführung der Kaliber wurden die Formen von Hand mit der Schere ausgeschnitten. Auch bei orthopädischen Handschuhen, die zumeist Spezialanfertigungen sind, erfolgt in der Regel der Zuschnitt mit der Schere. Ebenso werden Nachbesserungen an den Ausschnitten manuell vorgenommen.

[11] Es wird zwischen einer Vielzahl von Nahtarten unterschieden. Diese können sowohl von Hand als auch mit der Maschine ausgeführt sein. Siehe für Nähtechniken Collins 1945, S. 109 ff. sowie Toomistu-Banani 2011, S. 129 ff.

[12] Zum Dressieren wurde früher der fertige Handschuh angefeuchtet und mit zwei langen Hölzern, den *renformoirs*, und einer kegelförmigen Vorrichtung gedehnt. Vgl. Latour 1947 III, S. 2629.

Ausgestanzte Handfläche und Daumen, Deutsches Ledermuseum
Cut-out palm and thumb, Deutsches Ledermuseum

Handschuhe bei der Dressur in einer Handschuhmanufaktur in Witney, 1930er Jahre
Truing the gloves at a glove factory in Witney, 1930s

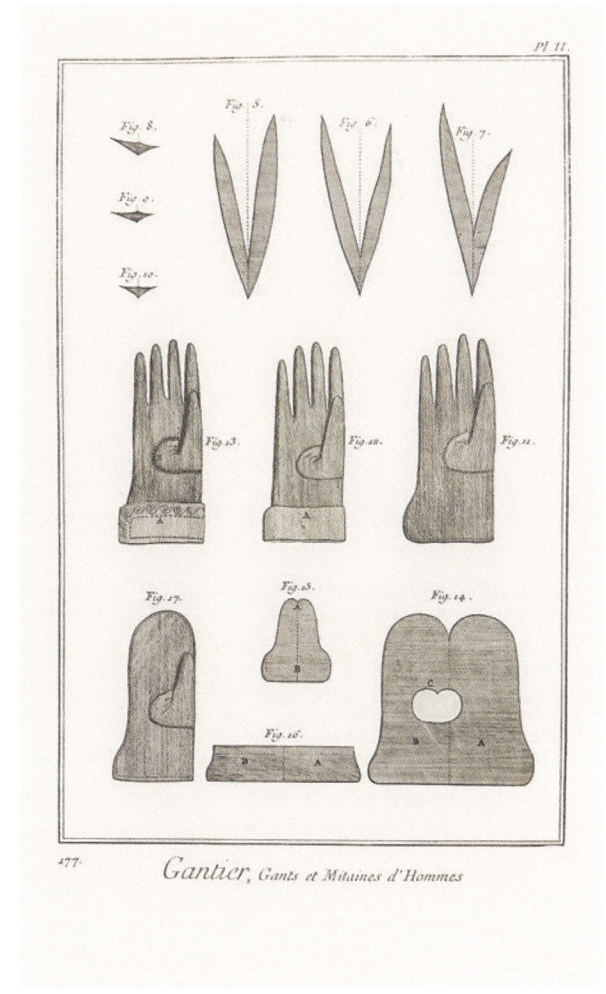

Zwickel und Schichtel (oben), Herrenhandschuhe (Mitte), ein Fausthandschuh sowie seine Bestandteile, *Encyclopédie* von d'Alembert und Diderot 1751–1788, Deutsches Ledermuseum
Gussets and finger walls (above), men's gloves (middle), a mitten and its parts, *Encyclopédie* by d'Alembert and Diderot 1751–1788, Deutsches Ledermuseum

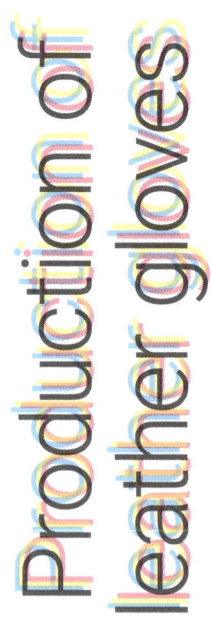
Production of leather gloves

Handmaking leather gloves is precision work with a longstanding tradition that can be traced back to the European Middle Ages, through the guilds that were formed at that time.[1] These days, only a few still master the ancient craft – since 2011, apprenticeships in glove-making have no longer been recognized as training for a profession in Germany.[2]

Depending on the fashion of the day, leather gloves have varied down through the centuries in terms of the length of the shaft, the width of the cuffs, and the type of leather or decoration. However, the method used to make them remained the same: Each glove was cut individually, with scissors, from carefully selected leather and sewn by hand with needle and thread.[3] Until the 19th century, this manufacturing process remained as good as unchanged.[4]

Groundbreaking achievements, such as the invention of the final cutting machine in the 1830s and the introduction of sewing machines in the middle of the century, revolutionized glove-making permanently.[5] Further innovations, such as devices for stretching and ironing the gloves, followed in the second half of the 19th century.[6] Mechanization simplified the steps in the process of cutting and sewing, but above all it allowed the production of higher numbers of gloves. Integrated into the manufacturing process, machines continue to make work easier for glove makers to this day.

There are numerous steps involved in making a well-fitting glove from a piece of leather, also known as a hide in technical jargon.[7] First of all, the hide is checked and selected with regard to quality, thickness, color, and elasticity.[8] To make the material easier to work with, it is wrapped for a short time in damp cloths to make it more supple. If it does not have a uniform thickness, it must be dolled, i.e., adjusted, by machine or by hand in the next step.[9] Before cutting, the moistened hide is stretched out in width and length. To do this, the glove maker pulls it vigorously over the edge of a table several times to stretch the material. Brushing with talcum powder makes any unevenness visible, which can be taken into account later during the cutting. For the cutting, the dimensions of the palms with the four fingers and the thumbs are measured out individually and marked on the hide using a yardstick. Cutting the hide into blanks, or square pieces, is done with scissors, then the edges of the leather blanks are smoothed. The blanks, or "etavillons", are then pulled and stretched again lengthwise over the edge of the table from the wrist to the fingertips before being worked on a cardboard cutting pattern. This is done for both the palm and thumb pieces.

---

[1] As professional associations, the guilds represented the interests of the glove makers. Until the trade was mechanized, they regulated the craft and the training and thus ensured the products' quality. The first known guilds arose in England in the 10th century. Cf. Green 2021, p. 45, and Redwood 2016, p. 14 ff. While craftsmen in France specialized in glove production at an early stage, for a long time in Germany it was boot makers and bag makers who produced gloves as a by-product. Cf. Latour 1947 II, p. 2615. In Germany, it was mainly the Huguenots, having emigrated in the 17th century and brought with them the knowledge and skills of glacé glove manufacture from France, who laid the foundations of the glove trade, which had its heyday in the 19th century; many French technical terms are still in use today. Cf. Latour 1947 II, p. 2621 ff.

For traditional centers of European glove production, see ibid., pp. 2615–26.

[2] Cf. Schleufe 2014.

[3] For production techniques of textile gloves, such as those sewn from linen, and knitted gloves, see Cumming 1982, p. 17 ff., and Collins 1945, pp. 112–24.

[4] Even before industrialization, glove production involved a gender-specific division of labor. Men processed the hides and handled the cutting, while needlework, such as decorating and sewing together, was done by women, mostly working at home and then later also in factories. See also Green 2021, p. 68 f.

[5] Various innovations at the beginning of the century made individual work steps easier, such as James Winter's comb-like sewing machine, also known as the *gloving donkey*. This was a wooden stand with a toothed clamp to obtain even seams. Cf. Green 2021, p. 57, and Latour 1947 III, 2631. For Jouvin's "final cutting" machine, see ibid. and p. 106 in this publication.

[6] Cf. Redwood 2016, p. 64.

[7] The procedure described here is a simplified representation of the production process. For a detailed description see, for example, Toomistu-Banani 2011, pp. 105–15, and Collins 1945, pp. 102–11.

Nähen der Handschuhe, in einer Handschuhmanufaktur in Witney, 1930er Jahre
Sewing the gloves, in a glove factory in Witney, 1930s

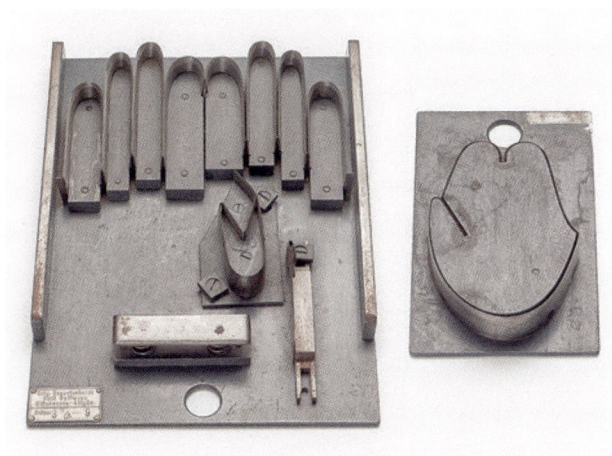

Stanzkaliber für Handfläche und Daumen, 20. Jh., Deutsches Ledermuseum
Caliper scissors for palm and thumb, 20th c., Deutsches Ledermuseum

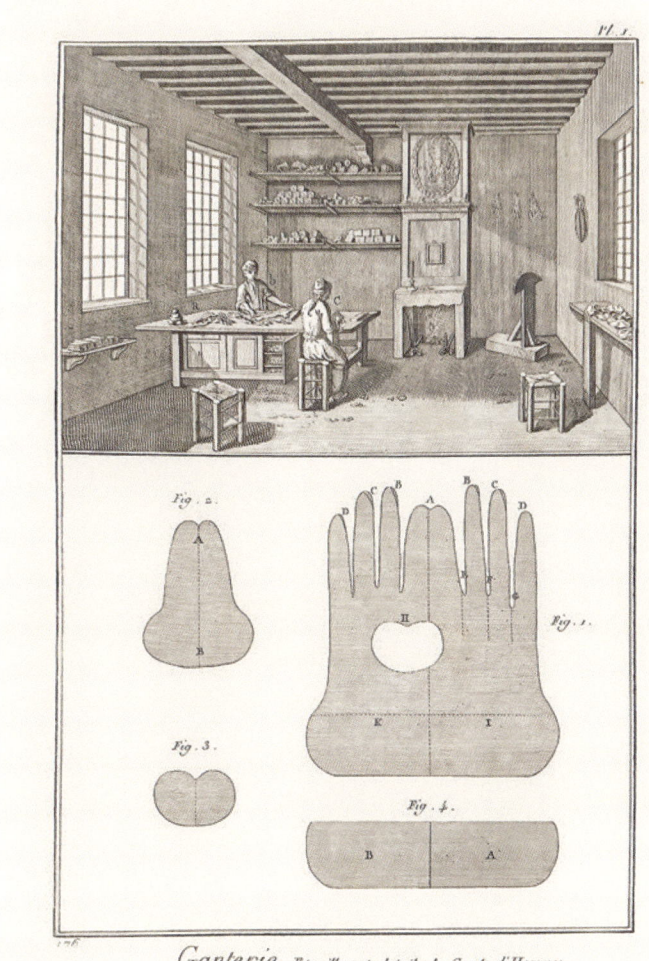

Blick in die Werkstatt, Vorbereiten und Zuschneiden der Felle, *Encyclopédie* von d'Alembert und Diderot 1751–1788, Deutsches Ledermuseum
View of the workshop, preparing and cutting the skins, *Encyclopédie* by d'Alembert and Diderot 1751–1788, Deutsches Ledermuseum

The glove receives its actual shape in the next work step. The final cutting is done with the punch press and hand-shaped cutters, the caliper scissors. In this way, the palms with the fingers, the thumbs, and the narrow, elongated side parts, the so-called "fourchettes", which are inserted between the fingers, are punched out.[10] Some models are also given diamond-shaped gussets, which are placed between the fourchettes at the roots of the fingers. Before the individual parts of the gloves are sewn together, the leather pieces are decorated, for example with the application of decorative stitching, pleats, embroidery, or perforations on the backhand. The glove pieces are then sewn together with different types of stitching, such as topstitching or double lock stitch, either by machine or by hand.[11] Final steps for lined gloves include tucking in the lining, hemming, and attaching buttons or other closures. To bring the gloves into shape, they are pulled onto electrically heated metal hands for smoothing or "shaping".[12]

This traditional method is still used for individual and series production by a few small companies and larger companies such as Dents in England or Roeckl in Munich. Glove makers in their own factories also offer custom-made products and can also respond to the individual design wishes of their customers or to specific anatomical considerations.

---

[8] While, today, ready-to-use skins are purchased from dealers, for a long time glove makers tanned and dyed the raw skins themselves or had their own tanneries where they worked as needed. See Latour 1947 III, pp. 2627 f. and pp. 2632–5, and Redwood 2016, pp. 21–6. The most common types of leather used in glove production come from goats, sheep, cows, pigs, and deer. Depending on the tanning method and finish, they are used as nappa, glacé, mocha, suede, or chamois leather. See also Collins 1945, p. 86 ff., and Toomistu-Banani 2011, p. 115 ff.

[9] Nowadays, this is usually done by machine and prior to the purchase. In the past, dolling was done by hand with the aid of a broad-edged knife, with which the hide, spread out on a marble slab and stripped, was scraped on the flesh side. Cf. Latour 1947 III, p. 2628 f. Both tools are depicted in the well-known engravings of the *Encyclopédie* by d'Alembert and Diderot.

[10] Before the introduction of caliper scissors, the shapes were cut out by hand with scissors. In the case of orthopedic gloves, which are mostly custom-made, the cutting is also usually done with scissors. Likewise, touch-ups to the cutouts are made manually.

[11] A distinction is made between a variety of seam types. These can be executed both by hand and by machine. For sewing techniques, see Collins 1945, p. 109 ff., and Toomistu-Banani 2011, p. 129 ff.

[12] The shaping used to be done by moistening the finished glove and stretching it with two long pieces of wood, the *renformoirs*, and a cone-shaped device. Cf. Latour 1947 III, p. 2629.

Julia Suppanz, 2021, HS Pforzheim
DARE TO CHANGE (ARTIC GLOVE, JUNGLE GLOVE)
Leder, Mesh-Tüll / Leather, mesh tulle

Jennifer Laura Schmidt, 2022, HS Pforzheim
protACC
Kunststoffschaum, 3D Druck / Plastic foam, 3D printing

Özlem Gökce, 2022, HS Pforzheim
Protection
Jute, Draht, olivengegerbtes Leder / Jute, wire, olive tanned leather

Paul Kaiser, 2022, HS Pforzheim
Protection
Olivengegerbtes Nappaleder, Strick, Futterstoff, Füllwatte /
Olive tanned nappa leather, knitwear, lining, filling absorbent cotton

Samuel Bemmer, 2022, HS Pforzheim
Introvert/Extrovert
Anilinleder, Mesh, Stretch Fleece / Aniline leather, mesh, stretch fleece

Emma Maria Mayer, 2021, HS Pforzheim
Femined – Denim Collection
100 % recycled Denim / 100 % recycled denim

Rosalie Schele, 2022, HS Pforzheim
Lucid Dreams
Dupionseide, Organza, Lackstoff, Futterstoff, Vlies /
Dupioni silk, organza, lacquer fabric, lining, fleece

Rosalie Schele, 2021/22, HS Pforzheim
Layers
TPU, 3D Druck / TPU, 3D printing

Luca Giurcich, 2021, HS Pforzheim
Bergeri / Fiori
Veloursleder, Rattan / Suede leather, rattan

Ideas for a firm hold

Pantopia

What role do design and fashion play in a world ravaged by pandemic and war? This was the question posed by students on the Accessory Design course at Pforzheim University as they designed gloves not only with a view to aesthetic and functional aspects, but also while placing them in a social context with a current reference to time. Under the title PANTOPIA, they developed cross-semester collections in a balancing act between recognition of reality and the desire for human harmony, expressing their very own visions and expectations of a future yet to be shaped. At a time that seems more uncertain than ever, especially for the younger generation, there is a growing curiosity about what is to come, as well as a longing for permanence and reliability. The apparent contradiction intensifies the search for the possibilities of one's own effectiveness as a prospective designer.

Some dream – with open eyes and an alert mind – while others reflect on things that provide support and protection. With shapes, materials, and textures that you not only want to look at but also touch, the students show their love of detail in traditional craftsmanship on one hand, but at the same time break new ground in aesthetics and experiment with functionality – including with the use of future-oriented technological possibilities. The symbiosis of head and hand, concept and creation, utopia and feasibility is visualized in the glove as a free design object with effective symbolism and directly experienced by the students themselves in the creative process.

At this point, I would like to express my sincere thanks to the team at the Deutsches Ledermuseum, particularly Director Inez Florschütz and her co-curator Leonie Wiegand, who have supported our course of study with a high level of expertise and a great deal of passion for many years. In doing so, I also speak on behalf of the students, who were able to enjoy numerous inspiring visits and stimulating, informative tours at the Deutsches Ledermuseum. The opportunity to show selected student projects as part of the exhibition **THE GLOVE: More than fashion** is a special honor.

Finally, I wish all those reading the publication and all visitors to the exhibition at the Deutsches Ledermuseum stimulating experiences and an entertaining and insightful time.

Prof. Madeleine Häse
Head of Study Programm, Accessory Design
Faculty of Design, Pforzheim University

Pantopia

Welche Rolle spielen Design und Mode in einer Welt, die von Pandemie und Krieg heimgesucht wird? Dieser Frage stellten sich Studierende des Studiengangs Accessoire Design an der Hochschule Pforzheim und entwarfen Handschuhe nicht nur unter ästhetischen und funktionalen Aspekten, sondern setzten diese in gesellschaftlichen Kontext mit aktuellem Zeitbezug. Unter dem Titel PANTOPIA entwickelten sie semesterübergreifend Kollektionen im Balanceakt zwischen Anerkennung der Realität und dem Wunsch nach menschlicher Harmonie, die ihre ureigenen Visionen und Erwartungen von einer noch zu gestaltenden Zukunft zum Ausdruck bringen. Zu einer Zeit, die insbesondere für die junge Generation unsicherer denn je erscheint, wächst neben der Neugier auf das, was kommt, auch die Sehnsucht nach Beständigkeit und Verlässlichkeit. Der scheinbare Widerspruch intensiviert die Suche nach Möglichkeiten der eigenen Wirksamkeit als angehende Gestalter*innen.

Die Einen träumen – mit offenen Augen und wachem Geist – die Anderen besinnen sich auf Dinge, die Halt und Schutz geben. Mit Formen, Materialien und Texturen, die man nicht nur ansehen, sondern auch anfassen möchte, zeigen die Studierenden einerseits ihre Liebe zum Detail im traditionellen Handwerk, beschreiben aber andererseits neue Wege der Ästhetik und experimentieren mit Funktionalität – auch unter Nutzung zukunftsweisender technologischer Möglichkeiten. Die Symbiose von Kopf und Hand, Konzept und Kreation, Utopie und Realisierbarkeit wird im Handschuh als freies Designobjekt mit wirkungsstarker Symbolik visualisiert und im gestalterischen Schaffensprozess von den Studierenden unmittelbar selbst erfahren.

An dieser Stelle gebührt mein aufrichtiger Dank dem Team des Deutschen Ledermuseums, insbesondere der Museumsdirektorin Inez Florschütz und der Co-Kuratorin Leonie Wiegand, die unseren Studiengang mit hohem Fachwissen und großer Leidenschaft seit vielen Jahren unterstützen. Damit spreche ich auch im Namen der Studierenden, die zahlreiche inspirierende Besuche und mitreißende, lehrreiche Führungen im Deutschen Ledermuseum erleben durften. Die Möglichkeit, ausgewählte Studienarbeiten im Rahmen der Ausstellung DER HANDSCHUH: Mehr als ein Mode-Accessoire zeigen zu dürfen, ist eine besondere Ehre.

Abschließend wünsche ich allen Leser*innen bei der Lektüre der Publikation und allen Besucher*innen der Ausstellung im Deutschen Ledermuseum anregende Erlebnisse sowie eine unterhaltsame und erkenntnisreiche Zeit.

Prof. Madeleine Häse
Studiengangleiterin Accessoire Design
Fakultät für Gestaltung, Hochschule Pforzheim

Julia Suppanz

JUNGLE GLOVE

ARCTIC GLOVE

Jennifer Laura Schmidt

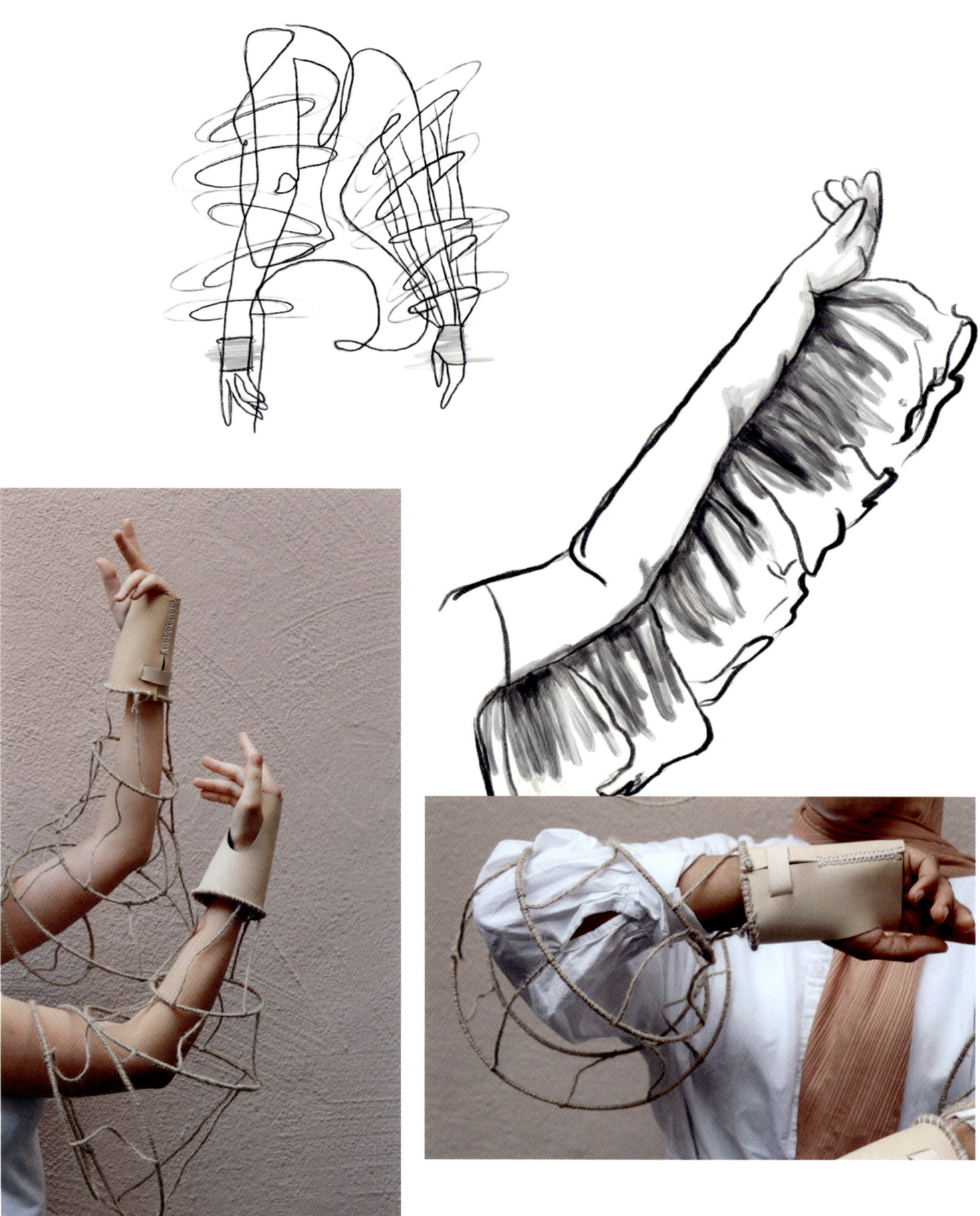

Özlem Gökce

PANTOPIA2.0

Die Menschheit ist erschöpfter denn je. „Gibt es noch Hoffnung?" ist die Frage, die sich jeder zur Zeit stellt. Nach einer jahrelangen Pandemie, welche die Menschen einschränkte, krank machte und sogar den Tod herbeirief, folgen direkt die nächsten furchteinflößenden Nachrichten. Krieg, Naturkatastrophen und Mangel an Nahrung in aller Welt. Was können wir tun? Und vor allem, wie können wir uns selbst schützen? Darauf basiert meine Kollektion in Zusammenarbeit mit Paul Kaiser.

SCHUTZ

Neben all den physischen Schmerzen, welche heutzutage immer noch Menschen erleiden müssen, habe ich mich mit psychischen Schmerzen auseinandergesetzt, denn sie sind unsichtbar. Somit zeigt sich in meiner Kollektion das Licht am Ende des Tunnels.

Paul Kaiser

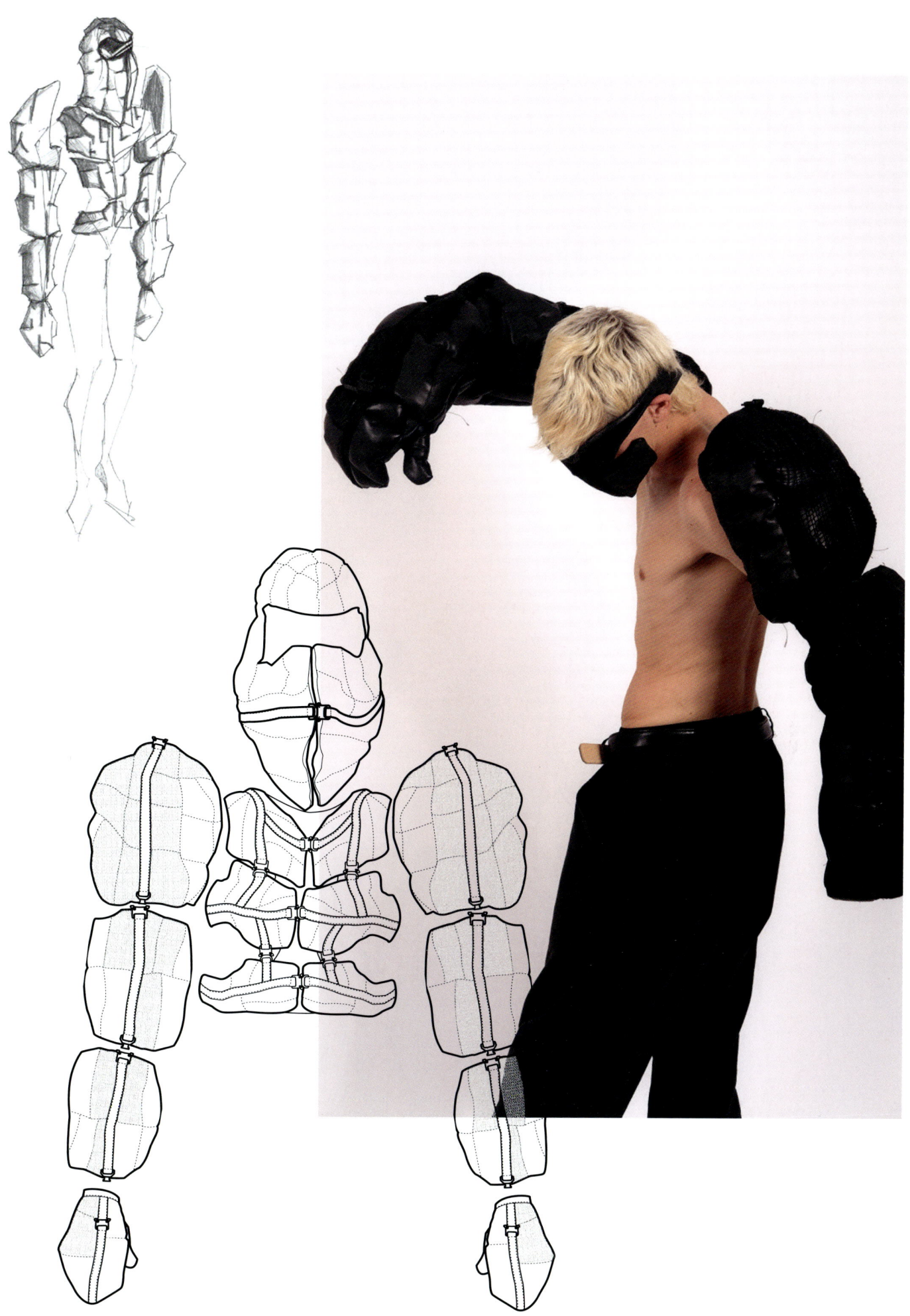

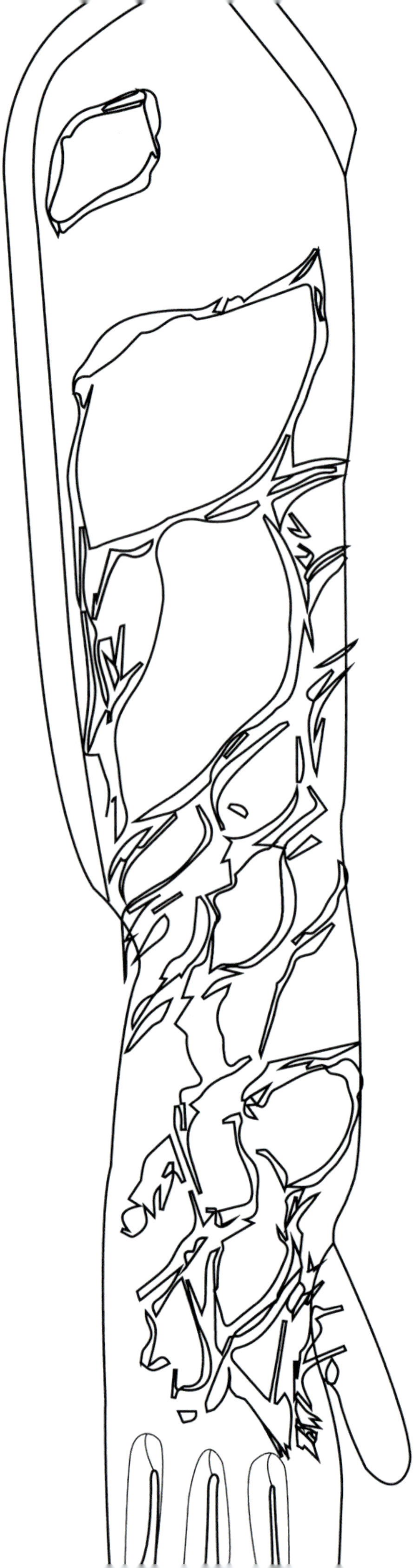

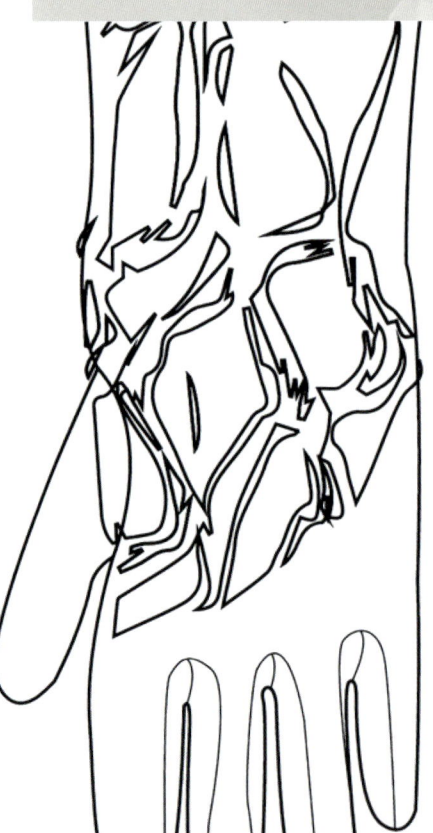

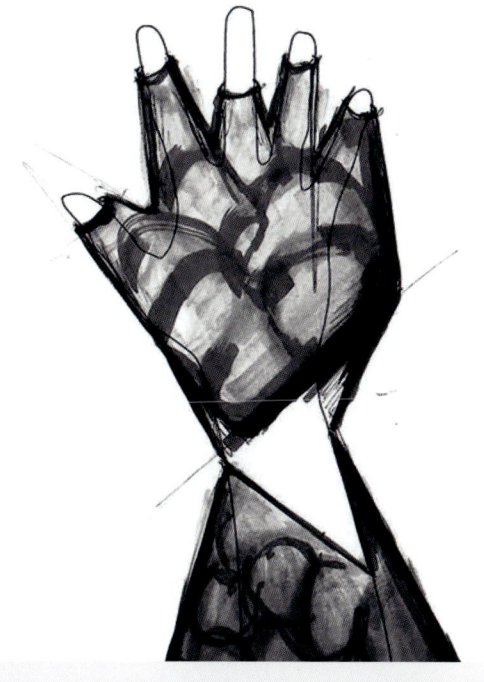

Samuel Bemmer

Emma Maria Mayer

GLOVES

→ Eigenverantwortung
→ Verpflichtung - anderen zu helfen, eigene Privilegien anerkennen und für andere nutzen

⇒ SENSE OF BELONGING

→ "Du hast es in der Hand etwas zu verändern"
 → POWER → im positiven u. negativen Sinne
Verbindung → Bewusstsein darüber, was für
zu allem ← Folgen (für andere) eigenes Handeln hat
 → ganzheitlich denken → und für den Planeten

FEMIN3D

GLOVES

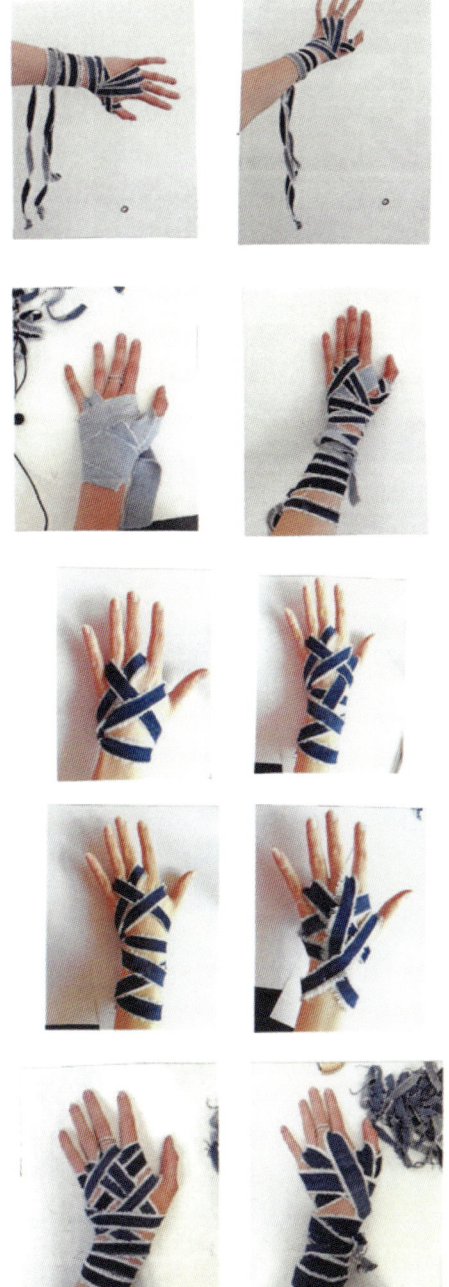

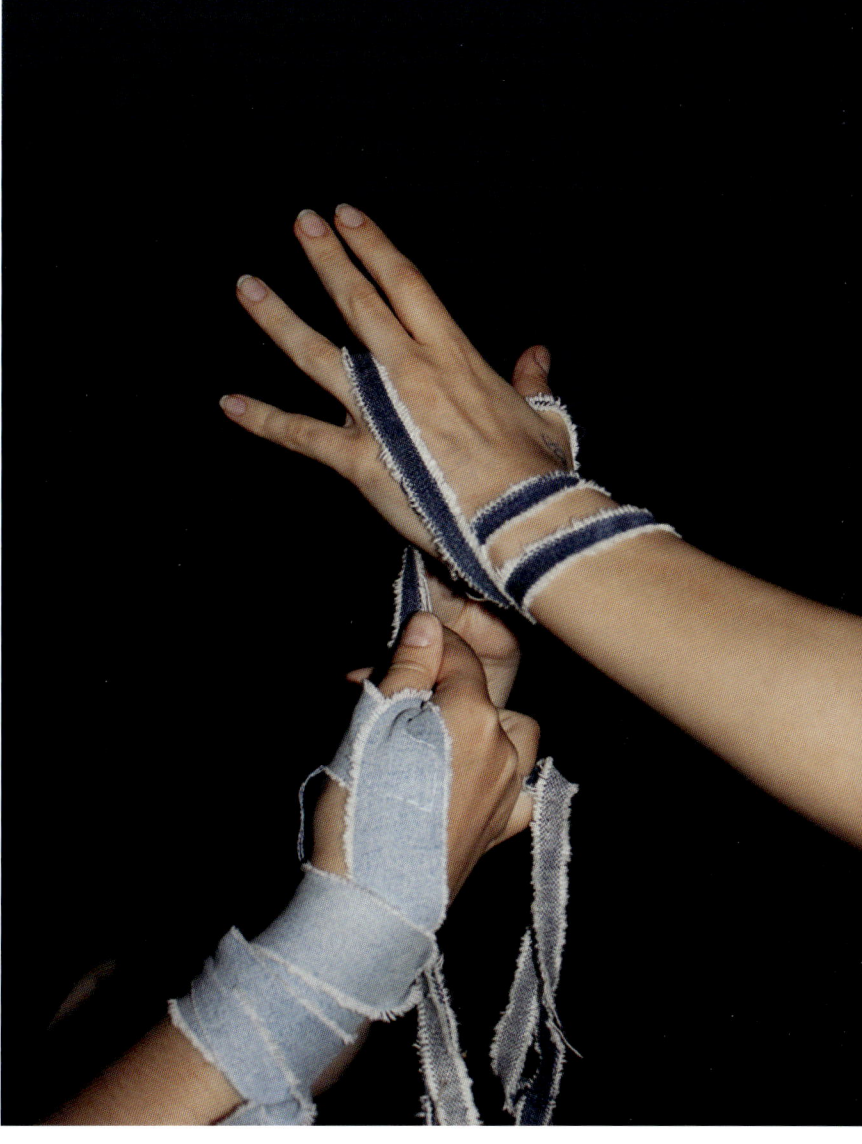

Rosalie Schele

Luca Giurcich

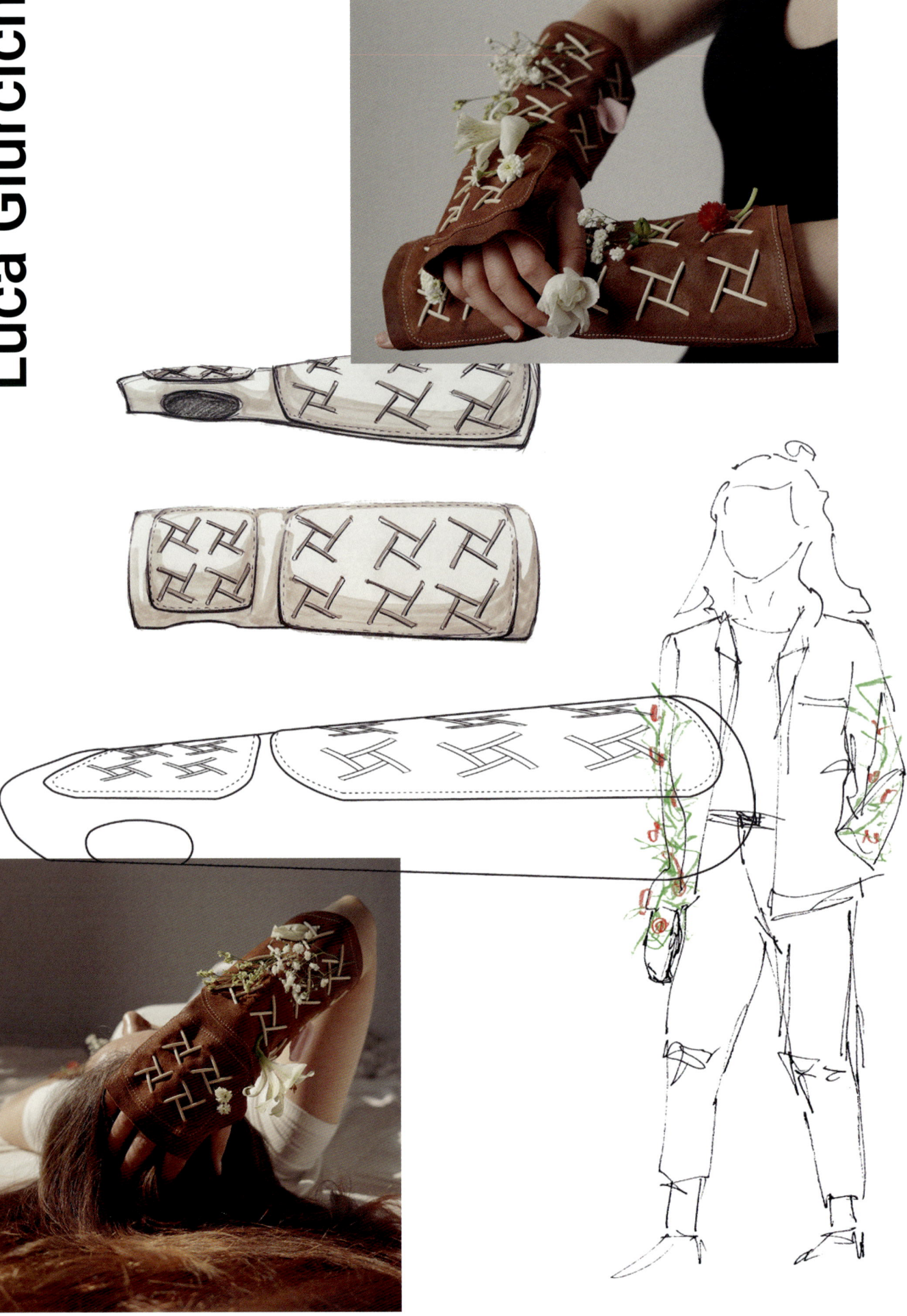

Bibliografie / Bibliography

Bayerische Versicherungskammer 1979
Bayerische Versicherungskammer (Hg.): Modisches aus aller Zeit. Accessoires aus vier Jahrhunderten. Fachsammlung Bayerisches Nationalmuseum München, München 1979.

Boehn 1928
Boehn, Max von: Das Beiwerk der Mode: Spitzen, Fächer, Handschuhe, Stöcke, Schirme, Schmuck, München 1928.

Collins 1945
Collins, C. Cody: Love of a glove. The romance, legends and fashion history of gloves and how they are made, New York 1945.

Colonel und Dalmasso 2022
Colonel, Audrey und Dalmasso, Anne (Hg.): Fait main. Quand Grenoble gantait le monde (Ausst.-Kat. Musée dauphinois), Grenoble 2022.

Cumming 1982
Cumming, Valerie: Gloves, London 1982.

Ebstein 1927
Ebstein, Erich: Zur Verwendung des Handschuhes in der Geburtshilfe im Jahre 1758, in: Monatsschrift für Geburtshilfe und Gynäkologie, Bd. 76, 1927, S. 39–40.

Ebstein 1926
Ebstein, Erich: Zur Geschichte der Operationshandschuhe, in: Monatsschrift für Geburtshilfe und Gynäkologie, Bd. 73, 1926, S. 341–344.

Frevert 1991
Frevert, Ute: Ehrenmänner. Das Duell in der bürgerlichen Gesellschaft, München 1991.

Gall 1970
Gall, Günter: Von der Schönheit des Leders. II. Der Handschuh. Symbol und Mode, in: BASF, Jg. 20, 1970, S. S. 118–124.

Göhlsdorf 2015
Göhlsdorf, Novina: Immer in Beziehung. Der Handschuh, in: Von Kopf bis Fuß. Bausteine zu einer Kulturgeschichte der Kleidung, hg. von Christine Kutschbach und Falko Schmieder, Berlin 2015, S. 278–286.

Green 2021
Green, Anne: Gloves. An intimate history, London 2021.

Kilchmann 2010
Kilchmann, Esther: Der Handschuh. Ein Accessoire der Leidenschaft, in: Passionen. Objekte – Schauplätze – Denkstile, hg. von Corina Caduff, Anne-Kathrin Reulecke und Ulrike Vedder, München 2010, S. 275–283.

Kment 1890
Kment, J.A.: Der Handschuh und seine Geschichte, Wien 1890.

Keupp 2011
Keupp, Jan: Mode im Mittelalter, Darmstadt 2011.

Latour 1947 I
Latour, A.: Der Handschuh als Amts- und Rechtszeichen, in: Ciba-Rundschau, Der Handschuh, 1947, S. 2608–2613.

Latour 1947 II
Latour, A.: Zentren der Lederhandschuh-Erzeugung, in: Ciba-Rundschau, Der Handschuh, 1947, S. 2615–2626.

Latour 1947 III
Latour, A.: Zur Herstellung des Lederhandschuhs, in: Ciba-Rundschau, Der Handschuh, 1947, S. 2627–2635.

Latour 1947 IV
Latour, A.: Vom modischen Wandel des Handschuhs, in: Ciba-Rundschau, Der Handschuh, 1947, S. 2636–2642.

Latour 1947 V
Latour, A.: Notizen zum Thema, in: Ciba-Rundschau, Der Handschuh, 1947, S. 2645–2650.

Loschek 2011
Loschek, Ingrid: Reclams Mode- und Kostümlexikon, 6. Auflage, Stuttgart 2011.

Loschek 1999
Loschek, Ingrid: Geschichte der Accessoires, in: *apropos: Der Charme der Accessoires, (Ausst.-Kat. Museum für Kunst und Gewerbe Hamburg), Heidelberg 1999, S. 8–41.

Loschek 1993
Loschek, Ingrid: Accessoires. Symbolik und Geschichte, München 1993.

Niesters 2012
Niesters, Horst: Die Kunst, mit dem Falken zu jagen, in: Die Jagd, hg. von Kurt G. Blüchel, Potsdam 2012, S. 162–193.

Redwood 2016
Redwood, Mike: Gloves and Glove-Making, Oxford 2016.

Schlegel 2021
Romeo und Julia, von William Shakespeare, aus dem Englischen übersetzt von August Wilhelm von Schlegel, München 2021.

Schwineköper 1937
Schwineköper, Berent: Der Handschuh im Recht, Ämterwesen, Brauch und Volksglauben, Berlin 1937.

Stallybrass und Jones 2001
Stallybrass, Peter und Jones, Ann Rosalind: Fetishizing the Glove in Renaissance Europe, in: Critical Inquiry, 2001, Vol. 28 No. 1, Things, 2001, S. 114–132.

Thalheim 2005 I
Schiller. Sämtliche Werke in zehn Bänden, Gedichte, Bd. 1, hg. von Hans-Günther Thalheim u.a., Berlin 2005.

Thalheim 2005 II
Schiller. Sämtliche Werke in zehn Bänden, Bd. 5, hg. von Hans-Günther Thalheim u.a., Berlin 2005.

Toomistu-Banani 2011
Toomistu-Banani, Evelyn: Nahkkinnaste Valmistamine. Labakud, sõrakud, sõrmikud. Practical Making of Leather Gloves, Tartu 2011.

ONLINEQUELLEN / ONLINE SOURCES
Abrufdatum: 9. September 2022
Retrieval date: September 9, 2022

Babayigit 2010
Babayigit, Gökalp: Michael Jackson. Der König mit dem Handschuh, 17. Mai 2010.
https://www.sueddeutsche.de/leben/michael-jackson-der-koenig-mit-dem-handschuh-1.601095

Burkett 2022
Burkett, Betty: Have you ever wondered why Mickey and Minnie wear white gloves? There's a reason or two, 17. August 2022.
https://www.disneydining.com/mickey-minnie-white-gloves-disney-bb1/

Duden online
https://www.duden.de/rechtschreibung/Schuh

Foresman 2018
Foresman, Robert Roy: History of the Glove Box, 29. November 2018.
https://www.linkedin.com/pulse/history-glove-box-robert-roy-foresman

Grathoff o.J.
Grathoff, Stefan: Fehde.
https://www.regionalgeschichte.net/bibliothek/aufsaetze/grathoff-glossarartikel/fehde.html

Green 2018
The Odyssey, von Homer, aus dem Griechischen übersetzt von Peter Green, Oakland 2018.
https://de.scribd.com/read/370154044/The-Odyssey-A-New-Translation-by-Peter-Green#a_search-menu_48786

Heinz Nixdorf MuseumsForum 2021
Heinz Nixdorf MuseumsForum: Power Glove – Zubehör des Nintendo Entertainment System, 26. November 2021.
https://nat.museum-digital.de/object/209573?navlang=de

Martin 2014
Wilhelm Tell. A Play, von Friedrich Schiller, übersetzt aus dem Deutschen von Theodore Martin, 2014.
https://www.gutenberg.org/files/6788/6788-h/6788-h.htm#link2H_4_0014

Irish 2002
Irish, Oliver: Now and then…boxing gloves, Observer Sport Monthly, 6. Oktober 2002.
https://www.theguardian.com/observer/osm/story/0,,803152,00.html

Levitt 1909
Levitt, Dorothy: The Woman and the Car: A Chatty Little Handbook for All Women Who Motor or Who want to Motor, 1909.
https://www.gutenberg.org/files/58956/58956-h/58956-h.htm#CHAPTER_II

Markham 1623
Markham, Gervase: Countrey Contentments; or The English Huswife, containing the inward and outward Vertues which ought to be in a Compleate Woman, London 1623.
https://digital.library.lse.ac.uk/objects/lse:heh898zor

Marsden 2016
Marsden, Rhodri: Michael Jackson's white glove: Rhodri Marsden's Interesting Objects No. 105, 19. März 2016.
https://www.independent.co.uk/arts-entertainment/music/features/michael-jackson-s-one-white-glove-rhodri-marsden-s-interesting-objects-no-105-a6934371.html

Mercedes Group 2014
o. A., 23. Juni 2014.
https://group-media.mercedes-benz.com/marsMediaSite/de/instance/picture.xhtml?oid=7533323

Neumayer 2020
Neumayer, Ingo: Boxen, 20. Juni 2020.
https://www.planet-wissen.de/gesellschaft/sport/boxen/index.html

Prüfer 2014
Prüfer, Tillmann: „Ich bin nicht intellektuell, nur ziemlich kultiviert", 21. Mai 2014.
https://www.zeit.de/zeit-magazin/mode-design/2014-05/karl-lagerfeld-interview

Stamp 2013
Stamp, Jimmy: The Invention of the Baseball Mitt, 16. Juli 2013.
https://www.smithsonianmag.com/arts-culture/the-invention-of-the-baseball-mitt-12799848/

Stokes 2005
The Glove, von Friedrich Schiller, übersetzt aus dem Deutschen von Richard Stokes, 2005.
https://www.oxfordlieder.co.uk/song/508

Stork 2019 I
Stork, Jeff: Why Driving Gloves Can Make Your Hands Happy, 1. April 2019.
https://www.caranddriver.com/features/a26946744/driving-gloves/

Stork 2019 II
Stork, Jeff: Glovebox History: When Driving Gloves Were a Necessity, 18. Juli 2019.
https://www.caranddriver.com/shopping-advice/a28335732/glove-box-history/

Voß 1990
Odyssee, von Homer, aus dem Griechischen übersetzt von Johann Heinrich Voß, Frankfurt am Main 1990.
https://www.projekt-gutenberg.org/homer/odyss23/chap024.html

Wittmann 2018
Wittmann, Andreas: Vom Ziegenlederhandschuh zum Doppelhandschuhindikatorsystem, 12. November 2018.
https://www.sifa-sibe.de/arbeitssicherheit/schutzausruestung/vom-ziegenleder-handschuh-zum-doppelhandschuhindikatorsystem/

WEITERFÜHRENDE LITERATUR / FURTHER READING

Cella, Cristiana: La mano, il guanto. Simboli, gesti, stili, linguaggio dell' accessorio più espressivo, Mailand 1989.

Der Handschuh. Ein Vademecum für Menschen von Geschmack, Berlin 1914.

Descottes, Nicolas: Gants, Paris 2007.

Le Gant (Ausst.-Kat. Couvent des Cordeliers à l'initiative de: l'association «Mètiers d'art de Paris» et de la Mairie de Paris), Paris 1994.

Le Reste, Fanche: Le Gant, Paris 1984.

Sydow, Johanna von: Moden- und Toiletten-Brevier: Unentbehrliches und Entbehrliches aus dem Gebiete von Tracht und Mode, Toilette und Putz, Zierrath und Schmuck, Leipzig 1877.

Dank
Acknowledgments

Realizing the exhibition and this publication would not have been possible without the support of the foundations associated with us. In this context, I am most grateful to the Dr. Marschner Stiftung, to the Hessische Kulturstiftung and to Sparkassen-Kulturstiftung Hessen-Thüringen, to Kulturstiftung der Sparkasse Offenbach am Main and to the Patrons of Deutsches Ledermuseum.

My thanks go to arnoldsche Art Publishers, and first and foremost to Dirk Allgaier and Julia Hohrein, for the professional management and realization of the publication. The publication and the communications media were designed by Antonia Henschel who most expertly transformed our ideas and wishes into reality. A cordial thanks is likewise due to photographer Martin Url, who with great patience and feeling produced new images of all the glove exhibits for the present publication. My thanks also go to Jeremy Gaines for the translations into English.

Like a publication, preparing an exhibition consists both of numerous individual tasks and fusing them to create a coherent whole. The different activities were spread across the various members of the Deutsches Ledermuseum team. As always, my heartfelt thanks go to all of them. Some of them bear special mention: I am especially grateful to Leonie Wiegand, co-curator of both the exhibition and the publication, who reliably and expertly helped drive the project. I am most grateful also to Natalie Ungar, who not only anchored the PR desk but was also responsible for the image editing for the publication. My thanks likewise go to our scholarly trainee, Sarah Vogel, who particularly in the final phase of preparing the publication provided us all with such stalwart support. She at the same time with great zest prepared the education program. I would like moreover to thank Nora Henneck who marvelously processed all the exhibits for our database, a task requiring great diligence.

I wish to express my great thanks to Susanne Caponi, my personal assistant, who as always discharged countless duties with great care and circumspection. Likewise, strong thanks are due to Lea Schmitz for providing graphics support in the museum. My cordial thanks go to Ralph Müller for skillfully and with great craftsmanship building the exhibition architecture and assembling it. I am very grateful to Vanessa Becker and Karina Länger for their exceptional careful work conserving and restoring the exhibits. Furthermore, thanks are due to Agnes Stutz for her reliable handling of all the administrative and HR duties.

Furthermore, I would wish to most cordially thank the following persons and institutions for their support, advice and help, and all of them contributed crucially to the success of the exhibition and the publication: Mario Lorenz, DESERVE Wiesbaden, who once again provided good and insightful advice on architectural matters. Deutsches Architekturmuseum's Director Peter Cachola Schmal and Registrar Wolfgang Welker for their unbureaucratic assistance. Then there were Annette Roeckl, Kristina Schreiber and Nathalie Stoeckl of Munich's Roeckl Handschuhe & Accessoires GmbH & Co. who were so happy to field our questions and respond to our wishes. Substantive information was gratefully provided by Viktoria Wilkens of Handschuh Schmidt, Magdeburg. I would also like to thank our colleagues at Historisches Museum Frankfurt, namely Laurence Becker, Beate Dannhorn, and Dr. Maren Christine Härtel.

I am deeply grateful to all the lenders for their willingness to make their pieces available to us for the exhibition. I would like in particular to mention Mandy Frenkel at Historisches Archiv der Roeckl Handschuhe & Accessoires GmbH & Co. KG, Munich; Dr. Wolfgang Glüber of Hessisches Landesmuseum Darmstadt; Falk Heinzelmann of Digital Retro Park, Offenbach am Main; and Hans Schwarz of Hans Schwarz Pelze, Frankfurt/Main.

Last but not least, my special thanks are due to Prof. Madeleine Häse and the students on the Accessory Design course at Pforzheim University as well as Isabel Groba Castro and Katharina Daunhawer for their coordination efforts. Their great dedication and tenacity produced remarkable results in the form of designs for gloves.

Dr. Inez Florschütz
Director, Deutsches Ledermuseum

Die Realisierung von Ausstellung und Publikation wäre ohne die Unterstützung der mit uns verbundenen Stiftungen nicht möglich gewesen. Dafür bin ich der Dr. Marschner Stiftung, der Hessischen Kulturstiftung sowie der Sparkassen-Kulturstiftung Hessen-Thüringen, der Kulturstiftung der Sparkasse Offenbach am Main und dem Förderkreis des Deutschen Ledermuseums überaus dankbar.

Für die professionelle Betreuung und Umsetzung der Publikation geht mein Dank an die arnoldsche Art Publishers, allen voran Dirk Allgaier wie Julia Hohrein. Die Gestaltung der Publikation wie auch der Kommunikationsmedien übernahm verantwortungsvoll Antonia Henschel. Sie hat auf äußerst kompetente Weise unsere Vorstellungen und Wünsche umgesetzt. Ein herzliches Dankeschön dafür. Dem Fotografen Martin Url, der alle unsere Handschuh-Objekte für die vorliegende Publikation mit viel Geduld und Gespür neu aufnahm, danke ich ebenfalls sehr. Mein Dank richtet sich auch an Jeremy Gaines für die Übersetzungen.

Eine Ausstellung wie eine Publikation besteht aus vielen Einzelaufgaben, die durch Zusammenfügung ein Ganzes ergeben. Diese waren auf das Team des Deutschen Ledermuseums verteilt. Ihnen allen gilt wie immer mein großer Dank. Einige Mitarbeiter*innen sind besonders hervorzuheben: Leonie Wiegand, Co-Kuratorin von Ausstellung und Publikation, die diesem Projekt verlässlich und mit viel Kompetenz zur Seite stand. An dieser Stelle ein herzliches Dankeschön. Des Weiteren Natalie Ungar, die neben der Presse- und Öffentlichkeitsarbeit auch für die Bildredaktion des Katalogs verantwortlich war. Hierfür danke ich sehr. Ebenso unserer wissenschaftlichen Volontärin Sarah Vogel, die insbesondere in der Endphase von Publikation und Ausstellung uns allen eine gute Unterstützung war. Zugleich unterlag ihr das Vermittlungsprogramm, dem sie sich mit großem Engagement widmete. Die Aufbereitung der Objekte für unsere Datenbank übernahm auf gewissenhafte Weise Nora Henneck, der ich dafür sehr dankbar bin.

Ein besonderes Dankeschön geht an Susanne Caponi, meiner Direktionsassistenz, die wie immer an vielen Aufgaben umsichtig und fürsorglich mitwirkte. Ebenso gilt mein Dank Lea Schmitz für die grafische Unterstützung im Haus. Für die gekonnte handwerkliche Umsetzung der Ausstellungsarchitektur wie für den Ausstellungsaufbau geht mein herzlicher Dank an Ralph Müller. Die konservatorische wie restauratorische Betreuung der Ausstellungsobjekte übernahmen auf das sorgfältigste Vanessa Becker und Karina Länger. Hierfür danke ich beiden vielmals. Auch danke ich Agnes Stutz für ihre zuverlässige Bearbeitung aller administrativen wie personellen Tätigkeiten.

Ferner danke ich herzlichst folgenden Personen und Einrichtungen für Unterstützung, Rat und Hilfe, die damit wesentlich zum Gelingen von Ausstellung wie Publikation beigetragen haben: Mario Lorenz, DESERVE Wiesbaden, der uns wieder einmal in architektonischen Fragen als guter und versierter Berater zur Seite stand. Dem Direktor Peter Cachola Schmal und dem Registrar Wolfgang Welker vom Deutschen Architekturmuseum für ihre unkomplizierte Unterstützung. Ebenso Annette Roeckl, Kristina Schreiber und Nathalie Stoeckl, Roeckl Handschuhe & Accessoires GmbH & Co. KG, München, die für unsere Fragen und Wünsche offen waren. Für inhaltliche Auskünfte danke ich vielmals Viktoria Wilkens, Handschuh Schmidt, Magdeburg. Dank auch an die Kolleg*innen im Historischen Museum Frankfurt: Laurence Becker, Beate Dannhorn und Dr. Maren Christine Härtel.

Mein großer Dank geht an die Leihgeber*innen für ihre Bereitschaft uns ihre Exponate für die Ausstellung zur Verfügung zu stellen. Hier möchte ich Mandy Frenkel, Historisches Archiv der Roeckl Handschuhe & Accessoires GmbH & Co. KG, München; Dr. Wolfgang Glüber, Hessisches Landesmuseum Darmstadt; Falk Heinzelmann, Digital Retro Park, Offenbach am Main und Hans Schwarz, Hans Schwarz Pelze, Frankfurt am Main nennen.

Abschließend möchte ich meinen besonderen Dank aussprechen an Prof. Madeleine Häse und die Studierenden des Studiengangs Accessoire Design von der Hochschule Pforzheim sowie Isabel Groba Castro und Katharina Daunhawer für die Koordination. Mit viel Engagement und Ausdauer sind hier beachtenswerte Ergebnisse in Form von Handschuh-Entwürfen entstanden.

Dr. Inez Florschütz
Direktorin des Deutschen Ledermuseums

Dr. Marschner Stiftung

hessische kultur stiftung

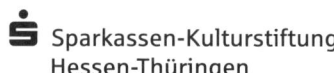

Sparkassen-Kulturstiftung Hessen-Thüringen

Kulturstiftung der Städtischen Sparkasse Offenbach am Main

FÖRDERKREIS DLM e.V.

Impressum / Imprint

Diese Publikation erscheint anlässlich der Ausstellung
This publication is issued on the occasion of the exhibition

DER HANDSCHUH: Mehr als ein Mode-Accessoire
THE GLOVE: More than fashion

Deutsches Ledermuseum in Offenbach am Main
12. November 2022 bis 30. Juli 2023
November 12, 2022 until July 30, 2023

PUBLIKATION / PUBLICATION

Herausgegeben von / Edited by
Inez Florschütz
in Zusammenarbeit mit / in cooperation with Leonie Wiegand

Redaktion und Koordination / Editing and coordination
Inez Florschütz, Leonie Wiegand

Bildredaktion / Image editing
Natalie Ungar

Texte / Texts
Leonie Wiegand

Übersetzung / Translations
Jeremy Gaines, Text / Translations

Englisches Lektorat / Copy editing English
Alexandra Cox, Coquelicot Translations

Arnoldsche Projektkoordination / Project coordination
Julia Hohrein

Grafische Gestaltung / Graphic design
Antonia Henschel, SIGN Kommunikation

Fotografie / Photography
Martin Url, Fotostudio Url

Offset Reproduktion / Offset reproductions
Schwabenrepro, Fellbach

Druck / Printed by
Schleunungdruck, Marktheidenfeld

Papier / Paper
Magno Natural 140 g/qm,
Magno Satin 135 g/qm

Buchbinder / Bound by
Hubert & Co., Göttingen

© 2022 Deutsches Ledermuseum, Offenbach am Main, arnoldsche Art Publishers, Stuttgart, **Studierende /** Students **Hochschule Pforzheim, Fakultät für Gestaltung, Accessoire Design und die Autorinnen /** and the authors
Alle Rechte vorbehalten. Vervielfältigung und Wiedergabe auf jegliche Weise (grafisch, elektronisch und fotomechanisch sowie der Gebrauch von Systemen zur Datenrückgewinnung) – auch in Auszügen – nur mit schriftlicher Genehmigung der Copyright-Inhaber*innen.
www.arnoldsche.com
www.ledermuseum.de

All rights reserved. No part of this work may be reproduced or used in any form or by any means (graphic, electronic, or mechanical, including photocopying or information storage and retrieval systems) without written permission from the copyright holders.
www.arnoldsche.com
www.ledermuseum.de/en

BIBLIOGRAFISCHE INFORMATION DER DEUTSCHEN NATIONALBIBLIOTHEK
Die Deutsche Nationalbibliothek verzeichnet diese Publikation in der Deutschen Nationalbibliografie; detaillierte bibliografische Daten sind über www.dnb.de abrufbar.

BIBLIOGRAPHIC INFORMATION PUBLISHED BY THE DEUTSCHE NATIONALBIBLIOTHEK
The Deutsche Nationalbibliothek lists this publication in the Deutsche Nationalbibliografie; detailed bibliographic data are available at www.dnb.de.

ISBN 978-3-89790-685-3
Made in Europe, 2022

AUSSTELLUNG / EXHIBITION

Idee, Konzept und kuratorische Gesamtleitung / Idea, concept and overall curatorial management
Inez Florschütz

Co-Kuratorin und Projektkoordination / Co-curator and project coordination
Leonie Wiegand

Wissenschaftliche Mitarbeit / Research assistants
Nora Henneck, Natalie Ungar, Sarah Vogel

Presse und Öffentlichkeitsarbeit / Press and Public Relations
Natalie Ungar

Grafische Assistenz / Graphic assistant
Lea Schmitz

Übersetzung / Translations
Jeremy Gaines, Text / Translations

Vermittlung / Education
Sarah Vogel

Teamassistenz / Team assistant
Susanne Caponi

Bildnachweis / Photo credits

Konservatorische Betreuung / Conservation
Vanessa Becker, Karina Länger

Ausstellungstechnik und Aufbau / Technical support and setup
Ralph Müller

Finanzen und Verwaltung / Administration
Agnes Stutz

Leihgeber / Lenders
Digital Retro Park, Offenbach am Main
Hans Schwarz Pelze, Frankfurt am Main
Hessisches Landesmuseum Darmstadt
Historisches Archiv der Roeckl Handschuhe & Accessoires GmbH & Co. KG, München

Studierende der Hochschule Pforzheim / Students of Pforzheim University
Samuel Bemmer, Pforzheim
Luca Giurcich, Villingen-Schwenningen
Özlem Gökce, Stuttgart
Paul Kaiser, Pforzheim
Emma Maria Mayer, Gerstetten
Rosalie Schele, Gengenbach
Jennifer Laura Schmidt, Ottersweier
Julia Suppanz, Bad Wörishofen

Abkürzungen / Abbreviations
l.: links; M.: Mitte; o.: oben.; r.: rechts; u.: unten /c.: center; b.: bottom l.: left; r.: right; t.: top

Umschlagabbildung / Cover photo
© Foto: DLM, M. Url und Gestaltung: Antonia Henschel

Deutsches Ledermuseum
15 © DLM, C. Perl-Appl; 17 (u./b.) © DLM, M. Özkilinc; 12, 13, 18–23, 28–31, 33 (M.l./c.l.), 36–39, 43 (u.l./b.l.), 44–46, 52–57, 62–67, 72–75, 80–83, 88–93, 98–103, 105 (M.r./c.r.), 107 (o./t.; M.r./c.r.), 108–111, 113 (u./b.), 115 (u.l./b.l.), 116–119, 124–129, 134–139, 144–147, 152–155, 160–165, 170–175, 180–183, 188–193, 195 (M.r./c.r.), 197 (o.r./t.r.), 199 (M.l./c.l.) © DLM, M. Url; 25 (o.l./t.l.), 133 (u.l./b.l.), 143 (o.r./t.r.), 195 (o.l./t.l.), 197 (u.r./b.r.), 199 (u.r./b.r.) © DLM

© akg images
49 (u.l./b.l.), 121 (o.l./t.l.)

alamy
17 (o.l./t.l.) © Shotshop GmbH/Alamy Stock Foto; 27 (u.l./b.l.) © PictureLux/The Hollywood Archive/Alamy Stock Foto; 40 (o.r./t.r.) © Art Collection 2/Alamy Stock Foto; 51 (u.l./b.l.) © Album/British Library/Alamy Stock Foto; 61 (u.r./b.r.) © James Caldwell/Alamy Stock Foto; 85 (o.r./t.r.) © Photo 12/Alamy Stock Foto; 123 (u.l./b.l.) © Shawshots/Alamy Stock Foto; 141 (u.l./b.l.) © Allan Cash Picture Library/Alamy Stock Foto

© Bally Schuhfabriken AG
133 (o.l./t.l.), 141 (M.r./c.r.), 143 (u.l./b.l.)

bpk-Bildagentur
25 (u.l./b.l.) © bpk/National Portrait Gallery, London; 27 (o.l./t.l.) © bpk/RMN – Grand Palais/Ayman Khoury; 27 (M.r./c.r.) © bpk/Bayerische Staatsbibliothek/August Beckert; 43 (u.r./b.r.) © bpk/RMN – Grand Palais/Franck Raux; 61 (o.l./t.l.) © bpk/Maurice Zalewski/adoc-photos; 61 (M.r./c.r.) © bpk/Herzog Anton Ulrich-Museum/B.-P. Keiser; 79 (u.l./b.l.) © bpk/National Portrait Gallery, London/Bassano Ltd; 87 (M.l./c.l.) © bpk/Kunstbibliothek, SMB/Knud Petersen; 133 (M.r./c.r.) © bpk/National Portrait Gallery, London; 141 (o.l./t.l.) © bpk/RMN – Grand Palais/Hervé Lewandowski; 159 (u.l./b.l.) © bpk/Hanns Hubmann; 177 (o.l./t.l.) © bpk/RMN – Grand Palais/Hervé Lewandowski

© bpk/adoc-photos
77 (u.l./b.l.), 131 (u.l./b.l.)

© gemeinfrei
123 (o.l./t.l.), 177 (M.r./c.r.)

Getty Images
35 (u.l./b.l.) © Photo Josse/Leemage/Corbis Historical/via Getty Images; 123 (M.r./c.r.) © Apic/Hulton Archive/via Getty Images; 149 (u.l./b.l.) © VCG/Visual China Group/via Getty Images; 151 (o.l./t.l.) © James Devaney/GC Images/via Getty Images; 185 (o.l./t.l.) © Paramount Pictures/Moviepix/via Getty Images; 185 (M.r./c.r.) © Jonathan Ernst/AFP/via Getty Images; 185 (M.u./c.b.) © Ethan Miller/Getty Images Entertainment/via Getty Images; 187 (o.l./t.l.) © Disney Channel/Disney General Entertainment Content/via Getty Images; 187 (u.r./b.r.) © Andreas Rentz/Getty Images Entertainment/via Getty Images

Hessisches Landesmuseum Darmstadt
47 © Foto: Wolfgang Fuhrmannek, HLMD

IMAGO
41 (M.r./c.r.) © IMAGO/Everett Collection; 71 (o./t.) © IMAGO/UIG; 97 (u.l./b.l.) © IMAGO/ZUMA/Keystone; 157 (M.r./c.r.) © IMAGO/StockTrek Images

© IMAGO/KHARBINE-TAPABOR
71 (M.r./c.r.), 105 (u.l./b.l.), 113 (o.l./t.l.), 121 (u.r./b.r.)

© IMAGO/United Archives International
87 (u.r./b.r.), 159 (u.r./b.r.), 197 (M.l./c.l.), 199 (o.l./t.l.)

© Mary Evans Picture Library
87 (o.r./t.r.), 167 (u.r./b.r.)

© ROECKL Handschuhe & Accessoires GmbH & Co. KG
107 (u.l./b.l.), 115 (o.l./t.l.), 115 (M.r./c.r.), 169, 179 (u.r./b.r.)

Scala Archives
10 DIGITAL IMAGE © The Museum of Modern Art, New York/Scala, Florence © VG Bild-Kunst, Bonn 2022; 131 (o.r./t.r.) © Photo Josse/Scala, Florence

© Sächsische Landesbibliothek – Staats- und Universitätsbibliothek Dresden
41 (u.l./b.l.)

© Staatliche Kunsthalle Karlsruhe
131 (o.l./t.l.), 179 (o.r./t.r.), 179 (M.l./c.l.)

© The J. Paul Getty Museum, Los Angeles
43 (o.l./t.l.), 159 (M.r./c.r.)

Timeline Images
79 (o.l./t.l.) © ullstein bild – Regine Relang/Timeline Images

© Timeline Classics/Timeline Images
85 (u.l./b.l.), 95 (u.l./b.l.), 177 (u.l./b.l.)

© Universitätsbibliothek Heidelberg
51 (M.r./c.r.), 59 (u.l./b.l.), 71 (u.l./b.l.), 159 (o.l./t.l.)

Einzelnachweise/ Individual references
25 (M.r./c.r.) © Schwedisches Nationalmuseum, Stockholm/Photo: Linn Ahlgren; 33 (o.r./t.r.) © Archiv des Instituts für Kunstgeschichte der LMU München; 33 (u.r./b.r.) © Galeria Colonna; 35 (o.r./t.r.) © Bildarchiv Foto Marburg/Albert Hirmer/Irmgard Ernstmeier-Hirmer; 41 (o.l./t.l.) © KHM-Museumsverband; 51 (o.l./t.l.) © Rijksmuseum Amsterdam; 59 (o.r./t.r.) © Bayerische Staatsgemäldesammlungen – Neue Pinakothek München, CC BY-SA 4.0; 69 (o.l./t.l.) © Klassik Stiftung Weimar, Bestand Museen; 69 (u.r./b.r.) © National Maritime Museum, Greenwich, London; 77 (o.l./t.l.) © Macgregor Goldsmith Inc./KeyMan Collectibles; 77 (M.r./c.r.) © Rijksmuseum Amsterdam/CC0 1.0; 79 (M.r./c.r.) © Matthias Kabel/CC BY 2.5/https://creativecommons.org/licenses/by/2.5/legalcode; 95 (M.o./c.t.) © Horace Walter Nicholls; 97 (o.l./t.l.) © The Pierce-Arrow Society/www.Pierce-Arrow.org; 97 (M.r./c.r.) © Mercedes-Benz Classic; 105 (o.l./t.l.) © Matthieu Riegler/CC-BY; 113 (M.o./c.t.) © FEMINA; 149 (o.r./t.r.) Städtische Galerie im Lenbachhaus und Kunstbau München © VG Bild-Kunst, Bonn 2022; 149 (M.l./c.l.) © The Internet Archive; 151 (M.r./c.r.) © The New York Public Library; 151 (u.l./b.l.) © The Chesney Archives of John Hopkins Medicine, Nursing, and Public Health; 157 (o.r./t.r.) © DASA Arbeitswelt Ausstellung, Dortmund/CC BY-NC-SA; 157 (M.u./c.b.) © Proglove, Workaround GmbH; 167 (o.l./t.l.) © Mattel Inc. 1989

Studierende/ Students
Hochschule Pforzheim
204 © Fotos, Zeichnungen/Photos, Drawings: Julia Suppanz, Model: Annalena Domke; 205 © Fotos/Photos: Jennifer Laura Schmidt, Model: Isabelle Barsch, 3D Print Entwicklung & Umsetzung: Matthias Seitz und Jan Schwellinger; 206 f. © Fotos, Zeichnungen/Photos, Drawings: Özlem Gökce, Models: Dahab Idris & Duygu Gökce; 208 f. © Fotos, Zeichnungen/Photos, Drawings: Paul Kaiser, Model: Aron Fickus; 210 f. © Fotos, Zeichnungen/Photos, Drawings: Samuel Bemmer, Model: Emily Körner; 212 f. © Fotos/Photos: Emma Maria Mayer, Models: Tiska Lambart, Jenny Thiess; 214 f. © Fotos, Zeichnungen/Photos, Drawings: Rosalie Schele, Model: Anastasia Polujaschny; 216 © Fotos, Zeichnungen/Photos, Drawings: Luca Giurcich, Model: Jasmin Aydogan

Alle Rechte bei den Künstler*innen/Urheber*innen. Die Redaktion hat sich bemüht die Urheber*innen zu recherchieren und die Bildrechte einzuholen. Für nicht verzeichnete Quellen bitten wir, sich an das Deutsche Ledermuseum zu wenden.

All rights reserved by the artists/copyright holders. The editors have made every effort to research the authors and obtain the image rights. For unlisted sources, please contact the Deutsches Ledermuseum.